The Height of Nonsense

'A fine adventure and delightful reading.'
The Irish Times

'A compulsive, educational, laugh-out-loud read, and one of the
most gloriously daft yet irresistible books I have ever read.'
Ferdia MacAnna, *Sunday Independent*

'For sheer pleasure, nothing I read beat *The Height of Nonsense*.'
Jan Morris, *The Observer*

'A book about turning off the motorway and heading for history
and legend. Take it in your car and you will discover parts of
Ireland you never dreamed of.'
Irish News

'A fascinating journey around the hidden corners of Ireland.'
BBC Radio

Burren Country

'Finely wrought language, lively engagement with interesting people.'
Michael Viney, *The Irish Times*

'Written in a carefree style, this is a love letter to the Burren that
digs deeper into the history, mystery and mythology of the
region – the author's avid fascination shines through.'
Belfast Telegraph

'A wonderful book that will brighten any day.'
Belfast News Letter

'A breath of fresh air, informative, funny and sensitive.'
Irish News

WANDERING IRELAND'S WILD ATLANTIC WAY

FROM BANBA'S CROWN
TO WORLD'S END

PAUL CLEMENTS is a journalist, broadcaster and writer. He is the author of a trilogy of travel books about Ireland: *Burren Country* (2011), *The Height of Nonsense* (2005) and *Irish Shores* (1993). *Romancing Ireland*, his acclaimed biography of the Irish travel writer, actor and singer Richard Hayward, was adapted for BBC television in 2014. He has written and edited two books on the travel writer and historian Jan Morris. A former BBC journalist, he also writes for three travel guidebooks to Ireland. He is a Fellow of Green Templeton College, Oxford, and the Royal Geographical Society, and lives in Belfast with his wife and son.

Keep up to date with Paul on Twitter: @clementswriting

To western wanderers who seek inspiration along the Way

WANDERING IRELAND'S WILD ATLANTIC WAY

FROM BANBA'S CROWN TO WORLD'S END

PAUL CLEMENTS

The Collins Press

FIRST PUBLISHED IN 2016 BY
The Collins Press
West Link Park
Doughcloyne
Wilton
Cork

The author wishes to acknowledge that the writing of this book has been
generously supported by the Arts Council of Northern Ireland.

LOTTERY FUNDED

A CIP record for this book is available from the British Library.

Paperback ISBN: 978-1-84889-260-6
PDF eBook ISBN: 978-1-84889-534-8
EPUB eBook ISBN: 978-1-84889-535-5
Kindle ISBN: 978-1-84889-536-2

Typesetting by Carrigboy Typesetting Services
Typeset in MinionPro 10.5pt/13pt
Printed in Sweden by ScandBook AB

Contents

Map	viii
Preface	xi
Author's note	xiv
Part I. The North-west: Donegal, Leitrim and Sligo	1
1 Donegal dalliance	3
2 The plain of hospitality	34
3 Magnetic pull of Leitrim	51
4 The sea god is found	81
Part II. The Midwest: Mayo, Galway, Clare and Limerick	105
5 The Klondike after the gold ran out	107
6 Powerful on land and sea	134
7 The road to Mannin Bay	160
8 Enjoying Guinness sensibly	200
Part III. The South-west: Kerry and Cork	239
9 The power of the black saucepan	241
10 Puckeroos play it their way	268
11 Whatever you seek is here	286
Valediction: Letter to Manannán	321
Bibliography	325
Acknowledgements	329
Index	331

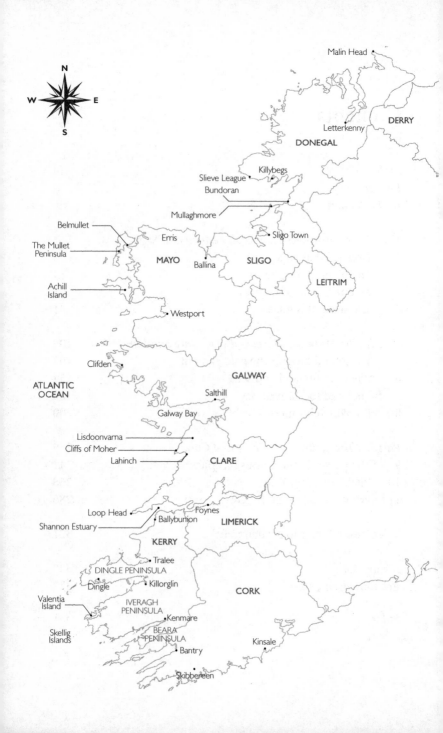

There is a perpetual mystery and excitement in living on the seashore, which is in part a return to childhood and in part because for all of us the sea's edge remains the edge of the unknown; the child sees the bright shells, the vivid weeds and red sea-anemones of the rock pools with wonder and with the child's eye for minutiae; the adult who retains wonder brings to his gaze some partial knowledge which can but increase it, and he brings, too, the eye of association and of symbolism, so that at the edge of the ocean he stands at the brink of his own unconscious.

Gavin Maxwell, *Ring of Bright Water*

Preface

THE NARROW ROAD TWISTS and spirals uphill for several kilometres to a car park at the Bishop's Viewpoint overlooking the north coast of County Derry. On a rocky outcrop, arms outstretched, stands the legendary figure Manannán mac Lir, the Celtic god of the sea. Tradition tells of the presence of a mythological sea god in Lough Foyle and the practice of making votive offerings to deities in Celtic times to Manannán, a fearsome figure who was regarded as the Irish Neptune.

Local people believe that his spirit is released during fierce storms and some are still to be heard to remark 'Manannán is angry today'. In folklore he is said to inhabit the offshore sandbanks between Inishtrahull Sound and the Magilligan waters. Fingers erect, he stands bearded and barefoot on a small wooden boat that resembles a washtub. His pacifying gesture appears to be calming the fury of the sea. A handsome two-metre-high grey fibreglass-and-steel statue, his belted dress and long robe fall behind. By his side is a sword, at his neck a brooch, and his head is plastered with bird droppings. Manannán's sword, it was poetically said, could cut through any armour, while his horse, Enbarr of the Flowing Mane, could gallop over water as though it were solid land. If I need a hero from the past for the journey I am about to start, then I have found a noble one at the top of this hill.

The horizons open out to Inishowen Head, and ten kilometres beyond to the Rhinns, while the isles of Jura and Islay lie to the north-east. The hills of the Inishowen Peninsula stand in long alignment from Raghtin More, Crockmain and Mamore down to the smaller tops of Urris. Beside me the distinctive headland of Binevenagh marks the western limit of the Antrim basalt plateau. Stiff-winged fulmars ride the thermals along cliffs while Magilligan Strand stretches for eight kilometres from Downhill to the narrows of Lough Foyle. A three-carriage train, looking like a Hornby set, rattles slowly along a track beside the water.

I have come to launch myself across the Foyle on a western odyssey, going where the meandering fancy takes me, peering into hidden places and boreens, and drinking in the Atlantic air. Rather than roar along the roads at speed, I want to weave in and out of spits of land, exploring at will. Larks pour forth their unceasing music as they climb skywards, and in competition with sheep, dominate the soundscape. An occasional raven adds to the 'caw-cophony'. I crunch my way back to the car through dying white-pink orchids, saxifrage, moss campion, wild thyme and harebell.

This location marks the starting point of a personal journey along the Wild Atlantic Way to discover unknown parts of the west coast and to pin down something of the area's genius loci. But I also wish to reflect on a trip that I made a quarter-century earlier when I hitchhiked the coastline for my first travel book, *Irish Shores*. My plan is to retrace my relatively youthful footsteps, but this time I do not need to wait by the side of the road, since I have my own wheels and control my own destiny. In 1991, I was thrown into a world of happenstance, gratefully accepting lifts from strangers and soaking up the wettest June on record.

At Magilligan Point the ferry prepares to set off across Lough Foyle for Inishowen. Twenty-five years ago I attempted to cross this stretch of water but was thwarted by bad weather and forced to sit out the storm with the Sunday papers in the Point Inn. The gnarled ferryman with his leather satchel speaks of poor business because of the weather. 'We've had a large number of wedding parties this year which keeps us afloat, although no funerals as yet,' he says. He points skywards. 'See that fella up there, Manannán, they call him – did you know that the Isle of Man was named after him and he was the first ruler of the island? He's supposed to have had a ship that didn't need sails or oars, and a boat that obeyed the thoughts of the sailors, or so they say anyway.'

Armed with a curiosity to see how the west coast has developed and to unravel the intriguing character of Manannán, I emerge into the afternoon Inishowen light to begin my western quest. Perhaps the force of this mythical sea god who has captivated me may be a presiding spirit on my journey, a protector to show me the way as the thrill of the open road begins.

Author's note

THE JOURNEY RECORDED in this book was undertaken in road trips spanning four seasons over a twelve-month period from autumn to summer. In a number of instances the identities of people have been disguised to respect their privacy.

PART I
The North-west

Donegal, Leitrim and Sligo

In doggerel and stout let me honour this country
Though the air is so soft that it smudges the words
And herds of great clouds find the gaps in the fences
Of chance preconceptions and foam-quoits on rock-points
At once hit and miss, hit and miss.

Louis MacNeice, 'Western landscape', *Collected Poems*

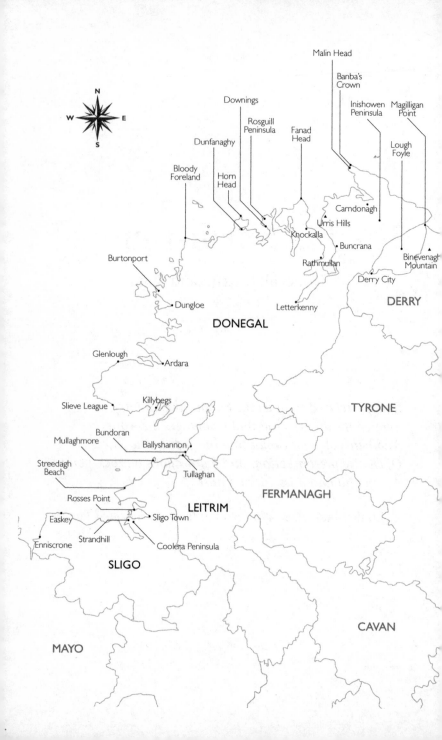

1
Donegal dalliance

THE DISTINCTIVE BLUE-AND-WHITE wavy logo signs of the Wild Atlantic Way are quickly in evidence as I drive from Greencastle through Gleneely, Culdaff and on to Malin Head. I am trying to catch the last of the daylight on an afternoon of heavy showers. My destination is the headland known as Banba's Crown, named after a mythical queen.

The Inishowen Peninsula is one of the least-known parts of the west coast, neglected by guidebooks and consequently tourists. Inishowen means 'Island of Eoghain', taking its name from Eoghain, one of the sons of a High King of Ireland, known as Niall of the Nine Hostages. Its isolated position means that it has been left behind, symptomatic of the wider county. In the initial plans for the designation of the Way, Donegal was not even considered. The tourist board devised a route from west Cork ending at Sligo until it was pointed out that, since Donegal was in the Republic, it should therefore be part of the signage. Wise counsel prevailed and the county now has no fewer than forty 'discovery points' and three 'key signature points'.

Donegal has long suffered from an identity complex. Its topographical situation confuses outsiders. Although the most northerly county in Ireland, it is not in Northern Ireland and is cut off from Dublin by dint of distance. Its people have to cross and re-cross a border (now largely unnoticeable on the ground at least) to reach other parts of the country. For many in Dublin or farther south, Donegal is, to paraphrase Neville Chamberlain, 'a faraway country of which we know little'. If Donegal is a faraway country, then Inishowen, which some think should be a separate county, is even farther. For many years it

Sheep and a sign for the Wild Atlantic Way, Inishowen, County Donegal.

has had its own 160-kilometre coastal drive which has now been incorporated into the wider Way. But the place has always felt out on a triangular limb, a bit estranged, more akin to Scotland than Ireland, given the historic connection amongst emigrant workers between the two countries. Twenty-five years ago I also had ignored it on my coastal hitchhike, bypassing the peninsula because my lift took me directly from Derry to Dunfanaghy. I am now making amends.

When I reach it, a squall is enveloping Banba's Crown, the farthest-flung northerly point in Ireland. Banba was one of three sisters, a divine trio of eponyms for Ireland, along with Ériu and Fódla. The name has often been used as a poetic reference for the country. A late afternoon mist creeps in over the water, restricting the view, but the sea hurls foam against the rocks, creating a visually spectacular start. The signal tower lookout post was built by the British around 1805 to guard against invasion from the French during the Napoleonic Wars. A century later, Lloyd's of London took it over to contact ships offshore, using telescopes and semaphores. Lloyd's hired the Marconi Wireless Company to set up a station in the tower and it was later used as a lookout during both world wars. Its masonry crumbling, it stands today forlorn and discarded, its door and windows bricked up. I survey the headland, inhale a deep whiff of ocean and enjoy the moment of being alone, until a car pulls up. A German couple steps out, steadying themselves in a cocktail of wind, rain and hail, grasping the car doors.

'Can you zee Zcotland?' the man shouts to me. 'Not today, you can see nothing apart from Inishtrahull and the Tor Rocks', which, I point out, are about to disappear under a wraith of mist. His wife jumps back into the car and he poses for a selfie before speeding off. The rain has become a deluge. Already, the Wild Atlantic Way is living up to the fulfilment of its name.

With the light draining rapidly, I make my way to the country's most northerly B&B at Ballygorman, overlooking Portmore pier. At the Seaview Tavern, owner Michael Doherty is welcoming diners, fielding calls and helping with meals. As a collector of considered and unconsidered trifles, or what Vladimir Nabokov called 'fluff' and 'straw', I know that Donegal contains one third of all Ireland's beaches and that a quarter of the landscape is bogland. One statistic I managed to pin down is that the length of the coastline is 1,500 kilometres, which includes small peninsulas and deserted headlands. With the best will in the world, I cannot visit them all. Browsing over dinner through a booklet about Malin Head produced by Donegal County Council, I discover a new acronym to describe places of interest: SEB or Site of Exquisite Beauty. The three listed are the Five Fingers Strand, Knockamany and Kinnagoe Bay. From the dining-room window, I watch two joggers in hi-viz jackets and with head flashlights splash past. In the distance, the measured rhythm of Inishtrahull lighthouse provides a reassuring beacon, silently signalling its message across the water.

Next morning a dilatory sun seeps through clouds, lighting up an unimaginably calm sea, reflecting the startling fickleness of the west's weather. After yesterday's washout there is a fresh energy to the morning. A small fishing boat, a half-decker, noses its way out from the pier, heading towards the Scottish coast in search of clams and whelks, a local name for sea snails. Barren rocks and islands stand out in glittering sharp focus. Geologists believe Inishtrahull island to be the oldest place in Ireland. The rocks have been scientifically dated to 1,778 million years old and are regarded as being similar to those of Greenland. On the wall of the breakfast room, a Highlands of Ireland map lists ships that foundered along this coastline. I ponder some of the names and dates: *The Venerable*, 1904, *The Laurentic* and *Justiac*, both 1917, *Thomas Hankins*, 1939, *The Prominent*, 1913, and HMS *Wasp*, lost with fifty souls after striking rocks in 1884 while on its way to collect taxes from Tory islanders. Leafing through tourism brochures, I identify locations to seek out along this section of the Way, a small *Itinerarium Curiosum* (Itinerary of Curiosities) of secluded beaches, wildlife habitats, cafés, pubs and … shark haunts.

Michael Doherty, known as 'Doc' to distinguish him from numerous neighbouring Doherty families, has long had a fascination for the coastline. After living and working in the United States, he returned to Donegal and promotes the area through his B&B and restaurant, as well as in his role with Inishowen Tourism.

'Seafood is our big business and there has been a crab explosion in recent years. Crab meat has a very delicate consistency and crab bisque is popular. Whelks are an acquired taste and are for overseas consumption. They are processed in Holland and sold to the Japanese market. It's tough for local fishermen. The trawlers from France, Russia and other countries have vacuumed that coastline.'

There is speculation that Malin Head may become a world centre, not only for basking sharks, but also for the most illustrious sea predator of them all, the great white. Michael tells me that a Californian marine expert, Dr Pete Klimley, has been to the area, concluding that it is ideal for the development of a protected zone for sharks. He described the waters around Inishowen as 'unique in the world'.

'Klimley is referred to under the soubriquet "Dr Hammerhead" as he is renowned for holding his breath while diving up to thirty metres in order to hand-tag hammerhead sharks with a dart gun. A shark park would be a great attraction and would bring more visitors. I enjoy telling people that the sharks always come for the marching season. They arrive each year on the Twelfth of July and stay until the end of August. Many people in the summer come in the hope of seeing them, so if it was controlled with boat trips it could become a big draw.

'A party of Spanish tourists here last summer was surrounded by twenty-five massive basking sharks which astonished them. The sharks follow the Gulf Stream from Cork and feed on the plankton-rich waters. People have the wrong idea about them as they don't bask but are quite active and thrash around. They can also grow up to eleven metres long and are regarded as being like the tiger on land. We frequently have dolphins leaping and jumping in and out of the water in front of us. Other species include blue sharks and common skate, while you sometimes see pods of orcas.'

Michael refers to Malin as a 'Holy Grail' for ornithologists. The birdlife ranks amongst the best in Ireland. He suggests two coastal spots for me to visit: the Wee House of Malin and the beach at Ballyhillin. Around the coastline at Malin Well a cave is built into the rock beside a church. The Wee House, as it is known, was thought to cure disease. Legend has it that a hermit once lived in the cave and no matter how many people entered, there was still room for more. This morning I have the cave all to myself, although five people would be a crowd. A shag zips low over the water, while, higher up, a curlew heads off on a mission, passing a tumbling waterfall. At the water's edge, gulls bicker restlessly, releasing a tirade of shrieks. Out of the blue, comes a symbolic high-speed fly-past of three closely bunched oystercatchers. I interpret this as a 'hello' greeting related to the Power of Three, a number charged with supernatural significance in Irish legend.

Beside the cave, in a glass-fronted niche, stands a one-metre blue-and-white devotional statue of Our Lady of Inishtrahull, originally from the island's school. When the school was closed, the statue was removed to the Star of the Sea Church, restored and placed here in 2001. Head bowed, palms open peacefully, she welcomes visitors, who have placed coloured stones, shells and jewellery. Walled remains of the small church are engulfed in foliage. An information panel, quoting James McParlan in the 1802 *Statistical Survey of County Donegal*, states:

> Near this old church, a famous pilgrimage is performed by dropping a great number of beads while whispering prayers: but the ceremony finishes by a general ablution in the sea, male and female, all frisking and playing in the water, stark naked and washing off each other's sins.

At the stony beach, sprawling sea mayweed, with its daisy-like flowerheads, grows in clusters. Beach detritus includes plastic milk bottles and bags, Ribena and Lucozade bottles, Nivea baby sun lotion, an empty packet of Mayfair sky-blue cigarettes (with Greek lettering), a tangle of blue fishing nets and sea rods mangled together. The rods are vegetation that resemble walking sticks but which are soft and pliable.

Famed for its semi-precious stones, Ballyhillin beach, at the foot of the tower I had visited the day before, is bookended by fields. My arrival along a mucky lane coincides with a burst of cackling fieldfares, which give the appearance of having just dropped out of the sky from Scandinavia. A jittery mob, they are busily searching for beetles and earthworms. Without warning, they explode into spring-heeled flight, their backs a rich chestnut as they move at speed, with their *chack-chack* call, to another part of the field.

I climb over a stile and crunch my way across a shingle beach strewn with a million pebbles. A paddling of ducks jostles on the waves. I am struck by the dazzling array of round and ovoid stones and by the silky lustre of their colours, looking like a milk chocolate selection box: chalk, silver, fawn, dove grey, dirty white, gold, jade green and a leopard-skin lookalike mottled with yellow, reddish-brown and dusty pink spots – irresistible pebbles that demand to be picked up, smelt and felt. My guidebook identifies them under their gemstone terminology with names such as agate, cornelian, jasper and serpentine. They are smooth to the touch; some have hairline cracks. Hunkering down, I make a ritual selection of three hard, veined ones with delicate swirls of light blue. I revel in their petrified coolness and, like a shoplifter, slip them into my pocket.

My attention is diverted by the nasal *rronk* of large skeins of Brent geese that have swept into a field at the far end of the beach. A flock 200 strong spends a few minutes finding its bearings before rising, heading out to sea, circling around, swinging back and settling into another field, wings gleaming and flashing in the sharp light. Through binoculars I watch them feeding. Many rest contentedly before lifting off again with their massed cries. I savour the moment. It has been an exhilarating autumnal morning of natural theatre-in-the-wild but I have covered only a short distance of the long Way ahead.

The blinding sun has me reaching for shades around the west side of the peninsula where a large 'S' on the Way logo indicates south to Malin town and Carndonagh. A traffic- and puddle-free single-track road wraps itself around the headland. The only signs of animal life are sheep, a lone donkey and an inquisitive hooded crow on a fencepost. I glimpse a buzzard spiralling over fields. Trees are still in riotous autumn glory along with small clumps of gorse, but the heather and fuchsia are past their colourful best. Newly built pebbledash bungalows sit hard by the roadside and three cats cuddle on the porch of a cottage with vivid green window frames.

From Knockamany, wide coastal views open up and I pass a complex of white buildings: the operations room of the Irish Coastguard Radio Station at Malin Head, which coordinates search and rescue. Its tall transmitter in the garden is surrounded by a high fence. The Meteorological Office's weather station has also a base here. Sea Air Malin is famed for its inclusion in the litany of BBC Radio 4 shipping forecast names beloved of poets, as well as bands such as Blur and Radiohead, and parodied by everyone from Frank Muir and Denis Norden to Stephen Fry.

A public revolt is under way in Donegal because of the imposition of water charges and the plan that a single public utility should develop the water system. As in other parts of Ireland, the belligerent mood amongst the community is reflected in newspaper headlines. Large marches against the proposed water charges have taken place in Letterkenny, Ballyshannon and Lifford. Countrywide protests have been organised by a group known as Right2Water, set up to encourage a campaign of civil disobedience, with non-payment of charges at its centrepiece and opposition to the installation of water meters.

The scale of anger is apparent on a Highland Radio phone-in. One listener complains that it is yet another sign of the country going to ruin. 'We've had everything here,' he says, 'backhanders, cronyism, nepotism and a country full of jiggery-pokery.' A news report carries the story of a tense confrontation in which two water meter installers were turned away from houses in Annagry and Meenaleck in west Donegal. An unrepentant local councillor stood on top of a manhole cover, refusing to budge, telling the workmen 'You are not wanted or needed here.' Some residents parked their cars over stop-valves to prevent engineers from accessing their water supply.

In need of a caffeine fix, I pull over in the Diamond at Carndonagh. On my journey I want to seek out the best places to recharge and consider how west coast café culture has flourished in recent years to become such an integral part of the fabric of Irish life. Café Donagh, run by a Frenchman, Pascal Thomas-Trabac, originally from Bordeaux, is a surprising find. The business has been part of the Carndonagh cognoscenti café circuit for several years. A peak-capped Pascal tells me the café is renowned for its chowder as well as its Croque Monsieur and Madame. He discusses his coffee in hushed tones as if it were a Sancerre or particularly fine Bordeaux.

If a café is to be judged on its snickers cake and the quality of its cappuccino – two shots of Sicilian Caffè Miscela d'Oro served in a mug like soup – then Café Donagh rates high in any customer satisfaction survey. Here they embrace artwork, books, newspapers and humour. Beside me, a Recipe for Happiness: '1 bag of smiles, 2 cups of sharing, 2 lb of positivity, ½ cup of humour, 1 bag of self-esteem, 2 spoonfuls of simplicity, 1 dash of goodwill, 4 drops of easy-going and a packet of life-caring.'

I glance at a story in the paper. 'A coffee a day keeps Alzheimer's at bay,' says the headline. It is based on new research which has found that drinking three cups of coffee a day can reduce risk of dementia and delay the onset of Alzheimer's disease. The research shows that older adults with mild memory impairment who drink three cups a day will not convert to Alzheimer's. I search my jacket and shoulder bag for my car keys but cannot recall where I put them, so decide on another coffee.

Fifteen minutes later, reunited with my keys which had slipped down a hole into the lining of my jacket pocket owing to the weight of three stones, I rejoin the Way curving around the sweep of Trawbreaga Bay to Ballyliffin and Clonmany. Rising inland, the rounded, peaty dome of Slieve Snaght is visible in its entirety on a day of unbroken sunshine. Road signs feature a drawing of a swan while another warns motorists: 'Caution Ride Slowly, School Children Are Crossing'. In this part of Donegal the traditional whitewashed cottage has largely given way to modern bungalows or two-storey farmhouses, some guarded with ornamental life-sized imperial eagles on gateposts. At Dunaff the wide prospect from this GCR (my newly coined initialism for Great Coastal Road) showcases an elongated chain of hills running from Raghtin More, across Mamore hill to the undulating line of the Urris Hills sloping down to Lough Swilly.

Two BAMBIs (Born Again Middle-Aged Bikers) vroom past me at breakneck speed on a corner. Fortunately, the steep road that zigs and zags up Mamore Gap comes with passing places at crucial bends. Sheep, crimson markings on their backs, speckle the boggy hillside. At the top of the gap, twenty towering white wind turbines, their rotating blades whirring industriously, come into view. These are the new controversial superstructures of the landscape, reinforcing how the skyline has shifted in twenty-five years. They have denatured the countryside, troubling the souls of many. Disputed claims and counterclaims over health effects from the turbines continue to be the subject of focus in many parts of Ireland.

On the other side of Buncrana, a road sign reads: 'Thank you for visiting Amazing Grace Country.' Blithely unaware that I had passed through it, I discover that it refers to a sailor, John Newton, who was caught in a violent storm in the Atlantic in

1748. He survived for weeks in the wreck of the ship, at the mercy of the ocean, before finding a haven in Lough Swilly. When he stepped ashore in Inishowen he found a new faith and years later wrote the words to the hymn 'Amazing Grace.' The enterprising tourism authority has exploited a tenuous link. They have created an annual festival to celebrate the connection and, in his honour, revitalised a scrap of waste ground into a park.

From Burnfoot a straight road leads to Inch Levels, an area of reclaimed farmland where a flock of more than 150 whooper swans feeds voraciously in a huge field close to passing traffic. Inch Levels are an internationally important staging post and this is a November highlight of the natural world. Under a European Union birds' directive it is also a Special Protected Area for the swans that have flown from high northern latitudes. For 3,000 of these avian giants this part of north Donegal is the first landfall after their 1,300km-long flight. They pick and peck cautiously, tiptoeing delicately across the ground, glad to be on the terrestrial sphere again. The triangular splash of bright yellow on their wedge-shaped black bill stands out. Five lie folded, exhausted from the journey. Cars and vans pass, oblivious to this spectacle. One driver pulls up, lowers the window of his Vectra and cuts the car engine. He squints into the sun and asks where I am from.

'You're after the Wild Atlantic Waay...?' his question trails off. 'Well, we've had the Inishowen won-hun-derd here for forty bleedin' years promotin' our coast and no one took a blind bita notice of it. Now these johnny-come-latelys have stuck a few fancy signs on top of it. They're a bit late cashin' in on our coastline. We don't want tourists clutterin' our countryside – we already know it's the best in the country – just ask the swans.'

He adds a note of derision, protesting about what he regards as the route's misnaming: 'It should be called the Wild Swully Waaay as it's not even the ocean here.' We turn our attention to the swans. He is impressed, up to a point, by their power. 'Aaanywaaay, they're a lovely sight but they're clumsy big brutes all the same when you see them flying t'gither like that, aaaren't they?'

On cue, a gangly dozen take off westward, quicksilver white in the autumnal light, necks stuck out, wings beating vigorously, a honking chorus line over our heads. The air pulsates with their shouts, their bugle-like calls echoing across farmland, roads and hills. For most of the winter, the swans roost as long-stay guests in the waters of Inch. Tourism marketing gurus refer to the length of time that holidaymakers spend in one area as 'dwell time'. While most people stay only a few days in this part of north Donegal, the 'dwell time' of *Cygnus cygnus* extends up to four months. The swans possess a powerful mythological symbolism because they are comfortable in the three habitats of water, land and air. Their love of the rich culinary offerings of cereals and crops, and the wet grassland that provides a safe roost, combine with the invigorating climate to make a recipe for whooper happiness, nature graced by raw beauty.

Swanning around Inishowen for longer than planned has delayed me. After a break in my journey, the next stage leads me early in the new year to the Fanad Peninsula, sidestepping Letterkenny, a town unrecognisable since 1991 because its population has more than doubled. In a Fáilte Ireland survey in 2013 Letterkenny was nominated as one of the top ten towns in Ireland for making a difference to tourism and followed this up in 2015 by winning the accolade of Ireland's tidiest town. The awards ignited fresh enthusiasm and encouraged new business. But the developments also led to a series of roundabouts and dull strips of approach roads filled with burger joints, pizza parlours, tyre companies, car washes, motorbike and car showrooms.

The vernacular buildings of this part of the Donegal countryside and its small towns are redolent of the nineteenth century. Warehouses, corn, flour and woollen mills stand four-square, some derelict, others repurposed for 21st-century use. Deep-rooted connections are reflected in shops and pubs with traditional fronts in bright colours. Despite the closure of many properties and the proliferation of charity shops, they show a sense of civic pride.

In Rathmullan, Belle's Kitchen Bistro is tuned firmly into the modern era and enjoys a thriving early January trade. Two wall hangings draw me in, exhorting: 'Drink Coffee: Do stupid things faster with more energy' and 'Coffee that hits the spot served here'. That coffee is Java but I am more attracted to their farmhouse beers, bottled by Kinnegar Brewery, with such names as Scraggy Bay, an India Pale Ale, an amber ale, Devil's Backbone, and Rustbucket, made with rye and barley malt. The pale ale Limeburner catches my attention and I discover from the bottle's label that it is named after a 45-metre-high undersea pinnacle hidden in an area where Lough Swilly meets the North Atlantic. The bright light of Fanad Head once illuminated the limeburner, guiding passing ships. The logo shows a bouncing rabbit with the tagline: 'Follow the Hops.'

The barman says they have done 'serious' business since the launch of the Way. He points to the beers. 'Our coffee is popular but we can't get enough of this stuff for our customers.' On his advice, I pour a large glass, paying silent homage to the divine chieftain Manannán mac Lir who washed down his food, legend has it, with the 'ale of immortality'. There is an otherworldliness about Lough Swilly which probes deep into north Donegal from the Atlantic. I can imagine how it would have appealed to Manannán, usually seen as 'Lord of the Otherworld', a land that lies beyond the mortal gaze, perhaps on a magical island, or under the sea with the limeburner.

Frequently, Lough Swilly slips beneath the tourists' radar because many see it as too remote and hence it does not attract the same number of foreign visitors as the southern half of the county. On important global migration routes for fish and birds, the lough's diversity of wildlife includes whales, dolphins and porpoise, known locally as the 'Inishowen tumbler'. Nevertheless, it is popular with Irish holidaymakers for the standard of its Blue

Flag beaches and for the quality of its history. The Flight of the Earls from this area in 1607 is well documented. Schoolchildren know the story of how the Gaelic nobility, led by Hugh O'Neill, Earl of Tyrone, and Rory O'Donnell, Earl of Tyrconnell, left to seek refuge in Europe following defeat at the hands of the English, later paving the way for the Ulster Plantation. Down at Rathmullan waterfront, a tall and evocative bronze statue of the earls saying goodbye to their people commemorates the event.

Less well known – enshrined in local memory but largely uncelebrated – is the 'Flight of the Parrot' in the same lough more than 200 years later. On 4 December 1811, HMS *Saldanha*, a Royal Navy frigate of 38 guns and crew of nearly 300, was patrolling the water as part of the naval war between Britain and France. Violent storms, driven by a north-west gale, forced the ship on to rocks off Ballymastocker Bay. More than 200 bodies were washed in, and the wreckage littered the strand. One of the most prominent among the drowned was Captain William Pakenham, son of the Earl of Longford of Pakenham Hall in County Westmeath and brother-in-law of the Duke of Wellington. Several months later, the only survivor, the ship's parrot, was captured near the site of the wreck and identified by a medallion around its neck engraved with the name *Saldanha*.

Fortified with a steaming breakfast bowl of Flahavan's porridge oats, topped with creamy carrageen moss, I set off early from my lodgings at Rathmullan House. The winter warmth has returned, prompting the waitress to reflect on the topsy-turvy weather. 'We're having June in January this year and who knows what the spring will bring,' she says. My route takes me past a rash of holiday homes on the outskirts of Rathmullan: two-storey mock-Tudor houses with red and black bargeboards, holiday chalets, cottages and small developments. Even though I am heading north, I pick up a sign for the Way indicating south. The road uphill follows a central unbroken white line. With the exception of splashes of gorse and red berries, colourless hedgerows line the roadside. Birds are busy, skittering here and there at speed, enjoying the pin-bright morning. The hillside heather has turned a deep terracotta. Small clumps of leafless trees stand amongst granite outcrops.

As I reach the higher ground of Knockalla, views unfurl across Lough Swilly, sparkling in the sunshine. The weather is bizarrely balmy – perhaps I have just been lucky. The road is turning into a GCR, rising, swinging around and traffic-free, apart from some stray Fanad ewes. At Ballymastocker Bay, a viewpoint beside Saldanha Head provides an outstanding position to look down on the three-kilometre curve of Stocker Strand, also known as Portsalon beach. It is divided into three separate sections by two streams flowing through rocks into the lough. Tight-lipped waves roll in slowly and from my elevated perch I can hear what sounds like a rumble of distant thunder. Fanad's beaches are amongst Ireland's finest and this one, with its immaculate gold-tinted sand, was once voted the second best beach in the world. This morning, not a dog walker, jogger or swimmer is to be seen; not even a solitary gull or oystercatcher combs the beach.

Directly across the water, overshadowed by the sharp outline of the Urris Hills, stands the bulbous promontory of Dunree Head with its fort. This stretch of coastline is noted for its defensive forts, while inland, the whole way down to Kerrykeel, lies the spread of Knockalla Mountain, known as the 'Devil's Backbone' of Fanad. Twisting like a giant letter 'S', the road is reminiscent of a smaller version of the Col du Tourmalet in the French Pyrenees. Three horses, clad in thick purple winter overcoats, peer over a five-bar gate as if to welcome me to Portsalon, albeit with a degree of suspicion. One nods his long head sagely, vapour breath steaming into the still, icy air. From a fence, a pied wagtail chuckles along with me at the fact that triplism reigns again.

North of Portsalon the landscape lurches into a different character with stone walls dividing fields until the Atlantic comes into view. The population appears to thin out as few houses dot the countryside. The white-walled Fanad Head lighthouse is a prominent historic building and a place of strategic importance. For many it was a poignant reminder of ships leaving Donegal with emigrants bound for a new start in a foreign land. In 1975 the lighthouse was automated and is now the base for helicopters supporting lighthouses on Tory Island and Inishtrahull. It is gated and locked, and a sign says 'Keep Out'. Scaffolding surrounds the building and a JCB digger lies idle beside piles of stones and slates. In a deep gorge waves swirl and slush against the rocks. Beside the lighthouse, the grey windowless ruin of a former coastguard station adds a further ghostlike dimension to the landscape.

Less than two kilometres away, the Lighthouse Tavern looks unprepossessing from the outside; inside, however, the welcome is warm. 'We've perfected a great way of dealing with the storms up here,' owner James Waldron delights in telling me. He motions to a small picture of a colourful drink on the windowsill. 'We serve Dark 'n' Stormy, a cocktail which helps us through the freezing days. It's made of Jamaican rum and ginger beer served over ice and garnished with a wedge of lime, and it slips down a treat. It's a taste of the tropics, so it helps us through the winters. We've perfected the ratio of rum and ginger beer to make it a Swilly special. How many would you like?'

James has been running the bar for six months and is planning to extend by adding en suite bedrooms for guests. Even as a blow-in from County Mayo, his feeling for the place is evident. A window sticker proclaims 'I Love Fanad'. He explains why he has become such a fan of Fanad.

'I like the storms – for me, the stormier the better, which is why I have chosen to settle here. If the power goes off at night, our generator supplies five hours of energy, then the candles take over. We bring out the camping stove, the cocktails are mixed and it's highly atmospheric. This is a small, unspoilt piece of paradise on the north coast that is neglected. We have all modern comforts here but in traditional surroundings. Of course, with the Internet there's nowhere that is all that isolated these days and we have our regular deliveries, so we are not really all that remote.'

Parts of north Fanad have a special designation, which he says is vital to ensure that the habitats are properly protected. From Ballyhoorisky to Fanad Head these include vegetated sea cliffs, shingle beaches, sand dunes, reedbeds, heathland, freshwater marsh, and lakes with rare aquatic plants. I remark on how sparsely populated the area appears to be compared to the southern part of the Fanad Peninsula, a point that James acknowledges.

'It has not been overdeveloped here, unlike some places, and is zoned as a special area of conservation. In other parts of Ireland you can't even see the scenery because the landscape has been scarred with so many developments, but that can't happen here. We need a balance between nature and tourism and that's how we want to keep it. More people will come when they open the accommodation at the lighthouse, which is why there is work going on there at the moment.'

Ambitious plans are under way to transform the lighthouse and build a visitor centre. James tells me the building is being reroofed and renovated by the Commissioners of Irish Lights as part of a new all-Ireland Lighthouse Trail. This will tell the history of Lough Swilly and surrounding coastline. It will also emphasise the significance of the link to the local community and its location within Gaeltacht Fhánada, Ireland's most northerly Gaeltacht community. A large photograph of the lighthouse on the wall carries a simple declaratory verse:

> Like a guardian angel
> The lighthouse stands
> Sending out hope in the night
> Like a faithful friend
> Reaching out a helping hand
> Bringing comfort, truth and light

From Fanad Head the road winds through farmland to Kindrum before looping around crests and dips across the northern tip of Mulroy Bay. Hereford and Limousin cattle pull mouthfuls free from a compressed bale of silage. At Leat Beg the road drops down to the Blaney Bridge, which spans Mulroy Bay, linking the Fanad Peninsula with Rosguill. A vast panorama of mountain, island, lake, rock, moor and bog bursts before me, encompassing the entire north-west highlands. For some peaceful horizon-scanning I pull over at a lay-by but my idyllic reverie is broken by a horn-blaring cavalcade of wedding-party cars gatecrashing the space. The bridal party is recording the day, using the backdrop of far-reaching views unfolding across the western arm of Mulroy, over to Sheephaven Bay and Horn Head, then southwards to the jagged skyline of the Derryveagh Mountains. The newly weds happily pose, at ease with the wonder of it all; it is not hard to see why photographers are enraptured with this location, known locally as Between the Waters.

I had not previously travelled this road and regard it is an example of how the Way, linked to the new bridge, has opened up little-known parts of the county. At 340 metres long, the bridge is the biggest in Donegal. Opened in 2009, it is named in honour of Harry Blaney, then a public representative for the area. Although the sun is on the decline it still has sufficient strength to produce reflections in the watery light. The result is a harmonious moodscape that has all the colour and tonality of a dramatic James Humbert Craig painting in its bare and raw winter glory; or a vista grand enough to adorn the cover of a proud bride and groom's wedding album.

After the unexpected winter sunshine a change of weather is on the way. The airwaves are filled with warnings of the west coast about to be hit by a cyclone called Storm Rachel. There had been talk some weeks earlier of a 'Weather bomb' but this did not materialise and I was sceptical of another major 'weather event'. Through crackly reception on the car radio, key phrases jump out: 'sub-zero temperatures ... mercury levels dropping to double-negative figures … Status Red severe weather warning for exposed coastal areas … considerable volumes of rain … stay indoors.' A few kilometres from Carrigart, an elderly man flags me down through heavy rain, waving a broken umbrella. I feel a historic empathy of identification with his hitchhiking plight.

'Where you headin', yungfella?' I warm immediately to him.

'Nowhere in particular, just cruising the Wild Atlantic Way. Looking into things.'

'You'll not get lost then.'

'Do you want a lift?'

'Just to Downings, or Drownings, as we call it. My daughter's makin' me dinner – that's wild enough for me but there's a storm brewin'.'

His face is blue from the wind. He proffers a wet hand. 'The name's Jack but they call me Jim or sometimes Jay-Jay. The wife died three years ago and I got cheesed off cookin' for myself. It's hard thumbin' these days.'

The reason he is hitching, he says, is because there is no longer a decent bus service since the closure of the Lough Swilly company. For more than 150 years 'the Swilly' operated a combination of train, bus and ferry routes throughout north Donegal.

'My father useta travel on the trains when they ran from Derry to Buncrana and Letterkenny. They were full of cattle, coal and passengers. The line to Burtonport was fifty miles but the train avoided towns and I remember him sayin' the Swilly stopped where nobody lived. During the war, when eggs, butter and milk were rationed, the women in Derry useta smuggle them across the border by stickin' them up their clothes. They weren't pregnant when they left in the mornin' but on the way back they said they were. Now you can't even catch a Swilly bus which is why I rely on lifts from strangers. Musta run outta money. Tough times.'

I drop him in Downings and look for accommodation. It is getting darker and stormier by the minute, road conditions are treacherous for night-time travelling and I am running out of options. The B&Bs are firmly shut for the winter but the lights in the bar of the Beach Hotel attract me. Although it is closed for guests, the owner looks me over and agrees to give me a room for the night. The wind rattles around the windows and doorways. She shows me to my room and brings an electric radiator for extra heat. 'We are used to it – it's a standard winter gale up here, but you'll need this to get you through the night,' she laughs.

In the bar, the television news reports that the National Co-ordination Group on Severe Weather has met in emergency session to discuss Storm Rachel. The advice is to avoid all unnecessary travel, and stay away from fallen wires and the coast. Snowfalls in some areas have caused serious disruption, with hundreds of schools closing early. Flights and ferry services have been cancelled and power has been cut to thousands of homes. The high seas have affected sailings to Tory Island and supplies and passengers are unable to travel. The King of Tory himself, Patsy Dan Rodgers, who had been on the mainland, was whisked back to the island by the helicopter coastguard.

The sombre weatherman warns that the storm will be at its most ferocious in the north-west, and in particular in Donegal, which will bear the brunt of it. Two men at the bar glance up at the screen. The apocalyptic warnings wash over them. A gravelly voiced one says, with seen-it-all-before resignation, 'It's the only time they ever mention us. You'd think 'twas a monsoon on the way.' The other, with a cold-engine cough, nods to me. 'Welcome to Donegal,' he splutters. 'Yo-yo weather. Wet day, dry day, stormy day, warm day – take your pick.'

My bedroom overlooks a caravan park that leads on to the darkness of Trabeg beach, watered by Sheephaven Bay. I open the window an inch, which is as wide as it allows, and a fierce, high-pitched whistle reverberates around the room. Hailstones spit against my face. Rachel is trying to get in and has turned violent. To escape her tongue-lashing, I retreat to the bed and settle down to read but am distracted by the net curtain swirling like a ghostly dancer. Rain flings itself against the window and joins forces with sleet. The churning sea is accompanied by all manner of booms and rumbles. Just as the wind reaches a banshee-like pitch, a power cut plunges my room into darkness. It is often said in Irish folklore that if you hear a banshee wailing there is good chance you might be dying, or already dead. Life returns when the lights come on again, then flash off and on several times as though a weary publican is declaring closing time. Bare trees in the caravan park are bent at arthritic angles and sway in the gusts. It is the first time I have experienced the true rage of Manannán, who has gender-transferred his anger to Rachel. All night long, I sleep and wake, toss and turn, while the moaning wind maintains its momentum, accompanied by regular clatters of rain and hail. Around 4 a.m. it reaches a shrieking climax.

By early morning, nature's onslaught relents although the storm is not entirely over. Power has been restored. I walk to the beach through the caravan park, sidestepping fallen branches. The tide is in and I am almost gusted off my feet. Downings is a scattering of hotels, pubs and summer holiday shops. The evidence left by rampaging Rachel is strewn around: roof tiles, guttering and debris ripped off buildings, upturned chairs and picnic tables, upended flower tubs, recycling bins tossed along the street, their contents strewn on the roadside, and signboards blown over. True to its nickname, the main street of 'Drownings' is flooded.

The road around Rosguill – a much smaller peninsula than either Inishowen or Fanad – rises, falls, twists and straightens along its circuit. Its map profile looks like an upraised thumb. This morning, apart from delivery vans, it is empty of traffic and hitchhikers. But it takes more than a storm to disturb the workaday rhythms of this part of the north-west – never mind those of a Wild Atlantic Wayfarer. The breadman told me that he was forced to re-route as the Harry Blaney Bridge, which I had crossed the day before, is closed to traffic because of the winds. Before the words 'Wild' and 'Way' were appended to it, Rosguill boasted one of the country's original 'Atlantic Drives'. A tourist sign shows a large-scale map from when the route was developed by the European Regional Development Fund.

Many years beforehand, in the mid-1960s, this area, comprising Carrigart, Downings and Rosapenna, was a holiday playground for my family. As an eight-year-old, I was taken on summer weekend excursions in my father's two-tone Riley Kestrel 1100 when my youthful imagination was fired by the exotic world conjured up by 'Atlantic Drive.' A signpost can set off a chain of rich childhood associations and this part of the north-west reaches back into my past. Beach walks in the rain, sandcastles, seaside games and picnics, running over mountainous dunes, holding shells to our ears to hear the murmurs of the ocean, HB choc ices, red lemonade, and high tea in a fusty hotel – unchanged since the early decades of the twentieth century – are indissolubly linked with Donegal. There was also the back-seat game that involved being the first to shout: 'I see the sea and the sea sees me,' and the happy refrain, 'I see the sea and the sea smells me.' It was a world of elderly gentlemen in tweeds, snoring on sofas in hotel lounges or dozing over the *Sunday Independent* on capacious wing-back Parker Knoll chairs. A fug of tobacco and cigarette smoke got in my clothes and up my nose. No one worried, since the term 'passive smoking' had not been invented.

As I navigate the peninsula's narrow roads and water pools, I snap out of my flashback with the blaze of bright white spume from the waves at Doagh Bay resembling a giant bubble bath. The sun lights up a rocky landscape and I feel an Atlantic electricity in the air. A mixed party of about forty ducks and gulls crests the waves, rising up in salvoes of white wings, while a solitary redshank trots across the small beach. The road downhill past the Singin' Pub brings me into Carrigart and on to Creeslough where a search for a caffeine injection proves fruitless. Rain becomes sleet and sleet turns to hail, darkening the atmosphere. At a bridge over the River Lackagh, a cannonade of marble-sized hailstones bounces off the tarmac, whitening the road

Donegal café cappuccino for the Way.

and reminding me of Gerard Manley Hopkins' description as 'heavengravel'. For ten minutes they hammer down with intensity. My dashboard helpfully flashes up: 'Low External Temperature -3.' I pull off the road until it passes as swirling storms sweep in over Doe Castle Strand.

All roads lead to Dunfanaghy, a humming nest of cafés, but which, along with nearby Portnablagh, contains a vast accumulation of holiday homes and chalets to the disfigurement of the landscape. Café society in Dunfanaghy revolves around a number of different options. In Muck 'n' Muffins, a former grain store refashioned as a craft shop and café, I order coffee syrup, a cappuccino laced with caramel. As part of her foam artistry, the waitress serves it with a large chocolate 'W'. I ask if this is in keeping with the Way or the wildness of the day, but she replies that it is purely unintentional since she has not heard much about the route. She explains the character of Bailies hand-roasted coffee beans and their specific flavour profile. Retro glamour is reflected in a picture on a wooden sign of a woman with a 1950s perm, which admonishes: 'Coffee: If you're not shaking, you need another cup.' Poetry on the walls, books on the dresser and framed prints of local scenes with close-ups of livestock bring an appreciated warmth.

At the next table four women discuss New Year's resolutions, a three-month running plan and how they propose to embrace *Operation Transformation* through their attendance at ashtanga and hatha yoga classes. They stare morosely at the waterfront. Walkactive, formerly power walking, is the new buzz term. One woman wants to transform the way she walks 'into a flowing movement of maximum efficiency'. In their world of healthy eating, kale is out this year and kelp is in. The tasty seaweed is high in iodine and is said to improve thyroid function. Hammering hailstones stop abruptly and birdlife returns to the pier. Two hooded crows with jet-black heads and grey backs forage amongst the seaweed, attempting forlornly to crack open shells. They are disturbed by the shrill trumpeting of plump and aggressive herring gulls who look as though they too could benefit from *Operation Transformation*.

Between showers I scuttle around Dunfanaghy in a 'walkactive' tour to see how it differs from 1991. I had stayed overnight on the Horn Head road at a B&B long since closed. Even out of season, it has a mildly cosmopolitan feel. Craft shops, art galleries, cocktail and wine bars, bistros, stylish restaurants, a wholefood and fine wine store, vie for business. A shop in the square sells 'Pre-loved' vintage furniture beside a white-van man offering 'Local potatoes grown on my own farm, Fresh dug every day'. The Daylight Wobblies are performing tonight in Patsy Dan's where a sign on the bar door warns, 'No Large Dogs Allowed.' I guess you could bring all the small ones you wanted.

From east to west, the fourth and final peninsula of north Donegal, Horn Head, is the smallest but arguably most dramatic of all. The Irish naturalist Robert Lloyd Praeger described it as 'the finest headland in Ireland'. Before embarking on it, I watch a hungry curlew in a sandy inlet just beyond Horn Head Bridge. It appears to have the whole place to itself. Its long bill and head probe deep into the sand. Two worms are hoovered up in swift gulps. On its large stilt-like legs it takes a few steps, burrows again, sometimes successful, other times not. Always alert, it glances up with one eye on me, a curious figure standing with binoculars on a grassy bank filled with white hail.

At the tip of Horn Head the wind carries the seabird calls and the roar of the Atlantic, which spreads around the headland with thick foamy waves known as Manannán's seahorses. The inland backdrop is dominated by the triangular peak of Errigal and the flat top of Muckish. It is bone-chillingly cold. The wind is getting fiercer. I struggle to close my car door; the whole vehicle is not so much buffeted as rocked and shaken on its Japanese suspension.

The four major north Donegal peninsulas have been box-ticked but I need now to make progress through the main towns south to Ardara, my destination for the evening. The coastal road from Falcarragh and Gortahork leads to Bloody Foreland, so named because the setting sun is said to enhance the natural red of the granite cliffs. The weather has calmed and from the *Cnoc Fola* – 'hill of blood' – viewing point, the rounded hump of Inishbofin is spotlit in the sunshine while behind lies the faint outline of two smaller islands, Inishdooey and Inishbeg.

A party of twenty Blackface sheep with turquoise markings proceeds in orderly single file uphill to gorge on nuts and grains. Bloody Foreland surprised me in 1991 with its heavily populated countryside and since then its ribbon development has continued apace. Old cottages sit cheek by jowl with large dormer bungalows, L-shaped holiday homes fronting on to the sea, some Snow-cemmed, others with stone cladding or pebble-dash, and tall well-slated farmhouses; you can have any colour as long as it is white, with pyramids of turf stacked for winter fuel. I later heard it cynically described as 'Bloody Blandland'. The one building missing, I was told, is the Church of Our Lady of the Boom Years.

A succession of small towns passes in a blur along a crinkle-cut coastline, shaped, influenced and tormented by the sea: Derrybeg, Bunbeg, Annagry, Crolly, Kincasslagh and Burtonport, where I stop briefly for old time's sake to see if it has entered the twenty-first century. Two cars wait for the ferry to Aranmore Island. If anything, the intervening years have not been kind. Sadly, the village seems to be still haunted by the sinking of the trawler *Evelyn Marie* with the loss of six men near Rathlin O'Birne island in 1975. A fortieth-anniversary event has just taken place.

Sixteen kilometres south in Dungloe, a Pat the Baker van parked at the roadside reminds me all those years ago of having been given one of my best-ever lifts. The driver covered more than fifty kilometres and went out of his way to help me. The best that can be said for the sludgy coffee in a café in the main street is that it is uneventful.

'It is *scaringly* quiet with us,' says the waitress when I ask about business. 'Tourists come to Donegal town, screech to a halt, turn around and drive south again. Few of them ever venture any farther north, but they don't know what they're missing. We have a new Daniel O'Donnell centre here and although I haven't been in it myself, 'tis very popular. Tourism has changed dramatically, many businesses simply can't cope with the commercial rates, property taxes, water charges and all the other bills, which is why we are seeing the protests.'

She raises her ultramarine eyes heavenwards. 'Just look at all the hotels that are shutting. Five major ones in this part of the county have closed in the past year, so there's not much optimism. The fishing is wiped out, the young ones have all emigrated and those who have stayed aren't coming out to spend money. We need more outdoor attractions and amenities as people don't just want to sit in a pub all day. Most accept the weather is the way it is. Donegal is a bit like a woman – she has many different personalities and you have to love her in all her moods.'

Someone who loves Donegal in all her moods is the county's singing son Daniel O'Donnell. The sharp-suited and clean-cut grinning figure looks down from the gable wall of the former National Irish Bank, now the eponymously named visitor centre that showcases his career. Originally from Kincasslagh, O'Donnell has become a poster boy for an Ireland long vanished and is as big a hit with North American audiences as he is in Ireland. The *Donegal Democrat* once claimed 'Daniel O'Donnell is to Donegal what Tourism Ireland is to the whole country.' At the doorway of a pub a multi-chinned smoker stamps his feet, shaking the cold off his bones. He smirks at me and looks up at the picture. 'One a' these years they'll be carving his face on the side of Errigal.'

Street lights flicker on as I leave Dungloe and head south for the Gweebarra Bridge that will take me through Portnoo, Narin and into Ardara. Distant mountains are visible in the dusky outline and birds sit in treetops in jostling silhouettes. After an hour's drive through velvet darkness, the orange glow of Ardara's lights beckons. Flurries of snow lend the place an evening chill. A small queue forms at Watcha McCollum's hot-food van.

On the edge of town, John Yates is the gregarious owner of Woodhill, a history-soaked coastal manor house dating back in parts to the seventeenth century. It was formerly the home of the Nesbitts, local landlords and Ireland's last commercial whaling family of the nineteenth century. John has opened a room in converted stables for me for the night.

'Woodhill is an old Plantation house, so we are sitting on history,' he tells me. 'We cherish the past and I enjoy restoring the property. The coach house had trees growing through it. We also kept the original stone walls, and the old walled garden is popular with our guests. Because of the whaling connection, at one stage there would have been a whalebone arboretum and I once found a piece of whalebone rib.'

John runs what must be the ideal guesthouse. It comes complete, not just with 400 years of history but with its own funky lounge bar. Beside an ash-log fire his son dispenses drinks from a small semicircular theatrical-style wooden bar with a copper top. Although supportive of the Way, John has some criticisms. 'I feel that the strict policy of Irish-only signs in the Gaeltacht areas is not working. I am all for the signs but it is shooting yourself in the foot to have them only in Irish as people get lost. If you are a retired American driving the roads and it's getting late, then it is stressful and you don't like getting lost. They get very nervous about our narrow roads and lose confidence. That is the feedback that I get from many customers. They are fascinated with the names and with how to pronounce them but they should be in dual language so they need to rethink the signage. The linchpin is firstly getting people into the country and then we have to get more people here because all we are doing with the Way is channelling people into one route. But it was a clever initiative from Leo Varadkar who was then Minister of Tourism and had a practical approach to things.'

I had seen guided walking tours of this part of south Donegal advertised at Woodhill House. One tour, led by Peter Alexander, follows in the footsteps of Dylan Thomas. The poet spent two months in the summer of 1935 living in an isolated cottage at Glen Lough, north of Glencolmcille. As a devotee of Thomas, I join Peter for a Sunday morning walk across swathes of ochre bogland and purple hills. We start from a potholed road marked on the map as *Sli Cholmcille* beside Lougheraherk. Eighty years on from the poet's visit, the tours focus on the forgotten Thomas connection to Donegal. A knowledgeable and amiable guide, Peter has researched the story of his sojourn here.

Under a metallic wintry sky and surrounded by staring sheep we head uphill. Scottish Blackface, Swaledale and Galway and Mayo 'Westies' speckle the slopes. Our route takes us past placid lakes before we join the Old Glen Lough road, a rough path of granite stones and gleaming white quartzite. Talking as we walk, Peter explains the background to Thomas' arrival in the area at the age of twenty-one. His first slim volume, *18 Poems*, published in 1934, had been critically well received.

'Thomas had been drinking heavily in London and developed a serious skin rash. An Irish doctor in Harley Street advised him that he needed a holiday. He suggested that he take a long break in Donegal and keep off alcohol. The opportunity arose to stay in a cottage, a former donkey shed that had been converted in 1927 by the American artist Rockwell Kent, who loved wilderness.'

We pick and slip our way across peaty ground, skirting several turquoise-coloured circular boglets. 'You don't want to fall down those as they are very deep,' Peter cautions. 'Don't forget, Thomas made his way around them in the dark. Years ago Glen Lough was renowned for its old caves with poitín stills, so it was the last place anyone would have come to.'

After an hour's trudge, we reach the top of a hill of springy grass and look down on the wide, tranquil valley of Glen Lough. The grey remains of two buildings are just visible but, apart from a meandering river, there is little sign of life. The air is utterly still and clear. Peter points out a sea stack called 'Edge of the World', which would have appealed to the young poet since there was a certain finality about this destination. As we make our way over to the cottage, he explains that on Thomas' walks he saw puffins, gannets and seals at the Rossaun cliffs. We drop down to the stone-walled remains, last occupied in 1967. Since then the roof has caved in and the surviving walls are covered in fence wire and strangled weeds. A pink mug, rusted kettle, brown beer bottle and a jam jar sit on the shelves of a wooden dresser. A stopped clock stands at 3.33. On all sides we are hemmed in by mountains: Port Hill, Glen Lough Mountain, Straboy and beyond it Slievetooey, comprising four summits. A mix of mountains, cliffs, sea and sky, it is the idyllic sequestered writerly retreat.

'This is an extremely remote and harsh place, ideal for escapism. But it was a very basic cottage with no electricity and no means of cooking. Luckily for Thomas, a farmer, Dan Ward, and his wife Rose who owned it and lived in the house nearby, made him his meals. Rose used to crack his eggs for him, the same as his mother had done as he had been mollycoddled as a child.'

Thomas spent two months at Glen Lough and at the start of his stay in July was accompanied by his friend and fellow poet Geoffrey Grigson. Most of the time it rained and they built turf fires. Grigson taught him to fish and in Lough Anaffrin Thomas caught small trout which he later ate, but mostly he lived on a diet of potatoes, oatmeal and buttermilk. The Glen Lough River drains Anaffrin, a sizeable lake where in penal times Mass was recited. Both men roamed the hills and walked to the cliffs overlooking the pounding ocean. Grigson sang 'The Ram of Derbyshire' to the birds, and on one occasion they frightened themselves when they shouted to the mountains 'We are the dead', and waited for the echoes to repeat 'We are the dead ... are the dead ... the dead', the words reverberating around the valley back to them. After two weeks Grigson returned to London but Thomas stayed on and grew a beard.

'It was an atmospheric place with sea mists and constant rain. There were long hours and days of solitude and Thomas gradually became less enchanted with it and self-absorbed. He was quoted in a letter as saying, "I'm lonely as Christ sometimes". To pass the days, he built a makeshift bridge of stepping stones over the river. Even though he was not supposed to be drinking, he got stuck into the poitín and once a week walked the fifteen kilometres to the nearest porter bar, O'Donnell's in Meenaneary. Don't forget this was a man who once said he would "drink anything that goes down my throat", and of course before he died he famously quipped "I've had eighteen straight whiskies. I think that's a record."'

Thomas' stay here was not entirely unproductive. Working in the cottage by candlelight, he managed to write six poems and a vampire story. This resulted in the long, surrealistic sequence of sonnets 'Altarwise by owl-light', as well as two of his most acclaimed poems: 'And death shall have no dominion', and 'I, in my intricate image'. They were published in his second book, *Twenty-five Poems,* in September 1936.

Although Thomas interacted with the mountains, he appears to have found the moorland dispiriting. In a letter to a friend he outlined how he was failing to engage on a deep level with the place: 'I find I can't see a landscape; scenery is just scenery to me ... in this wild unlettered and unfrenchlettered country, a poor and dirty land where the pigs rot and scrabble in the parlours.'

The locals, he said, were 'lazy and vocal, superstitious or mad, whining or boring.' Thomas fell out with many of them, including the postman. He had ordered *The Times* and had to have it delivered – a distance of eight kilometres each day for the postman. After two months he had had enough and at the end of August packed up his belongings, leaving quickly on the bus for Belfast. The exact reasons for his sudden departure are not known but he got into a brawl in Ardara and left penniless. He had been getting his tobacco for his cigarettes on tick and left an unpaid debt to the farmer, which Grigson later paid.

Peter and I return to Ardara and Nancy's Bar, a place I had last visited in 1991. It was then in the seventh generation of the same family and has now moved to the eighth. Little has changed apart from the addition of a small dining room and an extension at the back, as well as a smoking area. They also now sell their own farmyard cider, unfiltered and naturally unfermented, but the essential character of the place remains unchanged. Scores of Toby jugs still hang from the ceiling, along with historical memorabilia, and the fire glows as brightly as ever.

The remoteness had got under Dylan Thomas' skin. After he returned to London, he wrote that he had been too far from Ardara, 'a village you can't be too far from'. By midnight the moonless town has gone to bed and, as Thomas himself might have put it with a lyrical swagger, 'You can hear the houses sleeping in the slow, black streets of the town.'

2
The plain of hospitality

LYING AT THE EXTREME south-west of the county, almost falling off the edge of the map, Teelin is a history-soaked part of the Donegal Gaeltacht. It was one of the first settlements to appear on the map of Ireland. A walk around the pier stirs up the past. Built between 1881 and 1883 at a cost of £3,000, by the 1890s it was the leading cod-fishing port, outranking neighbouring Killybegs in terms of volumes of landings. The walled remains of a coastguard station destroyed in the War of Independence in 1922 overlook the small harbour where a pair of ducks paddle silently.

Several boats are tied up for the winter and the pier is deserted. Rust-eaten lobster cages sit beside a wall, while *The Nuala Star* waits for its first customers of the year to cruise the cliffs. *The Golden Fleece*, *Caoimhe Star* and *Mirror of Justice* are locked and docked. A square memorial plaque commemorates the fact that fifth-century monks left from here to sail to Iceland. A kneeling brown-cowled figure clasps his hands in prayer alongside a sailing boat. The memorial is on a large stone pillar in the middle of the remains of what was once a church and is now part of a factory. The Ordnance Survey map marks a church but no traces of it survive today. In its place stands a shed.

Slieve League, 'the mountain of the flagstones', with its towering cliffs, dominates the high ground and is coated in frost. A hail shower, like a mini-tornado, rattles down the valley through Shanbally and Lergadaghtan, bearing down on Teelin Bay before sweeping across to Kilbeg and Tawny on the other side over the small hill of Derrylahan. My 100-year-old Ward

Lock & Co. *Illustrated Guide to Donegal* notes that this area was once known as the 'Lair of the Whirlwinds'.

It is a precipitous drive up to Carrigan Head for the car park at Cunniltragh. The road clings to the cliff edge in places and is not for the faint-hearted. When I reach the top, it is surprisingly calm and sunny. A newly tarmacked path leads to a fenced-off viewing platform and information signboards on the cultural and social history of the area. Cliffs skirted with scree rise sheer. A giant view opens out across the bay where rain-laden clouds gather over the hills of Sligo and Mayo.

The combination of tangy sea and mountain air has given me an appetite. The Slieve League Cultural Centre is run by Paddy Clarke who serves the best Illy coffee this side of Teelin, if not all of Donegal. It was named after Ernesto Illy, an Italian coffee merchant who helped introduce espresso to the world by using nine different types of Arabica beans. Illy believed that espresso 'painted the tongue' and he regarded milk and sugar as contaminants. Paddy offers me a regular coffee, and despite the purists, I add a squirt of Donegal milk. He says the establishing of the Way has not just spread the love but has brought a more even spread of tourists.

'There is no doubt that it has democratised the west since everywhere is now being promoted equally by Fáilte Ireland. It's a fair way of doing it and at least we are getting our share. It has helped us with tour coaches and has coincided with a worldwide upsurge in tourism.'

I eat apple sultana pancakes with a maple-syrup butter followed by home-baked carrot cake washed down with several cups of Illy. That evening I make for the Rusty bar in Teelin where ten musicians and a couple of singers gather under a large Dunville Whiskey mirror in a crowded room. Fast, rippling reels and double jigs flow furiously but effortlessly from fiddlers, guitarists, accordionists and a banjo player. 'The Bunglass Lass and Mrs McGinley's' is followed by 'The Cock's Tail', 'The Five Mile Chase' and 'George White's Fancy', while 'The Fintown Girl's

Killybegs Harbour, County Donegal, in winter.

Lament' brings out the *ssshh* police. Several more reels, 'Drowsy Maggie' and 'The Black Fanad Mare', enliven the atmosphere and two hornpipes, 'The Soldier's Joy' and 'The Drunken Sailor', jump-start foot- and finger-tapping. Without warning, a thickly lipsticked woman with overpowering perfume and a dramatic décolletage, who had been sitting pensively beside me, erupts full-voicedly into 'The Rambling Boys of Pleasure'. She silences the bar and earns a sustained round of applause.

My route through Carrick and Kilcar feels like crossing out of another age. These small country towns are in an area that does not seem to have changed in a hundred years. Sheep, scattered like sweet wrappers across the fields, huddle together for warmth. A man in a supermarket in Kilcar tells me there was uproar at the start when their coastal stretch of road through Kilbeg and Ballyboy was left out of the Way. He leans over the counter, speaking in a confidential tone: 'We had several meetings but there was nothing we could do about it – we were powerless. It has brought in more people and was badly needed, but why didn't they do it twenty-five years ago? This place was on its last legs, although things seem to be looking up but you have to whisper that quietly.'

The road twists around Donegal Bay to Killybegs where the smell of fish is blowing in strong. I check into the historic Bay View Hotel, recently reopened after a three-year closure. Previous guests included Michael Collins and Éamon de Valera. Killybegs markets itself as Ireland's premier port; fishing is still the lifeblood of the local economy. My first stop is the no-pretence Melly's café, which serves fish and which I had last visited a quarter of a century ago. The café opened long before that in the frugal 1950s, and I form the impression that very little has changed since then. From other tables I hear conversations about the weather, the state of the fishing, marine diesel engines and football. The café is run by Michael Melly, who says the business has endured because of the consistently high quality of what they offer. Haddock, plaice, hake, calamari and cod are all on the menu which nowadays also includes kebabs, burgers, panini, chicken curry and salads. Sheltered at the harbour, twenty boats are stuck in port because of the bad weather. A hullabaloo of gulls comes from the rooftops. The lights have come on and Killybegs-by-night bears all the resemblance of a floating, neon mini-city.

Sunday morning, 1 February, and St Brigid has delivered snow for her feast day. Warily, Mass-goers make their way up Chapel Brae to answer the call to prayer at St Mary of the Visitation Church. Frost coats the footpath. Arm-in-arm, a young man oxter-cogs an elderly woman uphill. At the harbour a man flings slices of white bread into the water for gulls to squabble over. Two seals surface out of nowhere, quickly slinking away in tandem. Skim ice has formed on top of puddles but there is little movement.

Allusions to two classical gods, Poseidon and Neptune, are represented in the boating nomenclature – something of which Manannán would surely have approved. I had read that he is usually portrayed as a handsome and noble warrior, evoking these gods. And from the towering image of his statue it is clear this is how he has been interpreted. *Neptune*, a large navy-blue and white pelagic trawler, is tied up side by side with another similar-sized and identically coloured trawler, *Áine*. A man named Pat Gallagher, who works in a fish factory, tells me that they are partner vessels and put to sea together. This connection seems entirely apt given that Manannán – known as the Neptune of the Irish seas – had a relationship with Áine who, in Irish mythological circles, was the sun goddess and became a fairy patroness of love. Various texts offer different versions but some suggest that Manannán is either the father or husband of Áine.

Pat says the two boats will be heading out soon to fish for blue whiting, herring, mackerel and horse mackerel destined for markets all over the world, including Asia and Africa. A crew member who has just arrived shouts over to him that they have been told there is good fish 'just six hours away' and they intend to go out later in the day. 'St Catherine's' is stitched on to Pat's black bobble hat and black fleece. Since the fifteenth century, St Catherine of Alexandria, the patron saint of seafarers, has had strong links to Killybegs, and a church, graveyard and holy well are still used in her name. Pat does not appear to be in any hurry and is biding his time until the bookies open. I explain the purpose of my visit. From his pocket he produces an iPhone with a Marine Traffic app and shows me how he monitors the positions of the trawlers. 'You couldn't have done that back in 1991 and the boats would have been much smaller then,' he says. 'You can see where the movements are and track who is going where at any given time, so it's a very useful tool. A transmitter on some boats also allows fishery regulators to monitor their location – some fishermen compare it to tagging a criminal.'

Contrary to what people might think, Pat says, there are probably as many, if not more, fish factories today than twenty-five years ago. The port has moved with the times, opening a new harbour centre in 2004. He talks me through the buildings on the other side of the water and points out the new €50 million sheltered deep-water harbour which is also being used to target offshore oil and gas. There is an impressive assortment of stores, sheds and offices in the distance related to the industry: fish-processing factories, boatbuilding and engineering works, marine joinery, plant hire, maintenance and repair yards, cargo and freezer storage, laboratories, shipping offices and agents, stevedoring and cranage, ship chandlery, such as net manu-facturing and fishing gear, a training school, and even a museum of fishing history where for €1 you can skipper your own boat using an audio-visual simulator.

'Last week a cargo ship from China with a crew of twenty-seven docked in the new pier. It was one of the biggest commercial vessels we've ever seen here – it was as long as two football pitches. I heard them saying it was 53,501 tonne. It was carrying wind turbines and definitely boosted confidence in the harbour. It could be a catalyst for others. We also get cruise liners – up to ten calling into the port every year, which is good for the businesses.'

The sun has come out, producing warmth to melt the snow. The fishing boats, the town and Crownarad Mountain covered with a fresh layer of frost create a photogenic scene. One of the biggest changes, Pat believes, is in how the fish are sold. Years ago it was done by auction to the highest bidder. Now the transactions are all online.

'Fish processing brings added value and is now mechanised so it is not as labour intensive but there's still a need for manual labour and there are as many factories now as in the early nineties, just employing fewer people. There's also talk of a bio-marine plant opening soon near the new pier. But the main difference has been in the introduction of bloody awful EU quotas which has resulted in Ireland losing control over its rich territorial waters. The general view is that Irish fishermen were sacrificed for Irish farmers. What the EU gave to farmers, it took away from fishermen and all this has had a big effect on the number of days that fishermen can put to sea. In the 1990s fishermen could catch whatever they wanted; it was called open fishing and led to serious overfishing. But now some trawlers may go out for only between fifty and sixty days a year, or even less, so their income is halved which is why the men take on other jobs. A few of these vessels are just scraping a living and one or two are in the hands of the Receiver. Only twenty per cent of Irish fish lands in Ireland; the rest goes abroad. At different periods throughout the year there'll be Spanish, Portuguese and Norwegian trawlers all fishing off this coast. On the other hand, some of the local boats are doing well and there is still good money to be made at sea. Despite the doom and gloom, Killybegs is surviving and I would say actually thriving. The Atlantic is still a valuable resource for us.'

The main road is clear of slush while the snow is confined to localised pockets around Dunkineely and Mountcharles. Sheep scrape their hooves through thick white frost which persists in places where it is shielded from the dim sunlight. On the car radio, Ocean Sound is playing Nathan Carter and John Farrelly's song 'The Auctioneer'. The presenter announces that bingo, whist drives and a sponsored charity wax night scheduled for the evening have been cancelled owing to the adverse weather. Near Donegal town, the countryside is green, with not a trace of snow, ice or frost.

Ballyshannon's cafés offer respite for my hunger pangs. Two of the dozen tables in Kate's Kitchen are occupied by six burly men in yellow hi-viz jackets. They are halfway through a selection from the burger menu and are giving their food the total attention it deserves, with occasional breaks to discuss rally cars. Ballyshannon – marketing itself as Ireland's oldest town – likes to promote its past which, in Kate's, leaps from the walls.

Black-and-white 1920s photographs show streets crowded with horses and carts, while thirty years later they have been replaced by cars. My morning cappuccino, a large mugful of the Italian Lavazza blend, comes with a smile and is decorated with a large letter M. Could it be for Manannán, I ask the waitress, or perhaps I am looking at it upside down. She replies, 'Manna? Is that from heaven? We could do with some of that right now. Sure maybe I'll clock the big one on the lotto one of these days.'

Many fanciful theories surround Manannán. According to legend he was a noted shape-shifter with the ability to change appearance at will. Apart from his many guises, he also moved through time and place, and was blessed with inexhaustible energy. He was associated with significant magical powers, especially rebirth. In one reference to him, he is said to have enjoyed a feast at Ballyshannon in the sixteenth century. The host at the party was the historical Black Hugh O'Donnell, who died in 1537. In memory of this, I order the Big Kate double decker with bacon, Thousand Island dressing and gherkin with a side salad. A couple of newspaper headlines catch my eye: 'Snowfall expected as winter sets in'; and a homophone from the *Donegal Post*: 'Arctic weather back – time to baton down the hatches again.'

A young couple with a baby row over cigarettes. Two sisters check Facebook, one gulps down her coffee and sermonises about her husband. Unannounced, a man at the window table breaks into song – 'I wish I was young again' – to applause from the diners. Not every morning is brightened up with a singing café, producing the theatre of the unexpected. 'Welcome to Ballyshanny,' he smiles, as I tuck into my feast.

A couple of doors up, Dicey Reilly's bar is a place where the past lives on in the form of wall cabinets filled with carefully curated clutter. Tins of grate polish and Old Holborn Blended Virginia tobacco share shelf space with bottles of Sweetheart Stout, Old Imperial Whiskey from Cork, and Ginger Lozenges. An Erne bus timetable from 1941 sits alongside Bundoran holiday brochures from the 1950s, a Kodak Instamatic camera, and an egg timer. The men's toilet door sign says 'Twilet Zone'. Behind the bar a sign: 'Age is not important unless you are a whiskey.' The owner, Brendan O'Reilly, runs a purpose-built brewery. He talks about the surge of interest in craft beers, explaining the background and setting the scene in the early 1990s.

'Back then you had a choice of wine, which was Liebfraumilch Blue Nun or Black Tower, or, if you were lucky, perhaps Mateus Rosé. But Irish people were travelling widely and they experienced new wines, which led to a boom in this country in the mid-1990s. This morphed into foreign beers. German wheat beers became popular in Ireland as many people had gone to work there and realised there was a market at home. We also had a cherry beer from Belgium, called Boon Kriek, which everyone liked.'

Brendan attended Sunderland University, then worked in England, when he began to drink real ale, later taking a course on ales in Dublin.

'Donegal wasn't ready for a microbrewery then but several had opened elsewhere. I sourced beer for the off-licence, started some home-brewing and decided to set up a microbrewery here in 2006.'

Six years later the Donegal Brewing Company was up and running. With no shortage of enthusiasm and ambition, he renovated the former coach house, which dates to 1856 and converted it to a brewery. He produces a bottle of their most talked-about product, labelled 'Donegal Blonde: A Delight to Spend Time With.'

'The Tuesday before Christmas 2012 we served our first Donegal Blonde, which was an immediate hit. It was a great entry-level drink with many things in its favour. Because of the hop profile, it is not bursting with flavour but is at the low end of the spectrum and so it was instantly popular. We wanted a beer that could appeal to all people and the reaction was amazing. Within two months we got it into Superquinn. Blonde women starting drinking it, asking why didn't we produce T-shirts or mugs. The branding is simple and demand has outstripped supply.'

His next craft beer was Donegal Atlantic Amber Ale. He places a bottle of it on the counter and pours a glass for me. It produces a frothy head with 'scrubbing bubbles' from the carbonation and the ruby hue of Smithwicks, my normal drink of choice. The cereal grain is barley, hops, yeast and malt. The distinctive taste brings out the malt character, a refreshing change. We discuss aroma, flavour, mouth-feel and aftertaste. The hops of my Atlantic Amber have a fruity flavour. Clearly, Brendan loves his job, as well as life in Ballyshannon, a place that the nineteenth-century poet William Allingham called 'a kindly spot, a friendly town'.

'I wouldn't like to live anywhere else,' he declares. 'We are never going to be a major hub as there are no big employers here. It is a historic town and its last golden era was in the late 1940s when the place swayed in a haze of affluence after the setting up of the hydroelectric scheme in 1946. But we have all the facilities we need as we're close to schools, beaches, shops and much more. We are recovering from the recession and getting back on our feet again, so there is a lot of optimism around. There are now sixty-two microbreweries all over Ireland. The Wild Atlantic Way is going to be good for us and we already hold a Wild Atlantic craft beer festival in August. Then, of course, there is our home-town boy Rory Gallagher, who has his very own festival in June.'

In the centre of town, cast in bronze, the Gallagher statue is the cynosure for many. With his long, flowing hair, classic pose and fingers plucking the guitar strings, he stands on a plinth inscribed with 'Follow Me'. The sculpture was made by David Annand in 2010. Underneath are the words: 'I want to plant a star in the sky / One you find at the end of the night.'

Candlemas Day signifies the halfway point between the winter solstice and the spring equinox, or the end of the 'solar winter', the three months with the lowest daily amounts of energy from sunlight. The date, 2 February, marks Imbolc, the Gaelic festival heralding the birth of spring and which Christians transformed into Candlemas. Sadly, spring seems a long way off. From the bedroom window of the second floor of the Holyrood Hotel in Bundoran, where I arrived late the night before, a grey murkiness greets me with a mess of snarling, unruly waves breaking in all directions. The hotel is strategically placed to enjoy sea views and to hear the gulls calling the town awake. The signs for what the rest of winter will bring, summed up in a short rhyme, are ominous:

> If Candlemas Day be fair and bright
> Winter will have another flight
> If on Candlemas Day it be shower and rain
> Winter is gone and will not come again.

Bundoran hunkers down between the Dartry Mountains on one side and the Atlantic on the other. To the west, the plateau of Arroo looms over it with a dusting of frost while, on the other side, ocean winds whip in off the volatile sea over the bridge and rush up the main street. It marks the final leg of my journey along the Donegal coastline. For generations the resort has been a favourite haunt of holidaymakers from both sides of the border. The tourist board ambitiously labels Bundoran 'Ireland's Capital of Fun', and has rechristened it 'Fundoran'. The place has worked hard to sell its big international draw: the quality of its formidable waves said to be the optimal size for the best surfing. In recent years they have attracted 'water warriors' from Hawaii, South Africa, Brazil, Australia and Germany. The other main draw is Waterworld, which opened in 1991.

Twenty-five years ago the resort was not on the itinerary of overseas tourists. In the eyes of many, it was a place to be hurried through on the way north. It sells itself nowadays as a major activity centre with 21st-century adventure sports. These include cliff jumping, stand-up paddle-boarding, surf and river kayaking, high-rope climbing (complete with a 'Leap of Faith'), go-karting and blo-karting. Along the promenade I watch foam build up on waves. The briny wind peels off snowball-sized suds, which skitter across the beach. Two women in a Nissan Micra stare out at the waves the way a cat stares at birds. The sky darkens and thunderclouds appear. Without warning, a clattering of fifty carrion crows and rooks lifts off into the high wind in a noisy, whirling Hitchcockian scene. With the arrival of hailstones, they settle on a patch of grass before dispersing to pillage black bags piled beside a brace of recycling bins. A herring gull and hooded crow indulge in a wobbly *pas de deux*, one hovering above the other, wings aflicker, trying to work out the hierarchy of scavenging.

The lights glowing in Waves café are a haven from the biting wind and an escape from the dreary main street. The café is a shrine to the world of surfing. Framed and mounted photographs of dramatic waves line the walls, including the renowned local one, 'The Peak'. Blue and green scatter cushions on black leather settees carry the words Surf / Eat / Sleep. A wooden numbered sign, shaped like a small surfboard, sits on each table, while coloured boards dangle from the ceiling and on the walls. Given all this, it is not hard to guess that the wave logo is traced as a foam-art pattern on the cinnamon of my Bewley's cappuccino. The waitress is not sure if the design represents a wave or if it is a fern that has turned out wrong. 'Whatever,' she shrugs.

As a self-appointed 'inspector' of linguistics and pronunciation, in that single word, I detect a non-native accent and enquire where she is from. 'Oregon,' she replies. 'Eastern Oregon. A place called Gateway that you will have never heard of. There's not even a store, it's so small. The post office closed in 1956. Madras is the nearest town and Bend the biggest city.'

I admit I have never heard of, nor visited, Gateway, but explain that I have been to Portland where I spent a day in Powell's bookstore, which brings a flicker of recognition. I ask how she likes Ireland.

'It's small. You could fit Ireland three times into Oregon.' My next trump card astonishes her, an amazing fact of which she is not aware. 'Did you know that the coastline of Oregon is just

650 kilometres which is roughly equivalent to less than *half* the coastline of Donegal?', which elicits the reply, 'Awesome.'

Our talk turns to the Way. 'It's just a wiggle on a line on a signpost and it's a bit ridiculous. I can't understand why they spent a lot of money doing that. It's simply pointing people to waves but we already know where they are.'

Next door, in Surf World, Patrick Timoney is monitoring those self-same waves and the weather's every nuance. He has written on Facebook that they are 'messy'. He muses, 'It's a stay-at-home day with a game of snakes and ladders.' The shop has been in business for twenty-six years, so on my previous visit the sport was about to take off, although locals had been surfing for years before that. I tell him how I had got a lift with two young surfers from South Africa who brought me a long distance around the coast in their van.

'These days,' he says, 'people of all ages are surfing. I had an eighty-four-year-old woman in last week for a surf lesson. She was very healthy and enjoyed it. It keeps people fit. It is a core workout for most people, using every muscle: legs, arms and back. But there is more to it than just the fitness side: there is a scenic side to it, then the thrill of riding the waves and the search for the perfect wave, as well as the social aspect.'

Participation comes at a price. Surfboards range from €320 to over €1,000 for high-performance surfers. Patrick points out the vast choice available in a back room, which includes short boards, long boards, soft boards, big boy flyers, skim boards, skate boards and hybrids. Clothing and accessories occupy a large room. Everything from thermal rash vests and Sticky Feet wax to Muc-off foam spray and wax combs is for sale.

'You have flexible wetsuits these days, which keep you much warmer than years ago. The boards are fibreglass or epoxy, which take more abuse and are stronger. The local surfing community is not just Irish but French, Spanish and South African along with a mix of New Zealanders and Americans. We get the more committed surfers coming here, forming their own community, looking for critical waves. The hard-core ones come from September to March.

'Bundoran is a great community but we need more facilities, such as shower blocks. If you go to European countries you will find that they have all the necessary facilities. There are initiatives here, such as Surfers Against Sewage and beach clean-ups. But the vibe in the water is important. In some places there can be a lot of aggro in the sea. There is a clear wave etiquette and here people show good manners, which is very welcoming – they wait their turn. In winter we are just hammered by the wind and rain, but the surfing generates income.'

With the wind behind me, I walk along the straggle of Single Street to the West End with a cluster of shops, bars, cafés and hotels. Amusement arcades, Star bingo hall, beauty salons, hairdressers, bookmakers, charity shops, a discount centre, ten-pin bowling and a cinema complete the picture. Many businesses are shuttered since they open only for the summer but clearly Bundoran affords as much entertainment as you can pack into it in high season. The Grand Central Hotel is derelict, the boarded-up Ulster Tourist House has not kept guests for many a year, and out on a limb on the Sea Road, the Great Northern Hotel stands regal but lifeless. As a resort it has remained unashamedly tacky. Even off-season, sticks of green, white and gold Bundoran rock – a touchstone of seaside authenticity – can be bought in the long-established American House: 'Lotto Agents, Souvenirs, Ices and Fruit.' The rock sits alongside smiling photographs of a waving Pope Francis, his greeting reshaped from the thumbs-up sign he gave to his audience shortly after his election and something which caused consternation among Vatican officials.

A place cannot be judged solely by the facades of its shops or its sticks of rock. Like any small town, the people who live in it are what make it tick. To try to get a sense of community and find out what it is like living by the sea in this part of Donegal, I call in on the women of the Afternoon Club. They meet every Thursday at 2 p.m. in the parish pastoral centre. A baker's dozen of women, kitted out in warm coats and hats, sit around in a semicircle led by the indefatigable Breege Connor. They welcome me into their friendly bosom; the Magh Ene parish, of which Bundoran is a part, means 'Plain of Hospitality'. Afternoon Clubs have been running for more than thirty years and bring together retired people to meet in companionship. Their activities include outings to plays and concerts. Guest speakers, storytellers and singers are invited to entertain them. During their meetings they practise yoga.

'Some people told me that yoga was sinful,' Breege says. 'But we are not chanters – that's far too advanced for us. The exercises are good for relaxing the muscles and helping the bones. Yoga can strengthen your spine and it stretches calves and thighs. Active retirement is our aim and we are affiliated to the all-Ireland group. We have to look after ourselves.'

Apart from yoga, the women enjoy activities such as the quickstep, waltzes and line dancing. They talk about Bundoran as a place to visit as well as somewhere to live.

'People come here for different reasons,' Breege says. 'Some like the walks or the swimming, while others enjoy the amusements, and there's never a day that you don't see strangers. The beaches are excellent. It may not be Bondi, in fact we call it Bundi Beach, and there's a Christmas-morning dip, although our swimming days are over.'

The general agreement about the biggest change in the past quarter century is that there are fewer B&Bs, cafés and shops. And today's caravans all come with satellite dishes. Breege is philosophical about the place where she has settled. 'Bundoran is simply Bundoran and will always be the way it is. Rates are high so shops are closed. The main street is one long mile and a bit. There is no real centrepiece so it's hard to see what you could do to develop it any more as it lacks a core.'

For many of the women, the sea is a therapy. Some live here out of choice, rather than necessity. Many retired from inland counties to be near the water. In 2014, they survived no fewer than thirteen storms. For Breege – born and bred in

Glencolmcille – the sea is familiar and she is well acquainted with its moods.

'It can be pretty nasty in the winter with severe storms and there are times when I'm afraid of being blown off my feet. But I find it difficult to live away from the sea and I feel secure in my home from where I can look out at the waves and enjoy the spectacle. It's healthy, you don't feel claustrophobic and there are refreshing walks too, which help your mood. Some years ago a GP with a practice in Bundoran used to say that no doctor here would ever become a millionaire as it's too healthy to live here.'

Another woman disputes this and quips that when she was at the clinic that morning it was packed. They all feel that one of the strengths of Bundoran is its clear, unpolluted air, which is reinvigorating.

'There is no industry, apart from a bit of fishing,' says one woman. 'We have no pollution or industrial smoke. We are in a valley between the mountains and the sea. Tourism was always the biggest employer.'

Other Afternoon Clubbers feel that since the bypass opened four years ago, Bundoran has been left behind. Tourists rush through, they agree, to the Slieve League cliffs or Glenveagh National Park. Towards the end of the meeting, pots of steaming tea are produced, along with tray bakes and cake. Large mugs with red dots are passed around.

'Eat up,' commands Breege, 'You're in your granny's.'

Over thickly buttered fruitcake, shortbread and chocolate biscuits we discuss age and accents. 'Donegal people talk in a fast, high-pitched and excitable way,' says Breege. 'I could identify most areas where people are from when they start to talk. Mind you, we're influenced by the seagulls in Bundoran and I do screech a lot. When I am not wearing my hearing aids I can be quite gully.'

I had read that the term 'old' is no longer acceptable, so suggest they describe themselves as 'middle youth' or 'recycled teenagers'. The new term for anyone over eighty-five is 'wisdom warrior', which produces a ripple of laughter.

'We're getting on in years,' Breege reflects, 'and don't have much choice about the ageing process. Meeting people is good, hearing bits of news and general conversation, and doing away with social isolation is very important in this day and age.'

I pass the fruitcake tray to a woman with wispy grey hair. She sets her mug carefully on the table and leans towards me. With a gap-toothed grin, she whispers that she has just recently 'qualified' as a 'wisdom warrior'. She adds with a wink, 'I could pass for sixty if the light is at the right angle.'

The women have helped place Bundoran in context. I leave them to their bingo and dancing. Two uncharacteristically quiet herring gulls on the wall of the bridge watch me watching them. Walking back towards my hotel, I detect an air of faded gentility. Bundoran may not be the prettiest town on the Donegal coast, but despite all the negativity written about it over the years, especially in guidebooks, the place retains some of its nineteenth-century glamour in its peeling buildings and elegant Sea View terrace. The Wishing Chair, the blowholes at the Fairy Bridges, the Money Multipliers, Dublin Yer Money Winner, Star Strikes, and the Triple Bars and Bells will continue to attract a certain type of euro-in-the-slot holidaymaker. It is unlikely ever to hit the cultural jackpot, but is a place happy in its own skin, loved by those who ride the Wilmot Waltzers. As Miss Jean Brodie once remarked, 'For those who like that sort of thing, that is the sort of thing they like.'

That night – my last in the long haul of Donegal – Candlemas Day draws to a close. As evening sets in over the rooftops and chimneys of Bundoran, I gaze at a star-filled sky and a string of constellations. Manannán is said to have travelled by studying the heavens and was able to predict the weather accurately by the motions of the stars. Tonight the moon glows like a snowdrop above the spire of the Church of Our Lady Star of the Sea. Close to Orion, the winter Milky Way stretches over to Cassiopeia, which appears for all the world to be shaped in the distinctive outline of W, or could it be M? Oh, to be in Bundoran now that February's here!

3
Magnetic pull of Leitrim

WHEN I HEARD THE NEWS story on the radio that Thursday morning I could scarcely take it in. The statue of Manannán mac Lir – the very one I had visited to mark the start of my journey – was stolen overnight from its mountaintop plinth. The police were investigating, but mystery surrounded its disappearance. Who could possibly have sabotaged such a statue and to what end? It was believed the theft was linked to Christian fundamentalists or religious zealots offended by Celtic idolatry. Those who carried it out used an angle grinder to cut it from its base in the small boat and left behind a one-and-a-half-metre wooden cross carved with the words: 'You shall have no other gods before me.'

At the breakfast table in the Atlantic Seafront B&B at Tullaghan on the Leitrim coast, another guest ponders the theft. Maureen Doyle from Kerry is working in the area for a week and has come across something similar in her part of Munster.

'They did the same thing to the high cross at the top of Carrauntoohil. But the locals later replaced it so maybe they will do the same there and, who knows, they might find it. Some of these people are very determined when they put their minds to it but you'd wonder they'd nothing better to be up to. At least they can justifiably call it a moving statue.'

Local people appealed for Manannán's return and spoke of their dismay since the statue had become a focal point. The artist, John Darren Sutton, was quoted as saying that, since it took a team of six to put it in place, it would have required several people to remove it because of its weight. He was, he said, sickened at the news as he had spent six months working on it.

In a mild state of shock myself, I try, over scrambled eggs on toast, to absorb the information. I feel bereaved. My protector from the storms, my moving spirit and guiding light has been destroyed, and I still have a long way to go. The puzzle over the mindless morons who carried out the theft stays with me for the rest of the day.

To shake off my car-cramp and escape from my metal crate, I set out to walk the entire coastline of Leitrim – all four kilometres of it. It starts just south of Bundoran and runs through Tullaghan to Bunduff Bridge. Leitrim has a softer profile than Donegal or Sligo, its Atlantic neighbours on either side, owing to the fact that the coastal stretch is so short. According to the map, Tullaghan comprises a post office, school, castle and high cross. It holds a unique position since it is the only village on the Leitrim coast. My guesthouse also holds a unique position as the only place to stay on the coast. Beyond Tullaghan roundabout, I pull over at a bridge across the River Drowes while I wait for a horizontal rain shower to run its course. The bridge marks the official boundary between Leitrim and Donegal. I am quadruply welcomed to the county with large signboards. One from Leitrim County Council is adorned with its coat of arms, a Fáilte Ireland sign states *Fáilte go Liatroim*, a third is from Breifne Tourism, and finally, the now-familiar blue-and-white Way sign indicates my route south.

Tullaghan is made up of new housing developments, a community centre and two pubs, while a Spar Express is the nerve centre. A lopsided grey Celtic cross stands atop a grassy mound. It is believed to date from either the twelfth or thirteenth century and is said to have been moved here from a monastery. Standing three metres tall and with stumpy arms, Tullaghan's main claim to antiquity is encrusted with a confection of bristly lichen and bedecked at its head with green moss. Tall verbascum plants in boxes surround its base.

My aim is to walk the Leitrim littoral in one stretch, seeing it as a single unit. Despite wearing thick gloves, two pairs of socks and hefty boots, I feel numbness in my fingertips and

Tullaghan Cross, County Leitrim.

toes. From the vantage point of a square coastal lookout tower on a promontory beside the county boundary, it seems to lack wildness. The area is called Pointinchose, which means 'the forward point', and is the most prominent feature of the coastline. Perfectly formed barrel-shaped waves are whipped by a knifing wind. Over the centuries this wind has eaten away at the stones in the signal tower, perched at the cliff edge. Wall rue grows alongside weeds and in crevices, and many stones are curiously pockmarked with yellow lichen. The tower is next door to a deserted estate. A stone wall through a field acts as a boundary to boarded-up outbuildings and a derelict two-storey farmhouse beside a smaller tower with stone steps. No signs indicate who lived here, but it has the impression of having been desolate for many years and wears an air of melancholy. I learn later that this area was part of the Tynte Lodge, built by a Captain Cauldwell, who fought in the American War of Independence and married the widowed Lady Tynte.

Before setting off I had studied the map with the intention of walking the route of the coastline along the shorefront rocks. But the on-the-ground reality makes this difficult. Barbed-wire fences divide fields. As I poke around for the best way to access the coast, it becomes clear that this will not be possible. The overwhelming roadside greeting does not extend to the coastline. Private farmland separates me from the sea where signs warn of electric fencing, no trespassing and keep out; on one gate a diagonal line is drawn through the figure of a walker.

Pondering this odd mix of welcome and exclusion, I instead opt to walk the narrow coastal track that runs parallel with the main road. It is within shouting distance of the shore and comes with sea views. The sun has made an appearance but the forecast, which had spoken of freezing Canadian-Arctic winds, is proving accurate since they carry a hint of the Yukon on their breath. Briars and thorny brambles cover stone walls. A golden retriever howls from the porch of a whitewashed cottage and in the distance a rooster crows. From my left comes the continual hum of out-of-sight traffic; on my right the thunder of the sea competes with it, marginally outgunning it in decibel level.

My tarmac-bashing leads past roadside farmhouses, modern bungalows, trim cottages, tin-roofed dwellings and locked-up buildings with cars (circa 1972) abandoned in jungles of long-dead nettles. Three walkers greet me with wordless nods. My slow pace allows me to discover a largely unseen world of nature with its accompanying aromas. In a rough field, devoid of grass, a young girl leads a gypsy cob across a path to feed him barley oats from a daffodil-coloured bucket. Her mother waits by the car and tells me the horse is called Todd. With purple coat and long shaggy hair, he feeds voraciously on the oats. She talks about the severe winds from Mullaghmore Head, which frequently lift their sheds off their foundations.

Halfway along the route, at Redbrae, a hen party is in full swing. Carrick-on-Shannon in south Leitrim is one of the hen-party hotspots in Ireland, but this little fragment of coastline has its own variety of hot chicks and no stampede of stilettos. Supervised by a noisy Dalmatian, a gang of twenty bantams and a couple of roosters form a loose column marching across a mucky field beside a farmhouse. Eye-catching Rhode Island Reds, with erect Venetian-red combs and rust-coloured feathers, sprint ahead of the group. Brown-and-red bantams, and smaller hens with white-and-grey tails play follow-my-leader. In groups of three or four they scratch and nibble, arguing over their pickings. As I watch their comical activities, Jerry Pye emerges, wellington-booted, from a cowshed. He has been attending to his suckler pure and full-bred herd of Aberdeen Angus, Limousin and shorthorn.

Jerry wears a black woolly hat, brown parka-style jacket and grey trousers. On the stem of his blue-framed spectacles the word 'Replay' is written. We sit on the low wall of his house and he talks about living beside the sea.

'It's bleak in the winter but completely different in summer and we don't appreciate the scenery until someone comes along and talks about it. You can't build on the seafront as it's against the law, although some people have tried to, but we keep it as natural as we can. This was once the main road and dates from the Famine. In my father's time all the houses along it were thatched. He was born in 1917 and I remember him talking about the War of Independence and soldiers coming in with bayonets, searching for people.'

Two bantams tug at dwarf daffodils beside the farm gate, then cross the road to join the others. As Jerry discusses his penchant for poultry, we watch the hen parade. There is, he agrees, something restful about them.

'The Rhode Island Reds came to us from a hatchery. They were five months old and on the point of laying. The bantams were from a friend and can be very independent because they like their own space. They lay outside, anywhere they can find a niche, such as a hedge or straw, and they like the sea air. The first clocker we owned had eighteen eggs under her and they came out beneath a bush. She was a bantam and they're a hardy breed. From February until November they lay their eggs with a white shell and lose their feathers. They forage for worms and snails, and will eat any type of food such as yoghurt or potatoes, leftovers from our meals and barley, so they are easily reared and adaptable. Bantams that eat well, lay well.'

The Rhode Islands, Jerry says, are docile and passive, while some of the bantams are noisy and aggressive.

'They fight occasionally and they are aware of the dangers, especially from night-time predators, such as foxes and mink. They come in overnight for shelter as there are a lot of mink along stretches of the two rivers at either end of this coastline. The mink are nocturnal and they'll take eggs and hens and anything else they can get their claws on. The bantams are handled every day and become very tame so they get used to you and they're friendly birds. Roosters could give you a bite but nothing serious. It is satisfying looking after them and we sell lots of eggs to the neighbours. The good layers could lay an egg a day, so you get perhaps up to two hundred a year. The shops don't take them because owing to regulations they have to be stamped.'

Jerry's mother, Nellie, pink-aproned at the front door, shouts, 'Are you not coming in out of that wind?' She makes a round of white-bread egg-and-cheese sandwiches and sets them on a delph plate on the plastic kitchen tablecloth, with a large mug of tea and a carton of Connacht milk. We spread the map on the table and Jerry points to Redbrae. 'That's us here. *Rúid breá* translates as "a lovely piece of land". It's well named as we have the sea on one side and mountains on the other.'

Jerry's father, grandfather and great-grandfather all worked the land here and he is proud of his farming heritage. His ancestors, he says, came in with the Plantation. The family name, Pye, is from the west of England. 'It's the same as the people who used to make radios but we're no relation to them. You'll find references to them in books and historic documents as to where they went or which countries they left for.'

He scurries off to find a book, *From Glack to Bunduff*, a history of Kinlough parish, published in 2013. A short section deals with features of the Leitrim coastline and throws up indigenous names, such as Mulleen, which is a bank of shale visible at low tide; Crannogue, from *crannóg,* an artificial island, is a rock left isolated by erosion; Pollawaddy means 'the dog hole', where locals disposed of unwanted dogs, and Carricknarone is 'the rock of the seals.' The book also contains a Dartry vocabulary, a glossary of forgotten expressive words and phrases. As he leafs through the pages, Jerry selects some that amuse him.

'"Britchel" is the back part of a donkey or horse harness. "Clauber" is wet mud, the hens could be covered in that. "Footery" means awkward or fumbling. "Glugger" is a rotten egg and I don't have too many of them. "Oxter" is your armpit or under your arm. A "skite" is a blow, so you might say "I got a skite from the cow's tail". "Trawhook" is a hook with handles for twisting rope from hay. And that road out there is "the long acre": the hens are on the long acre.'

Jerry returns to feeding his clucking good chickens, and back on the long acre my presence acts as a trigger, setting off dogs, cattle and birds, shaking them out of the lethargic depths of winter. Triadism follows me to Leitrim. Three cows, tails bannering in the wind, turn their heads in unison to gaze with a startled stare at the solitary walker. On the road, birdsong is amplified by the absence of traffic. From a fencepost, a tiny tail-cocked Leitrim wren unleashes a full-throated burst of long trills, which makes me think that perhaps spring is not far away. Nearby, a robin competes with it, while two blackbirds *chink-chink* at each other. Meadow pipits chase one another in jinking flight over fields and hedges. In the next field, two stoic chestnut horses, a foal and its dam, munch on rushes close to the waves. They raise graceful heads, shake their manes, and continue feeding.

At the far end of the road a fingerpost on a cast-iron sign points the way to *Tobar Phadraig*, St Patrick's Shaver's Well where the patron saint is said to have shaved. Curiosity leads me down the path to see the saint in his glassed-in cabinet, with shamrock rather than razor in one hand, staff in the other, and a melancholy expression filled with longing. Close by, a tractor trundles down a field, then turns, flinging out seed from the hopper trailing behind it.

After a wind-blustered return journey, I dodge the traffic to the Spar Express and Topaz petrol station for a restorative coffee and doughnut from Hortons self-service drinks station. A local woman, Rita Magan, sits down at my table for her afternoon scone and coffee with a copy of the *Irish Sun*. She is curious about my journey and talks about life in Tullaghan and changes that have taken place.

'This is the gateway into Donegal; you have to come through here to get there. But most people don't stop and the traffic is so fast on that road, it's a crime. People are terrified at the speed of the cars; in fact the place is destroyed because of that bypass and there's no reduced limit. We had a great village when my kids were small, with a lively community spirit and three times the number of people living here then compared to now. It's very difficult to keep yourself going because of the way society has changed. You miss things; they aren't what they used to be and there is no will to improve the area. The young people are leaving in droves and housing is a big problem. I can't even get my medical card because I own my home. They reckon I should be able to live on my pension so I still work three days a week. Tullaghan is a small place with about two hundred people. There's nothing to it – blink and you'd be through it before you know. We live in the shadow of Donegal but the whole of the west is full of places to explore. The towns are clean and you can get a good meal these days, sure what more would you want?'

There was high excitement in the local press when it was discovered that Leitrim had been left out of the Way's promotional material and signage. The *Leitrim Observer* led with the story of a local councillor complaining of neglect while the paper thundered an outraged editorial on the matter: 'We in Leitrim have few enough opportunities to promote ourselves but our beautiful scenery and countryside is one thing we do have. This is a great opportunity to promote tourism here and halt the continued slide of emigration by creating much-needed jobs locally.'

The neighbouring *Sligo Champion* was not so exercised, running the story at the bottom of an inside page. The controversy brought a welcome change of news from the other headlines of weekend bar brawls, stabbings, knife fights, alcohol-soaked arguments and general bloodletting evident in the past week in court cases:

MAN POURED PETROL ON BAR FLOOR AFTER BEING REFUSED DRINK
THREE INJURED IN SATURDAY NIGHT MELEE
WELL BEHAVED WHEN HE IS NOT DRINKING
HAIRDRESSERS TORE INTO EACH OTHER IN SALON SCRAP

From the little-known inland town of Kinlough, I drive along the shore of Lough Melvin on a scenic loop to Rossinver and around the north side to Lareen Bay. My route is blocked by a flock of frisky mountain sheep being scanned by a farmer to see if they are in lamb. A stray ewe races off and skulks by a bush, chased by a border collie; a series of commands, whistles and calls delivers her back to the main group.

Although the county possesses only a short coastline, water plays a significant part in Leitrim's geographical DNA. An old joke is that land in the county is sold by the gallon rather than by the acre. Rivers, lakes and waterfalls abound. Sweeping glens are a quintessential part of a countryside that includes topographical features such as Eagle's Rock, Ireland's highest free-standing tower shaped like a thumb, Fowley's Falls, the Captain's Grave and the Sleeping Giant whose body and legs are shared between Keelogboy and Leean mountains. John McGahern once wrote: 'There is nothing dramatic about the Leitrim landscape but it is never dull.' McGahern, who died in 2006, lived and farmed at Fenagh, near Mohill in south Leitrim and his stories were set deep in the soil. He missed out on the drama of the north part of the county, an area now bubbling with creativity and a place that is certainly never dull.

In the past fifteen years dozens of artists have set up home here alongside the lakes or at the foothills of mountains, creating a vibrant energy. The area has attracted figurative, ceramic and textile artists, jewellery makers, photographers, illustrators, writers and filmmakers, sculptors, woodcarvers, blacksmiths and designers. They enjoy the unspoilt countryside, which, although close to the coast, is still a safe enough distance inland to escape the lashing winds and high seas.

Despite being in the shadow of the bigger counties along the Way, Leitrim is determined not to be outdone. It has adopted an imaginative approach with events such as the Dromahair Wild Atlantic Matchmaking and Music festival in October. An entrepreneur has come up with a circuit known as the Wild Atlantic Butterfly route, a section of which I am driving. This embraces Leitrim, Sligo, west Cavan and parts of Donegal and Fermanagh, and represents on the map the outline shape of a butterfly.

On my way back to Tullaghan I follow the course of the River Drowes, twisting gin-clear like a silver ribbon through the landscape. At the Drowes Salmon Fishery, on the Lareen Estate, anglers sit silently beside their gear looking at the water with intense focus. Owner Shane Gallagher is selling a half-day permit and giving directions to a visitor. Wall signs in his fish-tackle shop say: 'The worst day fishing is better than the best day working', and 'Give a man a fish and he'll eat for a day, teach a man to fish and he'll sit in his boat and drink beer all day.' I peer into drawers where scores of different patterns of flies are made from threads intended to replicate a trout's diet, with names such as Apache Bottleneck, Silver Rat, and Red Assed Green Peter.

The fishery was set up by Shane's father in 1977 and he himself has worked in it since 1998. They redeveloped the overgrown grounds of an old estate and now rent eleven cottages. Visiting anglers come from Germany, Spain, the UK, as well as Japan and South America, with many repeat customers.

'We have an annual catch,' he tells me, 'of around a thousand salmon each year, which is greatly improved from what it was in the late 1970s, although it was slow to start this year because of the difficult weather conditions. Only one fish was recorded in January and just one in February up to Valentine's Day. Our visitors love being close to nature, meeting local people, getting to know them and fishing with them. It's not very touristy and when they go into a pub they are treated like the locals, not as tourists, since some of our fishermen have been coming for up to thirty years. I have a guy from Germany this week and he tunes into the death notices on Ocean FM to make sure all his long-time friends are still alive. And the shop comes to a stop when they read out the names every day.'

Shane emerges from behind the counter to show me a map of the route of the Drowes, which runs for eight kilometres from Lareen to the sea pools at Tullaghan. One of Ireland's premier salmon rivers, it also holds stocks of brown trout.

'There's a considerable amount of history connected to the Drowes. Part of it forms the border between Donegal and Leitrim, which is also the border between Ulster and Connacht. The Four Masters Bridge is where the Franciscan friars stayed while writing their annals on the banks of the river, and you can see there are about eighty named pools, such as those at a spa well or old mill. The bridges all have local names too. The top section of the river, from Lough Melvin to just below Lennox's Bridge has some great fly water. What makes us unique is that we have fresh salmon in the river so early in the season from the start of January. Out of the last thirty-eight years, we've had the first salmon caught in the river during thirty of those years which is unusual.'

To embrace the Way, Shane markets his business as The Wild Atlantic Salmon Run and, although the Leitrim connection with the Atlantic is small, he believes the impact of it on the county is significant.

'Some of the salmon will spawn in the river itself, others will go as far as Lough Melvin and spawn in the mountain streams. These salmon have come to feed from the Faroe Islands, Greenland and sometimes farther afield. Those coming in February don't feed in the freshwater but live off their body-fat reserves of energy and will spawn in the river or in the mountain tributaries in December and January next year.'

He explains the life cycle of the salmon, pointing out the different stages on a wall chart.

'They start off a silver colour and when they are in the freshwater for a couple of weeks they lose their silver sheen and turn red and brown. As they get closer to spawning time, the male fish – the cockfish – develops a battledress and gets ready to spawn. The henfish chooses a suitable area of gravel in the river, forms a nest and lays eggs. The cockfish fertilises it with his sperm and then the henfish goes upstream and uses her tail to cover the eggs with gravel. After a couple of weeks, they turn into fry and then parr. Then they spend about two winters in the freshwater river, and in the spring turn silver. At this stage they will make the journey to the feeding grounds in the Atlantic, which could be a journey of over three thousand kilometres to the Faroes. Some will spend one winter at sea while others will spend more than one winter, and they will come back as an average size of about five or six lb. Those who spend two winters at sea will be much bigger, perhaps ten or twelve lb and it's those larger salmon that we are fishing for at the moment. So they come back, not only to the correct river, but to exactly the same stretch, in the way that migrating birds return to the same area.

We're not exactly sure how they find where to go, whether it's by scent or magnetic pull.

'The big draw for the fishermen is having the opportunity to reconnect with nature. Even if they don't catch a fish they may see a kingfisher or have an encounter with an otter, which are not things they would ordinarily come across. Although we are an island, we've had our backs to the sea for too long so I would hope that we will now face it and for the first time perhaps realise that we have this incredible connection to the ocean. There is a massive narrative here with the Atlantic in relation to the salmon fishing and that is something we can all develop.'

The dawn crowing of Jerry Pye's rooster disturbs my slumbers at the Atlantic Seafront guesthouse so I arise early for the road south. The fast-flowing River Duff links Leitrim to Sligo. Birdsong seeps from banks of gorse, shrubs and trees along the riverside where it meets the ocean. At Bunduff Bridge, school buses, An Post drivers, bread-delivery vans, and commuters late for work speed their way to Sligo town. Roadside verges can be hostile terrain but in breaks in the traffic there is a pastoral feel. Although the new growth has yet to appear, primroses, mauve crocuses and snowdrops line the wayside, heralding the approach of spring. A run of dry days in late February has allowed farmers to spread slurry.

In Cliffony, at the turn-off for Mullaghmore, several white steeds have been spray-painted on to the gable wall of O'Donnell's bar. They are part of an advertising mural that includes surfers riding the waves. It is not hard to imagine Manannán in his chariot pulled by Enbarr galloping in full flight across the sea as though it were dry land. Since hearing about the desecration of his statue, I have been troubled by the sea god's disappearance. Several days on from the theft, despite an extensive search of the area, there is no trace of it. Newspaper headlines announce that a reward is being offered for information. A man who proposed to his wife beside the statue has put up a three-figure sum for

Horse and surfer mural, Cliffony, County Sligo.

its safe return. The story has captured the public's imagination and a campaign on social media has inevitably built up several thousand followers.

Sea gods and ocean heroes have long fascinated me. I had been told by several people about a woman in Mullaghmore who was described as an ocean heroine. Apart from the fact that I have my own hero in the form of Manannán, I had telephoned May Burns last night to see if I could meet her to talk about her role in keeping beaches clean. For many years throwaway detritus and floating dunnage has been suffocating the ocean but in Sligo they take pride in looking after their beaches. Coast Care, Tidy Towns coastal resorts, Leave No Trace groups, and others active in beach clean-ups are busily engaged in clearing litter.

May is a Sligonian and has been living in Mullaghmore since 2005. When I arrive she has just finished feeding her cat, Puddy, also known as Puddles. From her house overlooking the seafront, she explains how her interest in beach cleanliness started when she joined Mullaghmore Active.

'Initially we didn't have a focus on the beach because, like many people, we thought that the tide comes in and the tide goes out and it cleans the beach. But in recent years with more interest in the environment, people are concerned about the erosion from the banks of marram grass, known here as bent grass. We decided to do something about it and fenced an area to keep human traffic off it and gradually saw the grass growing and rejuvenating. We became more educated and began to see that there are two different types of litter: the stuff that people drop on the beach when they're having their picnic, and the stuff that's being washed in. We collect all sorts of things but the biggest items that we pick up are tyres and we know exactly where they come from.'

'Cars?'

'Yes, initially but the car tyres are used by fishermen as a buffer against the sea wall and on their boats as fenders, as moorings on the seabed. In the winter when the heavy seas come, it's a short journey from harbour to shore and they get washed up here. You would think that the fishermen would come over to pick up their tyres, but they don't. They access them easily somewhere else but just can't be bothered.'

'What do you do with them?'

'It's a big problem because the county council won't take them. After the last clean-up we piled them in an area not visible from the road. We told the council we had them piled up and told the fishermen that they might like to take them back – they're still there. The council told us they cannot find any recycling company that will take them.'

In the world of marine litter, plastic is another problem. Tens of thousands of plastic bottles in Ireland are discarded every day and during the 2014 coastal clean-up half a million individual items of litter were removed. May's group constantly finds plastic bags and drinks bottles, a catalogue of shame. Nurdles, which are plastic pellets and known as "mermaid's tears", are the raw material for most plastics, and commercial fish off the coast have been found to harbour the tiny plastic pieces. A recent survey on fulmars in the North Sea revealed plastic in the stomach of ninety-five per cent of the birds sampled. May also read about a whale washed up on the coast of Spain with sixty pieces of micro-plastic in its stomach.

'Somebody said to me that's quite small as other large sea animals have been found with much more. But in our clean-ups we pick up at least that many pieces of plastic so although it may be convoluted logic, perhaps we are saving another whale.'

'Why do people leave litter?'

'It's a mix of laziness, a couldn't-care-less attitude and a feeling that someone else should look after my rubbish. We took a conscious decision a few years ago not to have a wheelie bin at the beach. When we had the bins people who stayed in the holiday homes came and pushed all their rubbish into them when they were leaving and then the crows pulled everything out. The local authority didn't empty them often enough so it was just a mess. We have four clean-ups a year, producing up to a hundred bags of rubbish. Clean Coast have an initiative called the two-minute beach clean which encourages people to pick up what they can in each hand – it will only take two minutes and is a great help.'

'What other detritus do you find?'

'Everything from umbrellas to biros, bits of boats, bits of cars – everything you can think of – it all gets written down on our data forms. The most unusual thing we found was a stand for a television. There's a lot of illegal dumping that goes on as you drive around the headland. Charges for collecting rubbish came in a few years ago and people resent having to pay so they go to Mullaghmore cliff and throw it into the sea. They think the tide will take it out and it'll never be seen again but the tide doesn't take all of it out; some of it is washed up here so that could be where the TV stand came from.'

'What more would you like to see done?'

'It's all about awareness. We bring out schoolchildren for a fun day and get in a bit of education along the way. Kids are very open to learning and once they learn something they pass it on to the parents. The image of Ireland is one of an unspoilt place, which should mean unpolluted. But it's becoming increasingly difficult. Although the Wild Atlantic Way is a great idea, I wonder in the case of Mullaghmore if it is going to bring loads more visitors here and is that going to mean more litter left on the beach? Maybe that's inevitable but who's going to do something about it? Is it going to be left to our group? What about the people making money, the businesses? Why can't the marketing drive by Fáilte Ireland not have shown part of the responsibility that goes with it? I went to talks about the Way and I didn't hear one person mention what we should do about all the increase in the rubbish.'

'Are we in danger of destroying the very thing we want to protect?'

'There's a balance to be struck. But I remember saying to one man that I had reservations about the new route. He was appalled and said that was very narrow-minded thinking and terribly negative. They are all cock-a-hoop about it but there's another side to it.'

'On the night after a big storm, do you go down to the beach rubbing your hands in glee?'

'Well, I always think: oh my God, how many tyres are going to be washed up from the harbour? I love the big storms and looking at the seas but I'm never negative about it. What I notice more after the big storms is the natural stuff such as the sea rods, which used to be harvested. Just last week we found starfish washed in after a heavy sea. There were at least sixty of them and the seagulls were having a feast.'

Puddy is restless, clawing at chairs and looking at me inquisitively with green-yellow eyes. Some fresh mackerel helps pacify her while I complete my chat with May and ask about the most satisfying aspect of living in Mullaghmore.

'The views are wonderful, the walks show the visitor some of the best scenery in Europe and it's unspoilt, despite the rubbish. It is also a sociable place with just a hundred and twenty permanent residents; everybody knows everybody else. But you could end up getting very depressed in this type of work. You read about the billions of tons of all kinds of rubbish found in the ocean and what industries are pumping into the seas and you realise that that is not the way to go. Here is one bit of beach where we can make a difference. What is coming in is ceaseless but we concentrate on doing the best we can with this one.'

I set off to drive around the headland to see if I can spot any polluters. Signs around Mullaghmore Head warn: 'Danger: Deep Drop'. Lest anyone be in any doubt, the sign is accompanied by an image of a figure in a red triangle falling over the cliffs. Anyone throwing rubbish off here would need to be careful. Alarmingly, signs also warn of an oil spillage. Red-and-white cones have been placed along one short stretch. I drive down a steep, icy road with a degree of trepidation. Rainwater, frost and oil make for a potentially lethal combination for what turns into a high-octane drive. No one has thought to close the road, which glistens with a dangerous-looking blue sheen. Mist restricts views but, on the headland, layers of grey shale mudstone in between thick sandstone are exposed along with wave-cut beds of rock. At Carricknacarta, as I round a corner, Classiebawn Castle, the former home of Lord Louis Mountbatten, rises mysteriously through rain and hail on an isolated position. Built in the Gothic style, turreted and multi-chimneyed, it looks a little like Hogwarts, which invests in it a dreamlike quality.

On the main road south, a green flush spreads across the flat-topped profile of Ben Bulben. Formed by moving glaciers, it dominates the landscape. I stop for a closer look through binoculars. It bears a striking resemblance to the capsized hull of a ship. Crossing the sky, a long, shapeless mob of barnacle geese sounds like a pack of barking dogs. I tilt my glasses upwards, picking out their creamy faces, white neck collars and dark flight feathers. Lines from the Dermot Healy poem *A Fool's Errand* come to mind: 'From gaggle to skein / every evening / and next morning / back again / shouting directions to the next in line.' They appear to be heading towards Lissadell beach so I decide to follow them by road. It could be a wild goose chase but by managing to keep them in my horizon through the windscreen for a few miles, I track them to nearby fields at Ballygilgan. My quest takes me down a lane, better suited to a tractor, where at a nature reserve they are hidden in a hollow guarded by a 'Beware of the Bull' sign. I settle for listening to their yelping and chattering in the distance. The noise is intense and continuous. After fifteen minutes, a party of a hundred lifts off for the beach or perhaps the uninhabited Inishmurray Island, one of their haunts.

The car radio rummages through the stations – RTÉ 1 and 2, Raidió na Gaeltachta, Lyric FM, Newstalk, Today FM – but I choose Ocean FM where a news item catches my attention. The report states that part of a boat belonging to the Spanish Armada has surfaced on the beach at Streedagh as a result of the spring tide, the highest in forty years. The 'supertide', which happens when a rare alignment between the moon and sun produces a higher-than-normal gravitational pull, generates waves up to fifteen metres high. Low tide, the report adds, may expose more wreckage tomorrow.

I divert to Grange, which styles itself as a 'National Heritage area for the Spanish Armada', and head straight to the beach. As I pull up at the car park, darkness is enfolding the coast. A local man says the tide has covered the wreckage and there is nothing to be seen. 'Come back tomorrow afternoon around twelve thirty and you will have a good view of it.'

Back in Grange, I stumble across a musical evening at Barry's pub. The Firesiders, a group of singers and guitarists, are limbering up for what promises to be a convivial evening's entertainment. Candles glow on tables and on the mantelpiece. Moody photographs framed on the walls portray exalted names who have played here. Paul Brady, Shane MacGowan, Steve Cooney, John Martyn, and Ritchie Harris have all graced Barry's, which dates to 1874.

Outnumbering the customers, the musicians sit around in a circle while drinkers settle on high stools in anticipation. One at a time, each musician and singer takes his or her turn. Not a tin whistle, bodhrán or fiddle is to be heard; instead, it is the pure clear sound of acoustic and electric guitars. The music is a mix of American folk ballads, bluegrass, cajun and emigrant songs. 'The Lakes of Pontchartrain' is followed by 'Darling Girl of Clare' and 'Sweet Mystery'. To rousing applause, a bearded tenor reaches impossibly high notes in 'An Irish Lullaby', while a pony-tailed man and flame-haired woman merge for a duet about Grange. The small, attentive audience joins in the chorus of 'What a Wonderful World' and 'Hang Down your Head, Tom Dooley'.

After a soothing rendition of 'Bathe me in the Water', the group rises to take what a rosy-cheeked man beside me calls a pissin' posse break and a smokin' posse break. Noel Mooney is a gregarious sixty-something and says the last song applies to his life. For sixty years, since he was 'knee high to a grasshopper', he has been swimming in the sea every day. A retired ESB engineer, he lives near the foot of Ben Bulben. He has come along tonight to support his son, who is performing.

'That early swimming passion in Tramore in Waterford where I grew up stayed with me wherever I went,' he says. 'I have swum in many places all over Ireland but the difference is that I swim all year around, virtually every day. I miss very few and only because something untoward has happened. Any troubles that I have are lost very quickly once I hit the water.'

As a designated driver, Noel sips a pint of Miwadi, and we fall into conversation. He explains there are a number of different spots around the Sligo coastline, depending on tides and wind direction, from where he swims.

'In the winter I swim normally between eleven a.m. and three p.m., although I swam at half past five today when it was getting dark at Lissadell beach. At this time of year I would stay in the water for about ten or twelve minutes. The handiest beach to me is Streedagh but at the moment the sea has robbed the beach of sand so there are a lot of rocks which are difficult on the feet. With strong waves you can be easily knocked against them, so I'm waiting for the sea to come back and cover those rocks which it nearly always does in the spring.'

'How cold is it in the depths of the ocean?'

'The temperature of the main body of sea is eight degrees but it comes in over cold or icy land so what I am swimming in is about three or four degrees below the ocean temperature. At the moment it is very cold. Traditionally the coldest time of year is the St Patrick's Day swim, so if you are swimming for charity on Patrick's Day you'd be earning your crust.'

'Do people not think you are mad?'

'One day I was on a mile-long stretch of beach and the wind and sea were ferocious. There was a woman on it with five dogs. She started roaring repeatedly at me "You're mad, you're mad." I politely shouted back at her: "You're mad … you've got five dogs." So we agreed we were both mad. One February day I was swimming in the Shannon, north of Athlone, and someone described me as slightly eccentric, so I think that sums it up.'

'Why do you do it?'

'I feel energised by it. I get more out of it in winter than I do in summer because it's a greater challenge. You have to be very careful, particularly when it's wild and rough and cold. During the summer if you get into trouble, you've plenty of time to get out of it. But in the winter if you get into trouble, you don't have the time. Mostly I am on my own, although occasionally a couple of people might join me for a day or two, but essentially I am a lone swimmer. Last year I got hypothermia and fortunately my daughter was with me that day and she brought me back to the house. Because it was a sunny day, I'd stayed in the water longer than I should have and when I emerged I just collapsed – I couldn't get up, I couldn't kneel, I couldn't do anything and it took hours to revive me. In the winter I don't like to be out of my depth because if a rip catches you and pulls you out, you haven't got the time to get back in.'

'Are people aware of the dangers?'

'We get people from inland places and even if they just stand in the shallows they don't see the danger and then, after starting in an inch of water, they find themselves suddenly in two feet of water. So they begin to panic and when you panic in the sea you're gone. Some day I'll be caught myself but so far I've got away.'

'Are there any dangers from fish?'

'Jellyfish can be a problem but the most unpleasant fish is the conger eel – very dangerous. They bite you. Normally they are in little holes and crevices so you should never put your hand into a hole. I bring bread and attract shoals of little fish which are beautiful, so all this restores my faith in humanity and, despite our efforts to attain perfection, the madness still prevails. Don't forget the sea gives, the sea takes. And I will keep on doing it until the sea takes me.'

The musicians resume their seats around the fire. A young singer strikes up 'Do I Wanna Know?' by the Arctic Monkeys. 'Have you got colour in your cheeks? … Have you no idea that you're in too deep?'

Noel guffaws and whispers to me that the group's name and lyrics could well be his ocean signature tune.

At noon the next day, with a frisson of excitement, I walk uphill across stones and look down on a busy beach scene. The smooth

Uncovered shipwreck at low tide on Streedagh beach, County Sligo.

sand and rocks on Streedagh glisten for the tide is now far out. Sunbeams glide across it and a rainbow arcs over the bay. The news of the wreck being uncovered has brought more than fifty people for a closer look at the remnants uncovered by shifting sands. A boat's rudder, said to be from the Armada, washed up by a storm, was removed earlier by a farmer. The remains consist of what is thought by many to be the curved bow and stern of one of the ships. Those who turn up believe these remains are also from the Armada but there has been no official confirmation.

Like a row of jagged, rotting molars, dark wooden oak beams embedded in the sand protrude at a 45-degree angle, some wrapped with seaweed. Photographers jostle for the best shots, while dogs poke around moss-covered sections; a collie enjoys a bath in a pool of water surrounding the remains. Two children pose for a parental photograph on one of the projectile-like slats before slipping off it on to the sand.

The three Spanish galleons, *La Lavia*, *La Juliana* and *Santa Maria de Visión*, were wrecked during a fierce storm on 25 September 1588. The ships were trapped off Streedagh and washed ashore with up to 1,100 on board. Whether or not these are part of the Armada is not troubling those present, since a shipwreck – any shipwreck, whatever its pedigree – is a bond between strangers on a beach. People who ordinarily would not speak to each other exchange opinions, pose questions and listen earnestly to those of others, trying to make historic connections.

Vinny Blighe, who lives in Drumcliff, knows Streedagh well. He tells me that his father and grandfather are buried in Drumcliff church graveyard. He is especially interested in this beach burial that has come to light.

'For more than fifty years I have walked this beach and used to ride horses over this particular stretch many times. But I would never have suspected – in fact, no one would have suspected for a moment – that this wreckage was so close to hand. It was probably at least eight feet underneath me. It's quite extraordinary to think it was here all this time.'

Vinny believes that the combination of lack of air and the fact that it was in water helped preserve it for such a long period. 'It would have rotted away on dry ground. Who knows what will happen to it now, but it would be an embarrassment if we didn't do something with it.'

With a sense of awe, many hunker down to inspect the beams. Not only are they curious, they are also puzzled. Some are surprised at the scale of the wreckage; others speculate as to what will happen to it. Will DNA tests be carried out, a beak-nosed man asks me, as though I have the answer. A rucksacked woman tears off a piece of seaweed and shows it around. Citizen archaeologists ponder where the remains could be brought and if they will be excavated. Museums do not have room for these things, says a young man, although he thinks they should create the space.

Beside me on the sand, a local wit, undeterred by the exact origin of the wooden beams, has left an imprint: 'De Cuellar was here,' a reference to the Armada's famed captain who made a heroic journey from Sligo to Antrim and back to Spain. After ninety minutes, white-capped waves start to appear. People stamp their feet on the sand for heat. In spite of the sun, the wind is cold. Slowly the tide turns, the water flows towards us and waves are lisping in. A capricious one takes us by surprise, collapsing at our feet, spilling around the wreckage, soaking boots, trainers and paws. Curiosity satiated, people peel off in twos and threes, continue their walk to see what else they may uncover, or drift back to the car park. As I return to the car, surfers are preparing to take over from the photographers to capture the late afternoon waves. An information signboard says 'Sligo: Land of Heart's Desire.' Beside it is a brief history of the Armada boats alongside a quote from Captain de Cuellar describing the horror of the day: 'Such a thing was never seen: for within the space of one hour all three ships were broken in pieces so that there did not escape three hundred men and more than 1,000 were drowned, among them many persons of importance, captain, gentlemen and their officials.' Some months after my visit, four bronze cannon from the wreck of *La Juliana* were recovered at Streedagh and brought ashore at Mullaghmore, before being transferred to the National Museum.

Nobody in Austies bar is sure about the number of sea captains who came from Rosses Point. Neither is anyone sure about the provenance of the remains washed up at Streedagh but they are nonetheless commemorating the story of the Spanish Armada. I have driven out through the early evening dark along a short Sligo spur, whose thumbprint protrudes into Drumcliff Bay. The wind and slanting rain force me inside to seek refuge. Packed with the loot of the past and with the loot of ships wrecked off the coast, Austies is a living maritime museum.

Memorabilia brought back by sailors includes a ship's wheel sitting hugger-mugger behind the bar with a chronometer, barometer, telescopes, ships in bottles and navigation lights. Embedded in the counter is a giant antique binnacle compass. A ship's log and bell stand alongside port and starboard lights. The deal wood, panelling the snugs, is from the *Narayana*, a Norwegian barque that was wrecked on the west side of Coney Island in November 1886. The vessel's original plaque is attached to the bar. From the ceiling, lobster pots, fishing nets and corks dangle. Overseeing it all in a high corner roost is Polly, the stuffed parrot. And then there are the sea captains. Walls are lined with photographs of them, all of whom came from Rosses Point. One estimate puts the figure at more than fifty.

Along this coastline and in Sligo town evidence of the sea's perils is immortalised in memorials and in sculpture, but nowhere is the nautical past museum-ified in such detail as in this pub. Gathered around an oval-shaped wooden table in the Captain's Cabin snug, a group of musicians tunes up. The table was salvaged from a Greek vessel, SS *Diamantis Pateras*, shipwrecked in February 1925 on its way into Sligo Harbour when the pilot lost his marks. It was carrying 5,000 tons of maize from the River Plate and bound for Pollexfen's shipping firm. (The Pollexfens were the maternal grandparents of Jack and William Butler Yeats.) The ship, which grounded on a sandbank off Ballincar, was later beached and cut in two for scrap. The historic table tonight hosts a group of young musicians known as Moxie. They are performing compositions from the *De Cuellar Suite*, a musical composed by Michael Rooney about the Armada's engagement with the English fleet. They have just finished the first song 'Open Sea: The Coast of Cadiz.'

Sitting quietly by himself on a bar stool, soaking up the music, is a dapper Kieran Devaney, with blue sailor's cap, red scarf and red corduroy jacket; he could pass for an old seadog himself. For him, the bar represents a tribute to the seafaring tradition of the village.

'Everything in here tells a story,' he says. 'It's like a museum where you walk into your past. No matter how long you are dead, you are not forgotten in here. The people who died two hundred years ago are still talked about and their ghosts are here too. And in two hundred years' time they will still be talking about those men.'

Kieran was born in what he calls the 'east Dublin suburb' of Liverpool. During a chequered career, he was a reporter in newspapers and on television. He produced news programmes for TV-am, Channel 4, ITN, Sky News and CNN. For the best part of forty-five years, he has lived on and off in Rosses Point and now contributes to the RTÉ maritime programme *Seascapes*.

'It's a secret place,' he says. 'You have to go looking for it as it's not on the way to anywhere. We are surrounded by mountains on three sides, and the sea on the other. It's horrendous in the winter: you could walk down the street and see nobody, and most of the time the beaches are uncrowded. Some people say we should thank Fáilte Ireland for bringing tourists to Sligo town and for keeping them out of Rosses Point.'

Kieran's career in journalism and broadcasting spanned thirty years. In his reporting, he covered wars, conflicts and other major news stories.

'I was sent away to sea as a cabin boy. When I was fourteen, I went to France as part of a holiday job but I left school two years later to become a journalist – it was either that or the sea. I covered the Iran/Iraq war and specialised in going to countries where journalists weren't supposed to go, such as Burma, Senegal and Mauritania, making documentaries with hidden cameras. After that I became editor of TV3 Ireland. Although I've seen some horrific scenes, I always like to reflect on the fun side of the job. I used to produce Bob Friend on Sky News, who was a great mate. One day a report came in that two African presidents had died in a plane crash. Friend announced to viewers: "Some news just in, the Presidents of Rwanda and Botswana have been killed in a plane crash." He looked at one of the unpronounceable names with twenty-six letters and immediately said: "We can't bring you the names until next of kin have been informed.'"

Kieran sometimes regrets not sticking to the sea, but writes about it in his books that are brimful of maritime themes. He describes his novel, *The Drumcliffe Pilots*, published in 2009, as a black comic tale of betrayal, drunken licentiousness, treachery, sexual infidelity and unrequited love. Rosses Point, he says mischievously, is a ripe source for these topics. With concertina and fiddle, the table musicians have stepped up the tempo, echoing the tension of September 1588, providing an evocative soundtrack to our conversation. The exuberant jig 'War on Water' is followed by 'Storm at Streedagh', then a series of reels and laments featuring the harp, before the stirring 'March to Breifne'. An introspective look spreads over Kieran's face, helped by alcohol-induced nostalgia. He pours another glass of wine and pours out ancestral knowledge that he has carefully curated.

'Sailing is in our blood. My father, grandfather and great-grandfather were all called Tom Devaney and they sailed the seven seas. They all came from Rosses Point and were master mariners. In those days you either became a farmer or went to sea. Farming was a harsh life so most men opted for the sea. My grandfather was on a ship, *The Eldorado*, which was wrecked off the Canadian coast. They had a crew of twenty-five and trekked for a hundred days through the wilderness to reach the safety of the Canadian Pacific Railway line. They all survived, except for the captain's dog.'

He points to a shelf behind the bar where exquisitely produced model ships are displayed between bottles of Powers, Jameson and Bushmills.

'My grandfather made some of those ships and had a great talent for putting them together. That's why this bar is home for me. It's friendly with a warm atmosphere and is a place to escape from the winds. The minute you walk in here everyone knows you or, if they don't know you, they'll know you in five minutes. My father went to sea as a youngster and eventually joined the B & I Line, becoming Commodore of the MV *Leinster* while his brother Frank was captain of the MV *Munster*. My sister Maureen joined the Merchant Navy, rising to Chief Officer before she married the Chief Engineer. And my son has just signed on as an engineer on the last crab-fishing boat in Cornwall, so we're keeping it in the family.

'In Rosses Point there are eight young men who are going to sea, still carrying on the tradition. The reason the village has produced so many sea captains – whatever the figure is we can't be certain – is because there is a *grá* about the place. This is the true land of Tir na nÓg. Nobody ever grows old here; they might die but they are still remembered as youngsters.'

Around the Captain's Cabin table, the musicians reach a finale with 'The Route Home', which includes a song, 'Sailing to Santander', and a Galician polka, 'By Low Roads and High Seas.' Kieran takes me past them into a room off the main bar. One of the area's claims to fame is that the Yeats brothers spent all their summers here. Jack stayed in the area during his youth and many of his later paintings were inspired by recollections of his early years at Rosses Point. The wild Atlantic and the stormy skies appealed to him. He once said, 'Sligo was my school and the sky above it.' Kieran shows me a large framed watercolour hanging on the wall over the fireplace.

'That's a copy of a Jack Yeats painting, "Memory Harbour", originally done in 1900. The bearded pilot in the foreground with the blue hat, blue jacket and cigarette is a Kilgallon, who is a relation of mine. In the water you can see a cast-iron navigation beacon known as the Metal Man. He's dressed in the uniform of a nineteenth-century Royal Navy Able Seaman and is pointing with his right arm to the safe deep-water channel between Rosses Point and Oyster Island. They say he's the only Rosses Point man never to have told a lie. It's a busy scene with the row of white cottages, the boating activity and a horse ferrying people uphill. Jack Yeats loved white horses; for him they symbolised loyalty, intelligence and freedom. The original painting used to be in the National Gallery in Dublin. I went looking for it a few years ago but it couldn't be found so I think it is probably lost. One other connection is that W. B.'s poem "A Stolen Child" is set on the beach here. My grandmother met him a few times and her memory of him was that she thought he was away with the fairies.'

4
The sea god is found

DURING 2015 THE YEATS INDUSTRY is in overdrive to celebrate the 150th anniversary of his birth, designated National Year of Yeats. Sligo has just held the four-day Yeats Winter School, while events, ranging from tea-leaf readings to a street carnival, are planned for Yeats Day on 13 June. A special set of coins has been minted to mark the sesquicentennial and the Yeats Society has launched a new variety of rose named in his honour. Large municipal signs urge: 'For Yeats' sake, please do not drop your litter.' There is no escaping the Yeats connection and it has been poetically exploited by one of Sligo's best-known pubs, Hargadon's. The time-burnished bar, built in 1864, the year before Yeats was born, is run by chef and owner Joe Grogan, a friend of mine. Since 1 January, when the first poem was read by Senator Susan O'Keeffe, they have held a daily lunchtime Yeats reading by pop-up poets to bring his work to life. The initiative came from Joe and has attracted strong interest.

'We've had everyone from well-known poets such as Paula Meehan and Theo Dorgan to lesser-known shop assistants. Sometimes the same poem is repeated, but we've had American university lecturers, as well as regulars and staff. We also had a woman with a concert harp and another on a ukulele who played "Down by the Salley Gardens".'

Some weeks earlier Joe had asked if I would be interested in a reading slot so we agreed a date and I arrive at half past noon to acclimatise. Wood panelling, marble-top counters and snugs with tiny glass doors on hinges all lead to a conducive mood. As the appointed hour looms, I read through my lines alone in

W. B. Yeats mural, Sligo town.

a quiet snug. Far from being crowded with lunchtime Yeatsian aficionados, about a dozen workers on their break are enjoying tapas. A small, arty crowd arrives, double-kissing and, like long-lost friends, indulging in huggery. Standing on a shelf beside me are enamel Scotch Whiskey White Horse and terracotta pitchers, while a circular tin tray provides its own slice of poetic fun:

> He who, when his turn comes round
> Is deep in slumber dozing
> May fool at first but soon 'tis found
> He'll never last till closing.

Beside a lectern and in front of an Annie West print featuring Yeats outside Hargadon's, I launch into a short section of 'The Wanderings of Oisin', from the Everyman's Library edition of Yeats' *The Poems*. This is a useful book as it also supplies the answers at the back. Running to thirty-two pages, the poem is an epic narrative dialogue between Oisin and St Patrick, with references to Manannán. It reflects Oisin's stay on the Faerie Islands. The Otherworld of Faeries, the Good People, the Sidhe and the Tuatha Dé Danann fascinated Yeats. The section that I read is from the end of the second part and is set where Manannán's abandoned castle once stood:

> I held a sword whose shine
> No centuries could dim, and a word ran
> Thereon in Ogham letters, 'Manannan';
> That sea-god's name, who in a deep content
> Sprang dripping, and, with captive demons sent
> Out of the sevenfold seas, built the dark hall
> Rooted in foam and clouds, and cried to all
> The mightier masters of the mightier race; …
> And when he knew the sword of Manannan
> Amid the shades of the night, he changed and ran
> Through many shapes;

After a ripple of applause, interest is stirred in Manannán. A woman sharing a bottle of Pinot Grigio with two friends, speaks to me in soft Sligoese, saying she feels a kinship with the sea god. The police have just issued an appeal for information about a 'missing person,' which has appeared in that morning's paper causing much mirth: 'We are looking for a well known, six ft tall, striking local male with an athletic build. He has shoulder-length hair held back with a headband and has a beard. We have concerns for his health in this weather as he is bare chested with only a thin shawl held at the neck with a decorative clasp to keep his top half warm. Evidence at the scene suggests that he has injuries to his feet. He is a very striking fellow so if you have seen him please let us know.'

From the picture of him, the women agree he is striking. One of them says, 'We are all looking for those type of men but I can't fathom why anyone would want to steal his statue.' With outstretched arms, the stance is similar, she tells me, to the figure of a female bronze sculpture, 'Waiting on Shore', at Rosses Point, which was unveiled as a memorial to men from the parish who have lost their lives at sea but also honours the women who waited for their return.

My return journey to Sligo coincides with a weekend conference, 'Weather Beaten Archaeology', about the erosion caused to the coast by storms. Reflecting the fascination of the topic, more than 200 people have turned up for the gathering of archaeological clans at the Sligo Institute of Technology. Twenty-five speakers from Ireland, Britain, France, Iceland and Canada present case studies, share experiences, exchange views and trade tales on what is acknowledged as a catastrophic situation.

The welcome pack includes a bookmark with thumbnail photographs of fourteen implements used by archaeologists. I recognise only a shovel, bucket and trowel. In another life, I would like to have been an archaeologist but it is unlikely that I would have progressed far without the skillset to identify the basic tools of the trade, never mind cultivating a liking for plastic sandals and beards. Speakers are restricted to fifteen minutes, which means they must present their case swiftly and succinctly, a difficulty for some. The session, 'Inundated with data', lives up to its title. It is a morning of historic timescales, graphs monitoring erosion rates, digital shoreline-analysis charts, field-survey results and climate-change projections. Extremism has come to Sligo. We hear about extreme weather, extreme waves, extreme rain, extreme flooding and extreme surge events, as well as exceptional storms, rising sea levels and dynamic landscape problems.

One speaker, Dr Kieran Hickey from Cork, whose wide-timescale talk is on the history of storms in Ireland (AD 1500–

2014), confirms that the winter gales of 2013–14 were the worst on record. This includes such momentous events as the hurricane on the Night of the Big Wind, 6 January 1839, and the storms of December 1951, which reportedly came down the chimneys of houses. Other speakers refer to the fact that not only is the coastline being eroded, but significant portions of sites are being lost to nature. Since 2013, through relentless erosion, havoc has been wreaked on vulnerable coastal archaeological sites, with some washed away entirely. It is an unfolding scenario of stone forts falling into the sea, castles crumbling to the ground, collapsing masonry and piers. Shipwrecks, middens, fish traps, timber trackways and ancient drowned forests are being revealed for the first time in centuries. Burial grounds, including an important Early Christian one, have been damaged, with exposed graves yielding skulls, and skeletal remains littering parts of the shoreline. Beach profiles have been changed beyond all recognition and some declared no-go areas. On the positive side, in terms of the long-term weather prognosis, a futurologist from the Heritage Council predicts that by the 2080s autumns will be much warmer – a fact that underwhelms most of those present.

In the queue for some 'extreme' coffee, a maritime archaeologist, Auriel Robinson, helpfully identifies the items on my bookmark that puzzled me. These include pincers, tweezers, toolkit, sieve, and finds bags. Apart from her archaeological work, through her company called Seatrails, Auriel organises guided tours of sites such as Streedagh beach, the Carrowmore cairns, Strandhill and Knocknarea. Originally from County Meath, she came initially to Sligo for surfing, fell in love with the landscape and stayed. Auriel is also an ambassador for the Wild Atlantic Way. Although she is not wearing her ambassadorial hat, she talks about her involvement with the route and sense of pride in the area.

'I show people sites and give them access to places that they would never have known about or have found on their own. Sligo has so much to offer in terms of cultural heritage, music, literature, and the landscape. When I meet people at conferences such as this, I make them aware of where they should go to get the best out of their time. Sligo is under-explored so I introduce these gems with an eco-friendly approach. The Wild Atlantic Way has drawn attention to what is here and the special experiences you can have. New businesses are opening and people can see what is available without thinking they have to go abroad. It is a creative stage in the history of tourism. People realise for the first time what is on their doorstep and what great value it is. We are on a par with anywhere else in the world in terms of what we can offer on the coastline.'

I ask Auriel if she can shed any professional light on the large timbers from the boat at Streedagh that were exposed in the exceptionally low tides and have been creating a stir.

'It is called a butter boat and has always caused interest but very little has been written or is known about it. It was probably a merchant vessel with substantial timbers with iron nailings so it is most likely from the 1700s or perhaps is an early eighteenth-century wreck. At low tide throughout the year it is exposed and because of this it now appears much more than was previously the case. There hasn't been any scientific work done on the boat other than dendrochronology, but it would have travelled between Ireland and Britain carrying cargo and it's quite a heavy construction. There are a lot of wrecks in the intertidal zone and it is not an easy thing to preserve and conserve something like that. You need expertise as well as means and storage. The rudder that was found earlier came from the Armada and was farther down the beach.

'The Armada is something that still grips the imagination. It is a very important part of political history in Europe and is a fascinating story about King Philip wanting to translate Protestantism to Catholicism. Ireland might have become Spanish-speaking if they had been successful so there is huge story that appeals to people. Every ship has a history and if you were to excavate one of them you could, for example, get back to the actual home of the cannon maker and the house where it was made.'

When I mention my interest in Celtic mythology and the god of the sea, Auriel suggests I should call on Michael Quirke, a woodcarver in Sligo.

I skip the afternoon lectures on developing terrestrial laser scanning for coastal sites, the study of palaeo-landscapes, and threats to underwater cultural heritage, and head into the town centre. Gulls are circling over the tumbling brown waters of the Garavogue as I make my way across the Douglas Hyde Bridge. Tourists photograph each other in front of Rowan Gillespie's flamboyant bronze sculpture of W. B. Yeats draped in a flowing coat overlaid with excerpts from his poems. Erected in 1989 to mark the fiftieth anniversary of his death, the sculpture has been repaired several times and is now on its fifth pair of spectacles following what has been described as 'an unfortunate altercation with a motor vehicle'. When I reach Quirke's shop in Wine Street, a scribbled note on the window reinforces the problems with cars:

> Back at 3pm Traphic Permitting
> There should be no 'F' in Traphic

Examples of the carver's work are showcased in the window display of wooden characters labelled with name tags. Mythology is well represented in his art: Amairgin, Arch-Druid and Leader of the Milesian Celts; Conall Cernach, The Horned Wolf; Oisin The Ancient Returned from Tir na nÓg; the Girl of Many Gifts, and The Good Shepherd. Small cards contain philosophical questions: 'How can the Knower be Known?'; 'Where is Wisdom to be Found?'; the title of a Yeats poem is invoked: 'Who Goes with Fergus?'

To kill time for an hour, I wander through the commercial heart of Sligo, admiring its built heritage, which has always seemed to me to live in the shadow of the permanencies of the much-lauded surrounding landscape. The handsome Arts and Crafts building, which looks like a north Oxford house, is now home to the Yeats Memorial Museum. Traffic angst causes delays along the clogged artery of O'Connell Street where family-owned department stores are still a part of the shopping community. Wehrly's jewellers, Mullaney Bros., general drapers and travel agents, and Henry Lyons Warehouse (in business since 1835) retain distinctive fascia boards in traditional hand-painted lettering. Sligo has reinvented its waterfront, a place of pedestrian bridges, riverside walkways, outdoor cafés and an animated Italian quarter.

When I return to Quirke's shop, Michael is applying the finishing touches to a carving of a dog for a young girl. 'There you are,' he says, 'I've left the dot off over the letter "i" in Aoife as it looks better without it.' When I mention my interest in Manannán, he motions me to sit down on a stump of beech while he explains his background in carving. The shop was originally his father's, a butcher's, and Michael started work in it in 1957.

'I wasn't much of a butcher, and although I had no training, I always made shapes out of clay and plasticine and began to make figures. I did my first carvings in 1968 and still have pictures of them. One of the reasons I gave up the butcher's was that I had a slack period from Christmas to Easter and that was my time for inventing new characters. So I could do Fionn mac Cumhaill, Diarmuid agus Gráinne, and Manannán mac Lir, or any of the other figures.'

The floor and counter are littered with wood shavings. Beech, sycamore and ash are the commonest types of wood that Michael uses.

'They're windfalls, all super woods and you can do anything with them. You have to remember, Celtic mythology can be complex. Mac Lir means "son of the sea" and Manannán was a half-brother of the Children of Lir. He was associated with the Tuatha Dé Danann and affiliated with Tír na nÓg so he has an important place in our mythological history. Originally, as god of the sea, he was typically powerful. There's nobody as superstitious as seamen and fishermen because they're completely at the mercy of the ocean. But what happened in Ireland was that after the Spanish Armada in 1588 we lost contact with the sea. The English had complete control of the local seas and we became insular and in many ways inward-looking and landlocked. This meant that our old gods such as Manannán were less relevant and went underground. Land gods became more important so Manannán was banished to the sea. Before that Poseidon and Neptune were gods of the land as much as of the sea and the underworld. I think a lot of this is pure psychology but the reason why our stories are great is that they are funny. You're not going to get a laugh out of *The Iliad* or *Beowulf* – they're not humorous; but ours are darkly funny. Manannán was displaced by St Michael, so you have Michael's Mount in Cornwall, Mont Saint-Michel in France and Skellig Michael in Kerry. Don't forget, though, that in Ireland the goddesses are much more complicated. The Celtic fertility goddess had three aspects: the maiden, the mother and the crone, encompassing potential, fulfilment and death, which might seem to be three but in fact is only one woman.'

We speak about the Power of Three and how the personification of Ireland is sometimes represented as three goddesses: Ériu, Fódla and Banba. I ask Michael how he would make a carving of Manannán.

'I have done him quite a lot in the past. One of the things that intrigues me about him is his sword, the *Fragarach,* the Answerer or Retaliator. The sword is vital, justice is very important and it was never used to make the first strike. In exactly the same way as in the film *The Vikings* with Tony Curtis, Kirk Douglas and Janet Leigh, they made great play of the sword of Ethelred the Unready which was called Requitor – which is exactly what it means – to retaliate or answer, requite. There's a lot of detail about Manannán and I would place seaweed or watery stuff around him. I'd reflect his *Wavesweeper* chariot drawn by his horse Enbarr. And you'd have to try to include in some way his shape-shifting trickiness which was often emphasised to show that you can't trust him.'

Face down on the shop counter is *Selected Writings* by the French philosopher and Jesuit priest Pierre Teilhard de Chardin. It is published in the Modern Spiritual Master Series and is open at a section called 'Christified Universe'.

'It is very tough stuff,' Michael sighs. 'Essentially it's a commentary on his most famous book, *The Phenomenon of Man,* published in 1955. It would be wrong to say that he is a phoney. There is an awful lot of stuff in it that is way out but I enjoy reading him. My *main* influences would be Robert Graves, Joseph Campbell and W. B. Yeats. The fascinating thing about Graves is that he spent as much time in Sligo as Yeats and was just as Irish. His father and grandfather were clergymen down in Limerick. I have also read some of the work of Thomas Merton. I came across him relatively recently, and found an excellent translation from the Chinese of his "Woodcarver".'

Michael offers to make me a small example of his work as a gift. Manannán would take too long to carve, so he returns to his vice and, using a veiner, draws a sharp cut in a small block of sycamore. As he works, he tells me about some of the more unusual items that he has been asked to make.

'Animals are very popular. I've carved everything from an aardvark to an elephant. People are always wanting dogs and cats so I once asked a customer to come up with something a bit more original as long as I can imagine it. He suggested an aardvark, which is how it came about. You must have the idea in your head first before you start with a blank piece of wood. I have been modelling since I was three years old so that's nearly seventy years and if I don't know how to do it by now, I think it's time to give up.'

With delicate precision, borne of seven decades, he knocks and taps gently, carving out the intricate shape of a fish, driving the veiner with a small wooden mallet. Deftly, he uses a gouger to cut away what is not needed before completing the tail with a flourish. On the reverse side he carves my name and a curved outline of Knocknarea with a small bump symbolising Maeve's cairn.

'That is the *bradán feasa*, the salmon of knowledge, and is a good connection to the sea for your journey.' He gives me his business card with a line handwritten on it: 'Guide to the wine dark intensities in the wood.' I thank him for his delightful salmon carving, handcrafted to perfection, and for his knowledge. Master woodman, philosopher and embodiment of the wisdom of the west, I salute M. Quirke, still carving after all these years.

The relationship between the sea and the mountains has long drawn me to the west and in particular to Sligo. The limestone hill of Knocknarea, as outlined by Michael, encompasses both these attractions. Five miles west of Sligo town, along the busy Coolera Peninsula, the skyline is dominated by the clear-cut bulk of the shapely hill standing 327 metres above sea level, with Maeve's cairn on top. At the far end of the peninsula, Strandhill is just the way a seaside resort should be. It has also become seriously chichi. For those who like rose-tinted retrospection, it supports an old-fashioned ice cream parlour called MJs, a funky seaside café, surf school, beach stores, amusements and seaweed baths, as well as trendy bars.

Shells café is as close as I get to eating on the water without wetting my feet. From my window seat I watch disjointed wave trains lash foam against rocks. They look dangerously close but diners are nonchalant about them. With its lime-green and sky-blue mismatched chairs, colourful artwork decorating plain cream walls, it bears the hallmarks of a Cape Cod café. I note the apophthegms above the counter: 'We don't do fast food. We do good food as fast as we can.' 'Eat well, laugh often, love much.' Following the instructions, I eat a lamb bap accompanied by a large cappuccino and laugh to myself at my good fortune at ending up in Strandhill, a place with which you could easily fall in love – even on a stormy winter's night.

That is what happened to the owners Jane and Myles Lamberth who have stamped their personality on Shells. Jane comes from Dublin while her husband is from Cape Town. She explains how they ended up in Strandhill.

'We've lived a travelling life and our goal has always been outdoor lifestyles, either sea-surfing or snowboarding in the mountains. After five years we realised we needed to settle down and find a home, so it was either surf or snow. We looked everywhere – Australia, New Zealand, South Africa, America, France and Cornwall. We wanted somewhere that could provide an income and a great lifestyle so we discovered Strandhill. I was secretly delighted that it was Ireland and we were close to my family.'

Since taking over the café in spring 2010 and opening a shop, they have not looked back and have transformed a cottage nearby, where they live.

'The draw for us was coastal living and everything that goes with it. For me, being here is chasing the essence of being in the water. There's an amazing freedom of paddling out to the surf; it refreshes your soul. It's an essential part of our living in the same way as for monks it might be meditation; you need it and can't live without it because once you've tasted it, you have to come back for more.'

Jane glances out and talks about the storms. 'Today is wild, it's big, it's heavy and is not surfable because you'd be destroyed if you went out in that. With a high tide, full moon, winds and all the gravitational pull, we have had seaweed and rocks in the car park right outside our front door and have had our car washed. It's been touch and go, and when you see the debris and the seaweed you realise you are at the mercy of the sea.'

Jane compares the Wild Atlantic Way to the Garden Route, a journey from Cape Town to Port Elizabeth along the scenic south-eastern coast of South Africa.

'It's such a simple idea for a huge distance and in exactly the same way this route here gives tourists a purpose as well as a ready-made itinerary so they achieve something rather than aimlessly driving around. I think for Ireland, given that our climate is not great, to market a driving route is a stroke of genius.'

The Gaggia machine behind us is fuming and frothing. I order a Frappuccino, which comes in a large glass with a shot of espresso, two scoops of vanilla ice cream, blended milk, whipped cream and chocolate sprinkles. They serve McCabe's coffee, a family business based in Wicklow. One brand is called Monsoon Malabar, which is stored in open-ended warehouses during the monsoon period to achieve the special flavours. Jane says her travels taught her the importance of serving quality coffee.

'We were exposed to many different things and try to pack that into the café, marrying the coffee with the food. Our goal has always been to provide the best coffee we can find so that we can bring here the vibe of a cosmopolitan city. McCabe's has been in business for fifty years and everything is hand-roasted. The company is pushing boundaries in coffee. The one we've chosen for Shells is a dark roast, an Italian espresso. It's strong, solid, robust and flavoursome. It gives you a good kick and that's what we wanted. The milk is steamed to sixty-five degrees and we can offer a single shot if it's too strong, but you need strength on a day like that.'

Jane sums up her feelings for her adopted coastline at Strandhill. 'Living here is an adventure. The energy from the ocean inspires everyone. I've never before led such a fulfilled and active life as the one I lead here. You find your moment of peace on a secluded section of beach away from the chaos of the busy café so it's a rollercoaster of energy and fun. That's why it's called the "thrill of Strandhill".'

I embark on a twilight walk along the seafront with just a few yards of sloping black limestone and sandstone rocks separating me from an aggressive ocean. Long sets of menacing waves unfurl, sometimes engulfing one another, overtaking or passing, while plumes of spray are thrown high into the air. For a distance of about 100 metres the sea storm swells in a torrent, a seething inexorable mass of mushy foam, commingling in a confused tumble from different angles, known as 'churned-up washing-machine syndrome.' Spits of hail combined with a salty spray slam against my cheeks and lips. Hardy, or foolhardy, photographers stand precariously on a wall capturing the scene on their camera phones. Because of the piercing cold they stay no longer than twenty seconds. Others watch nature's furious display from the warmth of their cars. Braving the conditions, a pied wagtail hops along the wall, speckled with white flecks from the waves, flitting to the ground and swinging its tail violently up and down. Never mind the 'thrill of Strandhill', the chill of the place, accompanied by the powerful basso profundo of Manannán's hostile seahorses, is the big attraction.

Western Sligo is less discovered than other parts of the county. It lives in the shadow of the more celebrated northern section with its landscape drama and literary allure while south Sligo is noted as being the traditional music heartland. From Ballysadare the Way brings me through Beltra, Skreen, Templeboy and Dromard, places that seem only to get on the map because the cartographer had a blank space to fill. Ewes, heavy with lambs, nibble the grass. The road runs parallel to the long, hunched silhouette of the sombre Ox Mountains. Their slopes, which set the tone of the countryside, are heavily cloaked in Sitka spruce. A series of small peaks with rocky outcrops leads to a low ridge standing like a rampart, facing Sligo Bay. Green, russet and dun dominate the palette, with the disfiguring scars left by gorse fires. Rampant daffodils, reminding me of Ted Hughes' 'Guardsmen At attention', are part of the blooming road show along verges while bees breakfast on bright dandelions. In some areas, I had read, daffodils are grown for extracting galantamine, a drug used for treating Alzheimer's. A profusion of the flowers is said to be an ominous sign of an unsettled summer.

The newsagent in Easkey is philosophical about the Way. He says they experienced a *tiny* bit of extra business from it so far.

'This place is suffering very badly', he says. 'We have two pubs left but when I was growing up there were fourteen. There was no television, people had time to talk and make friends. There would have been hundreds on that street on fair days, filling the pubs, keeping them in business, telling yarns and making a deal. People were doing business and they stayed on for their céilí and danced at the crossroads. But the world has changed; not, in my opinion, for the better.'

Through torrential rain, the road to Easkey beach is deserted. The wind is whipping up malevolent waves. I pull up beside a VW in which a large surfboard occupies the back seat. The driver is closely surveying the water. When the rain stops, we both venture out into the chilly air. Paul O'Kane has come to assess the surfing possibilities but it is not a day for what some call the 'beautiful surfer people'. His life, he tells me, is based around the weather.

'I'm a bit like a farmer since I always pay attention to what the forecast is like for the next day. I study weather and tide charts, and wind- and swell-prediction charts which make it easier but still the main thing is to go and have a look. As I live only ten minutes from here, I've come to assess it but it's not good enough for me to bother surfing. We've got two waves – Easkey West and Easkey East – which are the staple waves and the most consistent in this immediate stretch of coast. Most of the time you will get a wave and as you branch out from here the waves get more fickle and don't break as often or as well as here. I was surfing all day yesterday, which was the complete opposite to this. The wind was offshore, the sun was out and I flogged myself to death.'

Paul grew up in the 1970s beside Bondi Beach in Sydney where the ocean was part of his life from an early age. When he rode his first board he was enraptured by the sensation of speed. Since then, his life has been dominated by the pursuit of waves and he has surfed in New Guinea, Indonesia, New Zealand and South Africa. Although his father was born in Australia, his family has Irish roots.

'He was always telling me about Ireland and after I married an Irish girl, I moved to Easkey in 1997 because of the surfing. We came for a honeymoon, travelled along the west coast but for some reason Easkey was the place we kept coming back to and we are still here. As it's a lot colder here you have got to be a bit tougher but twenty years ago it was also a lot quieter – that was the attraction and after growing up in a big city I was happy for a quietness in my life. I wouldn't move back to any city. I'm a culchie now and my son was born here. The curious thing is that we are still finding waves on this stretch of coastline. With surfers there's a desire to always look around the next corner.'

Paul's claim to surfing fame is that he was part of a group in 2010 that discovered and surfed the monster wave 'Prowlers', the biggest seen for many years, and a private realm.

'We didn't tell the press where it was and that got them all excited. They put investigative journalists on the case and they tried to trick us into telling them where it was. It started its own little firestorm.'

'Is it still a secret?'

'Not really, it's out at sea.'

'In County Sligo?'

'Yes. We liked the name Prowlers as it has a great ring and all voted for it so it was chosen by committee and it was funny that it was mentioned in the Dáil.'

'How do waves get named?'

'You can name a wave yourself but it must be taken on by popular culture. If no one is ever going to call it what you have chosen, then it won't be called that.'

'Have you named any?'

'One called Double-Ohs which is in Sligo – no other people surf it yet. I got barrelled twice on one wave so that's how it got the name and so far it's sticking.'

When Paul is not surfing he is involved in rescue work. He trains surfers, helps run competitions and works closely with the coastguard. His whole life revolves around the sea, in trying to understand it and the many subtle differences between the surfing rides.

'The ocean has a myriad of moods, at least a million different ones. Each one of these waves has its own characteristics and they're all completely different. One breaks left, one breaks right, and after that every wave is unique; it has its own water movements in the way it changes, the different swell directions, some favourable, some unfavourable, some will be difficult to surf, others easy, but they all present different challenge levels. It can keep you busy for a lifetime because no two waves are the same.'

'What is it like riding a big wave?'

'When you are surfing a big one at Mullaghmore the feelings are intense. I used to check it from the headland and would talk myself out of going. Before I get to Mullaghmore there comes a point on the drive where my stomach starts to churn with butterflies. That's a really stressful time and I don't know whether I'm going to throw up or not and that is because of the fear of the unknown. Then you get to the break and start your routine. I go quiet, get on with my preparation and go through a certain ritual. Then I join the others in the team and the first time I feel any calmness is when I actually get on the water and start going over the waves. My breathing settles into the rhythm and then it becomes a more calculated thing.'

We talk about the dangers involved, which Paul says are no worse than in motorbike racing or other sports. Bad things happen to surfers and they have to be tough. He has had several narrow shaves, including one occasion when his board smashed against his head, splitting his ear.

'I also came close to drowning at Aileens near the Cliffs of Moher. I didn't get the wave I wanted, I turned around and there was a giant behind it. Your worst nightmare. The wave was frightening enough and it broke twenty feet in front of me and the white water exploded up higher and I just remember thinking "I need to do more training". Friends rescued me so I escaped with their help.'

As a non-surfer, I am fascinated by what force drives them to dance on the water, and by the argot of the sport: barrels, bowls, tubes and take-off spots, sets and intervals are all part of the lingua franca. As we look out at the lacework of breaking waves that is his playing field, Paul explains why it is so important to him.

'It's the clarity of thinking that is the best thing about it. Coming in from a good surf you feel elated and each time is just as exciting or more exciting than the first time. You're chasing something that is completely attainable and you're improving and gaining experience at the same time. It's best explained with the big waves because it's more noticeable as it's exponentially blown up but my life is an oval of vision where my peripheral vision would be only eight metres wide in front of me on a wave, twenty metres long and that's my survival line. If I can get from here to there, I am going to survive this moment and then my heart starts beating and adrenalin kicks in – you're at the end of the wave in the channel, you're shaking hard. It's a crazy feeling. That was your world and that clarity comes from the fact that that was the only thing in your world; there was no worry about what happened yesterday, what bills I have to pay or the fact that my underfloor heating is not working – there is just nothing – your brain is working on a million different calculations and it's an exceptional feeling.'

Back in Easkey the Stranglers' hit 'Golden Brown' fills the Grub Hub where I have come in search of sustenance. The place is even more deserted than the beach. A cardboard box of Olé peat briquettes sits beside a stove at a stone fireplace, while overhanging it a sign says: 'Coffee, Chocolate, Men: some things are just better rich.' A large wall is dominated by a mural of Brendan Gleeson from *Calvary* released in 2014. Dressed as a priest, he is portrayed in the middle of the street amongst Easkey's colourful shopfronts. The actor played the lead role of Fr James Lavelle whose life is threatened in the confessional. Set in and around the town, it was filmed during a three-week period in the autumn of 2012.

Brendan Gleeson mural, Easkey, County Sligo.

On the plastic yellow tablecloth, the waitress places a three-cup cafetière alongside a white cup and saucer with a Douwe Egberts logo. Matching plastic flowers stand upright in a green vase. She looks up at the painting.

'It helped put the place on the map,' she says, 'but although it was classified as black comedy, I didn't find any humour in it. It was a serious film, not funny at all which I was annoyed about as I like a laugh when I go to the cinema but 'twas a bit too heavy for me. Mind you, Gleeson did well out of it and won awards for his acting although I don't really think it has attracted many people to come to the area.'

She says the Way has brought in people, especially German and French visitors as well as those searching for their roots. Out of the side of her mouth and with cupped hand, she adds sotto voce, 'Why would you want to come to Easkey?'

My final Sligo port of call, Enniscrone, a few miles south, is close to the Mayo border. The road to it is lined with stone walls. A humble farmhouse sign on a gatepost advertises 'Hay

Sale.' Three white onshore turbines, each with three blades wheeling lazily, harness the wind off the sea; not only do they clutter the horizon, but they bring a whole new meaning to the Power of Three.

In Enniscrone, I look out on a wide strip of beach. The only users are several dog walkers, waders and two paddle-boarders. The tide is a long way out. Portly oystercatchers, immaculately clad in black and white, line up in three-three-three parade-ground formation. Uncharacteristically becalmed, they peck and pause in the sand. They remain undeterred even by the nearby spectacle of a closely bunched murmuration of knot rising in a cloud, looping and dancing in the sky in mesmerising coordinated twirls.

The woman running the hotel tells me the resort has remained largely unchanged over the years. It is a popular destination with families for it offers a safe beach, miles of sand dunes and energetic walks. When I mention my walking being curtailed because of a sore leg from sitting in the car for long stretches, she suggests a hot seaweed soak in baths just along the shorefront. From sheer curiosity, I decide it might be worth trying.

The baths are in a square single-storey building that looks like Lego. For over 100 years Kilcullen's Bath House has attracted seaweed soakers. Before stepping into the bath, I sit for five minutes in a marine plywood steam box, using a small lever to regulate the amount, and end up releasing enough to power a small train. My head pokes out through the top of the door as if I'm a medieval prisoner in stocks, fortunately not subject to public humiliation. The bathroom decor evokes the elegance of an older age of quality: cedarwood panelling, Edwardian floral tiling, solid brass taps, a copper shower, and creaky plumbing sound-effects.

Cautiously, and after some apprehension, I step into a whale-sized free-standing delph bath filled with seaweed and saltwater straight from Killala Bay, heated to between eight and sixteen degrees centigrade. I cover myself with dark green fronds of serrated wrack, also known by its more expressive Latin name *Fucus serratus*. Initially it gives me the heebie-jeebies. Salty fronds fall into my mouth and I have trouble regulating my breathing. It feels slimy, especially on my neck and upper arms, so I close my eyes, lie still and let it wash over me. Gradually, after a period of wallowing and floating, the effect becomes soft and buoyant. My toes are tangled in a silky seaweed mangle and small clusters break off. After thirty minutes I heave myself out, gather up the seaweed, now broken up into loose strands, and place them in a bucket beside the bath. The most invigorating part of all comes from a cold seawater power shower from which screams frequently emanate. It easily wins the 'Coldest Shower of My Life' award.

Edward Kilcullen, whose grandfather started it all in 1912 as a modern seaweed bathhouse, is pleased to hear my positive report of bathing in the green stuff. We sit in the foyer of the building beside shelves of body-care products and boxes of Carraig Fhada Atlantic Seaweed selling for €10. A quotation, attributed to Einstein, hangs from a shelf: 'Great spirits have always encountered opposition from mediocre minds.' There has been, he says, a strong resurgence of interest in the baths in recent years.

'Enniscrone is a beautiful seaside place with about 600 people and very few are bothered about seaweed baths. But our catchment area covers Connacht and half of Ulster and we have our regulars who travel on a weekly basis from up to sixty miles away. A big proportion of our business is from people on holiday. We have grandchildren and great-grandchildren of the people who originally came here wanting to find out what it's like. It's a traditional place where families have come for years and is not over-commercialised. Unlike other places on the west coast, we don't suffer from over-development as Enniscrone is so expansive – it's got a huge footprint and with the large beach it means you are not hit by in-your-face developments.

By the 1980s it was on its knees because there had not been any investment for many years, and then it just seemed to turn.'

Seaweed baths developed from people looking for a cure, and in the Victorian era sea bathing became popular. Edward took over the running of the baths in the summer of 1989.

'We invested in it and in the early 1990s people were looking to alternatives again as they were disillusioned with the modern lifestyle. So it went well and we've now brought it back up to the levels that it would have been at in its heyday. It produces a mixture of curiosity and doubt. We get some people who turn their noses up at the idea of seaweed; some are squeamish and others are sceptical. They are more used to being wrapped up in fluffy robes in spas. An awful lot of people's perception of seaweed is formed by being on the beach as children during the summer and finding this horrible stuff with flies in it and getting caught up in it when paddling in the water. This is the notion that is ingrained in their head and while it is seaweed, it is totally different since it is in its natural environment rotted by the sun. We offer a rawer hundred-year-old experience and ninety-nine per cent of people leave converted so it does tend to silence the cynics because we aren't a gimmick.'

Every morning Edward rises early, makes his way down to the shoreline and pulls off the seaweed growing on the rocks in front of the bathhouse.

'When the tide is out, it exposes this growing marine plant and we harvest it fresh every day and bring it in. It is seaweed in its natural form. There's a big bucket in the bathrooms – there's nothing refined or pretentious about it since it's the way it has always been done – and we put the seaweed in that under a jet of steam for twenty seconds. This helps soften it and releases the natural gels which gives it the oily texture. In its growing process, seaweed extracts iodine from the surrounding seawater and concentrates it in its fronds to such an extent that some seaweeds have up to 20,000 times the concentration of iodine of the water in which they grow. It is something that has been handed down over the generations and is traditional, unprocessed and unadulterated.'

Back at the waterfront, the oystercatchers have been replaced by a party of six Brent geese, circling in the water, then riding languidly over waves. Over dinner at the Enniscrone Pizza Place, I relax in the afterglow of my *serratus* experience, concluding that I am best of 'fronds' with it. As I cut my Neptune pizza into slices, I wonder about his role as sea god. From an online news story I discover that there has been a dramatic twist to the tale of the stolen statue. Manannán has been found a half-mile from his original position. A group of ramblers walking through a forest near the summit of Binevenagh Mountain came across the statue lying on its back on the grass. They alerted soldiers on a training exercise who called in the police.

The 'casualty' was carried back to the road and taken away for examination. The base of the statue was smashed from where it had been detached and the back of his head was also damaged. Although now safely recovered, mystery still surrounds why anyone would have stolen it and what possible motive was involved.

PART II
The Midwest
Mayo, Galway, Clare and Limerick

Under six inches of water
pebbles, each one of them noble
in the heraldic colours of their ancestry.

Time sits weaving
and unweaving an endless tapestry
for a Ulysses who will one day come.

As I will – not this caricature
who wades in six inches of water.
My true self, my aimless wanderer.

I pick up a pebble and watch
its colours fade – and put it back. Full tide
won't dull its invisible shining.

Repulsive death washes into my mind.
It won't dull the invisible shinings there –
dead friends, noble in the last certainty.

Norman MacCaig, 'Low tide'
The Poems of Norman MacCaig

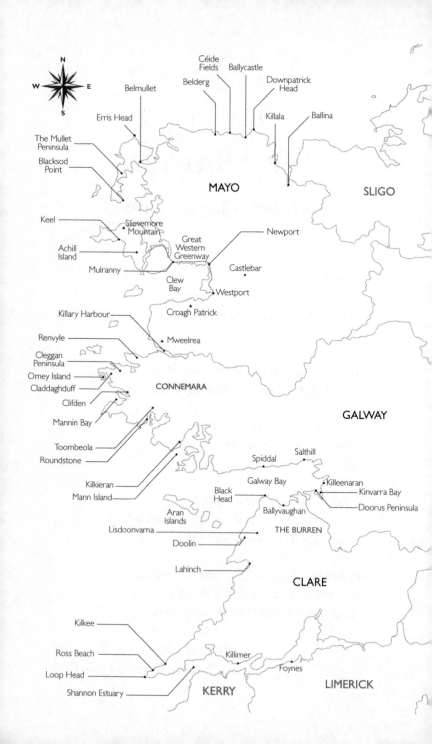

5

The Klondike after the gold ran out

WHEN THE NAME FOR HIS CAFÉ in Ballina was first suggested, Anthony Heffernan was not sure it would be accepted by locals. But since 2012, the Heifer and Hen name has stuck and you need to arrive early for a lunchtime table.

'It was the chef's idea,' Anthony recalls. 'I thought people would react wrongly to it but it took off. Originally we opened in 2007 and five years later, with a designer's help, we rebranded ourselves and haven't looked back.'

Cupcake-ification has come to Ballina and alongside these multicoloured treats, Anthony runs a butcher's, baker's, deli, salad bar and upstairs restaurant. Red-aproned waitresses with black shirts buzz around tables while diners tuck into vegetable soup, fish pie or lasagne.

'Our customers are very discerning, particularly about coffee, which is a huge thing now,' he says. 'We tried Fair Trade coffee for a change but it was not popular and we now use Red Bean Arabica. People don't like change; they like to be comfortable with what they're used to.'

His father started the business in 1961 and now Anthony has his own abattoir. 'In the 1980s there were five Heffernan butchers in Ballina; now there's just one. These days spring lamb is the big seller but rib-eye steak is popular. There's a big swing back with traceability, which is important for customers.'

Anthony says the Way has helped bring in visitors. 'The Italians love it here – they fly into Knock Airport and come up to Ballina. We're an anchor town with some fantastic scenery but are out on a limb so we try hard to build a return trade.'

Known as the 'Salmon capital' of Ireland, Ballina has been celebrating winning the prestigious Purple Flag award, which recognises excellence in town centres with a focus on the night-time economy. The idea is to help it become part of a growing breed of tourism towns. A signboard also records the fact that it was a Pride of Place winner in 2013.

Behind the wheel again, having completed my trip through LSD (Leitrim, Sligo, Donegal) it is time for a coastal exploration of the mid-west counties. I am beginning to feel like an addict; the west has become a potent drug, and I need to have it coursing through my veins as much as cappuccino. The winter-into-spring months have arrived and I am not sure what season it is. Along the minor coastal road to Killala, stone walls – one a Famine wall – line the west side of the Moy River. The men who built it in 1848 each received a bowl of Indian meal every evening as payment for their day's work. Food was ground up and served as a family meal called stirabout and, to this day, the wall running alongside Belleek Castle is known as the 'Stirabout Wall'.

The road bristles with energising birdsong. In quick succession tits, robins, a magpie and blackbird rise ahead of me off the tarmac. At a crossroads near Carrowkelly, a song thrush, its head cocked, pours out its loud repeating *tsip* call, drawing me into its melodic domain as it stakes out its territory. Other thrushes pace around looking for worms. Branches of bare trees are adorned with what are known colloquially as 'witches' knickers', a satirical term for windborne plastic bags. In Mayo they have a positive approach to the Way. An editorial in *The Western People* stated that it was one of the success stories of 2014, benefiting some of the more remote parts of the north of the county.

> The Wild Atlantic Way is an immensely clever piece of marketing and Fáilte Ireland deserves full credit in investing in it. In truth, there was not a whole lot of investment involved. All it took was a few signposts and some advertising, but that modest investment has certainly reaped dividends. Each of

the counties on the Atlantic coastline are magnificent in their own right, but when their strengths are pooled together they form a very formidable tourism product.

Killala is café-less and hotel-less, and its 'tourism product' is at first sight not obvious. Its streets with blind bends overflow with cars parked, or more accurately, abandoned at dangerous angles. Half a dozen buildings lie derelict or bear 'To Let' signs. Despite its run-down appearance, it has made strenuous efforts to bring in visitors by capitalising on its history through festivals. Maria Bilbow, who runs Avondale B&B on the quay road where I stayed twenty-five years ago, assures me that a new café is on the way. It is going to be called just that: On the Way. When I stayed here in 1991, her father, Michael Caplice, who now lives in Ballina, ran the guesthouse in a small dormer bungalow. Maria took it over in 1998 and has extended.

'We've had a few changes since your last visit,' she says. 'We've done six extensions in total. All the rooms are now en suite. Killala is a seasonal place and although we have a short tourist trade, there's tremendous history and it's a friendly place as people always have time to talk to you.'

The guesthouse overlooks Killala Bay with the low-lying Bartra Island, known as St Patrick's Cocklebank, sitting peaceably in the sun. The town is a long-established seaport, first mentioned in the 'Tripartite Life of Patrick' around 900. It is also well known as the first place to be taken by General Humbert and his French troops after their landing at Kilcummin in 1798. Three rusting hulks are moored at the tidal harbour alongside fishing boats: *Louise Joanne*, *Leah*, *The Huntress*, *An Déiseach*, *Anastasia* and *Brenda Joan*. A man power-hoses the floor of a fish shed. Chalked up on a trailer at the Seafood Shop, today's specials are Salmon Darne €2 each and Whole Plaice €1. Along quay road, a gang of six gregarious mallard with bright orange legs cross the grass with a tipsy waddle. They look inquisitively at me and retreat to the pebble beach, some attempting a half-hearted flight. Then it is time for aerobics class: they flick wings, swivel glossy green heads, flex white necks, wiggle tail feathers, stand on one leg and then the other, completing their workout with a conversation of soft gabbling quacks and grunts.

Rising above the harbour, the town skyline is dominated by the twelfth-century round tower, twenty-five metres high, and across the road, the spire of the Church of Ireland Cathedral of St Patrick. A long flight of steps leads to the tower standing on a plinth and built of oolitic limestone. Its round-headed doorway was positioned three metres above the ground for security. A noticeboard poses the question: 'Why were towers built?' In the time-honoured tradition of keeping all historical options open, no fewer than eighteen different possibilities and extant theories are outlined in the answer. These range from: fire towers, watch towers, granaries, forts, purgatorial pillars, phallic symbols, places of refuge, sepulchres, hermetical dwellings, depositories of valuables, radio antennae, astronomical marks and paramagnetic energy marks, astrological gnomons or pins, pagan *lithoi* or obelisks, or the theory that the towers are aligned with the night sky at winter solstice. For good measure, traditionalists argue that they are ecclesiastical belfries, hence the Irish name *Cloigteach,* which translates as a round tower, a steeple or bell-house.

At the other end of town, the Wolfdog Tavern is a daytime drinkers' bar. Suffering caffeine withdrawal symptoms from the absence of a café, I am in need of a coffee reboot. Two elderly men and a middle-aged woman perch on high chairs discussing the merits of whiskies such as Jameson, Powers Gold Label and Scotch. A man in a black fleece, his conversation sprinkled with oaths, indulges in banter with the woman and a blue-jacketed man. They argue over the taste of Crested Ten – too thin and too smooth for blackfleece, too much like sherry for bluecoat. The woman rummages in her handbag for a pink mobile phone, checking her texts and shifting on her chair. Everything falls quiet. Another round is ordered.

My bitter coffee is served at a window seat and poured from a silver teapot. Two young children draw at a table in the back room. The walls contain information on 1798 and photographs from battle re-enactments during the 2014 festival 'In Humbert's Footsteps' when locals dressed as pikemen. A copy of the 1916 Proclamation of Independence hangs beside a fireplace. The bar-counter small talk turns to the quality of shirts and their ironing, job contracts, work pensions, Killala's traffic jams and dilapidated buildings. A community action plan has shown dissatisfaction about the large number of derelict properties, as well as vandalism, an underage drinking culture and drug use. It also spoke of 'baneful negativity' and a lack of transparency on the community council.

'There's nothing for the young ones here, no jobs, no prospects, so it's no wonder they take to drink,' bluecoat says.

'I try to keep sober,' says blackfleece.

'You're in the wrong place for that,' the woman replies, scrolling on her phone.

En route to Ballycastle, a tailback of single-file traffic over the eighteenth-century Palmerstown Bridge causes me to stop, presenting the opportunity to check the bustling river for birdlife without having to step out of the car. Aloof in midstream, a heron, at its full height of one metre, stands on a grassy island. It plunges its sharp beak and the struggles of its prey throw up a shower of droplets. Sensing the presence of binoculars, it lifts off, slow-flapping a solitary path unswervingly low, disappearing around a bend into Rathfran Bay. According to *Brewer's Dictionary of Irish Phrase & Fable*, it is said in folklore that the chimera-like shape-shifter Manannán mac Lir used to visit women at night in the shape of a heron. The water traffic is quickly replaced by two grey wagtails taking up position on top of boulders. In some areas these birds are referred to as 'water' wagtails. Flirting with each other, they dart and hide, their short *stzit* call bouncing off the multiple-arch stone bridge. Their black throat and yellow breast belie their name while sulphur-yellow undertail coverts flash brilliantly in the riverine light.

The small towns of north Mayo, with family-run shops, are free of multinational chains. At least that is how I remember them from my hitchhike along this stretch of coast. But the 21st-century reality is different and some villages have lost their vigour. The corner shop, once the fabric of most places, is being replaced by the online community, tweeting and trending, clicking and collecting; no longer do they smoke away the gossip of the town at the crossroads. The reason for this decline is often the closure of a grocer, butcher, baker, bank or post office, the mainstays of the local economy. They were the nerve centre of the place and when the beating heart was removed, the town lost its way.

To say that Ballycastle is lacking in entrepreneurial confidence is an understatement. From the top of the town, the sloping High Street is a melancholy string of boarded-up or closed shops in dull shades of cream, grey, yellow or green. Net curtains guard privacy, while in other buildings windows are broken. At first I thought it was half-day closing. It is like stepping into a sepia photograph resembling an empty film set before the crew arrives to reconstruct an impoverished village scene from the late nineteenth century. April Thursdays in Ballycastle are eerily quiet, bordering on ghostly.

The only animation is a refrigerated mobile shop set up by Jarlath Tolan outside the post office. Part of a regular weekly ritual from 10 a.m. to 2 p.m., he sells home-cured bacon and ham. The woman running the Resource Centre says his is the only butcher's left. She suggests I speak to George O'Grady who lives at the bottom of the street. He is the go-to man for information on Ballycastle and has retired from running the last full-time butcher's shop, which is why they rely on a mobile visit. When I call at his house, George invites me in. A tall, thin man with a friendly countenance, he offers to boil the kettle. We sit at the kitchen table where the Sacred Heart of Jesus keeps a watchful eye as we sip tea. A turf fire glows in a stove. On the mantelpiece a sign with two flowers says: 'An old rooster and a young chick live here.' George's grandfather started the butchering business in 1910 and it was later taken over by his father.

'I left school at fourteen and was involved in farming until I was twenty-two,' he says. 'In the early years we had crops – potatoes and oats. We cut turf, saved turf, we ploughed and we had no money. Nobody had much money. I bought a heifer for £26 in September 1966, sold her the first week and made some money. The following week I bought another one for £22 and sold that within a week. The shop took off and people flocked to me. I started with my father, although he had more interest in farming than in butchering and I spent forty-eight years in the shop. In recent times, things had got quiet, so by March 2014 I had made up my mind to close and retired six months later.'

When he was growing up, lamb was popular but it was many years before pork and bacon products were sought. George invokes a threefold manifestation, known as tricolon, about the work involved.

'It was blood, sweat and tears, very hard work, but I was young. Everything was fairly primitive, especially in the slaughterhouse. I did the buying, the killing and the selling. I enjoyed it as I was making money so I was happy. The customers would sit on chairs along the wall. They talked about cows calving, about the mart, about football and politics – everything was covered so it was a great meeting place for single men living alone. They might have stayed an hour – they just wanted someone to talk to. Very decent people. A lot of them have gone to their just rewards. The shop was a hub and was open seven days a week. Sunday was a big shopping day. Everybody went to Mass and they were in no hurry home. After the early Mass at 8.30 a.m., I would run down to the shop and there would be maybe twelve or fifteen behind me, and then after 11 a.m. Mass there could be twenty people.

'In the 1960s everyone knew everybody's business. People would ask me where I got the meat from. It was a thriving town, full of shops. We had fourteen pubs, some with a grocery at the front, but now there are only three pubs and two shops. The pubs are taking a hiding; cheap drink in the supermarkets has finished them. We had three petrol stations and are down to one. We had a dance hall, which was booming every Sunday night when all the Northern bands came here. You could get anything you'd want in Ballycastle then. When I was growing up we had three blacksmiths shoeing horses, two carpenters, two dressmakers and a shoemaker. We had three butchers – I was the last to close – so I have seen vast changes. It's a totally different place and is becoming quite lonely. It's full of empty houses and places for sale. Mary Robinson came here once during her presidency and said it was on the periphery of the periphery.'

George now spends his time farming and keeps Charolais, Limousin, Belgian Blue and Salers. He refers to Ballycastle as 'a town of little museums' where some of the closed businesses such as his still retain their original fittings. His retirement after nearly half a century running the business was mourned. He brings me next door into the shop where the blinds are permanently down and the white tiles have lost their gleam. His maple-wood butcher's block, 'turned inside out and upside down', a band saw, and cold room are exactly as he left them, preserved in aspic. Many people were sad when he decided to hang up his pinstripe apron.

'I saw two women crying the day I closed,' he reflects. 'We had craic and fun and knew each other. But I wasn't in great health and had circulation problems in my hands so I have moved on. It was expensive to run. Times have changed and you have to go with them. I hate to be despondent but it's so sad when you look out and see an empty street. It is like the Klondike after the gold ran out.'

The forward march of the prospecting baristas and the movement known as the 'Third Wave of Coffee' has not yet reached Ballycastle. In Mary's Cottage Kitchen, an old-school café free of electro chatter – and one of the few bright spots – there is no danger of suffering cappuccino fatigue.

'We leased a cappuccino-making machine,' says Mary Munnelly, the owner, 'but it kept breaking down so we gave it up. Sometimes it would pack up on a Friday and if it was a bank holiday weekend we couldn't get it fixed until Tuesday so that was no use. We now serve Bewley's regular coffee. We are not an urban coffee shop: we are rural and we take pride in that.'

She motions to the fire. 'Where else would you get a café burning turf directly from its very own bog? Ours comes from Sralagga, just out the road. And where else would you find a sloping ceiling between two rooms?'

The character-filled cottage with its flagstone floor was built in 1825. Mary has run it as a café since 1997. Signs on the wall say: 'OMG: Mother was right about everything', and 'A balanced diet is a cake in each hand.' Her tasty, moist soda loaf is made with buttermilk. Mary speaks about the decline of Ballycastle.

'We are on a downward spiral,' she says pragmatically. 'Shops have closed but we have built up our business. Since 2008 we have struggled – there was no money in the area, the farming community don't have the money and the young people have left, but we have to keep going and do the best we can.'

Along a thin coastal road and over a cattle grid at Downpatrick Head a breeze ripples the grass like an invisible hand stroking hair. A necklace of breakers curls in, foaming across wave-eroded slate-grey flat rocks which look like kitchen-floor tiling with diagonal lines forming a square pattern. The sun lurches in and out of feather-like clouds. As I squelch my way past clumps of heath bedstraw, a red sign warns 'You are entering this area at your own risk of dangerous blowholes, rapidly eroding cliffs and subsidence risks.' The uphill path leads to a new installation, 'The Spirit of Place', by an American artist Travis Price. *Poll na Seantainne* blowhole is surrounded by a steel-rod flute fence with stone seating. Display panels feature inscrutable headings such as: 'Lapping turbulence weaves', 'Reflections forgotten', 'Surging eruptions unveil the Sea of Seeing.' A design metaphor, called 'The Crossing' is said to represent what lies 'Between the mystical and the material, between cultural history and the eternal sacred, and contradiction and paradox.' Through an arch, a large eddying whirlpool is filled with cappuccino-coloured spume. I knew the coffee allusion would catch up with me somewhere hereabouts.

Beyond the enigmatic artwork, a statue of St Patrick in a small enclosure lords it over the hill. Visitors have placed coins on the grass, which are embedded around the base. Three stiff-winged fulmars circle the air space, riding the thermals effortlessly, gliding, banking and following each other as if playing a game. From a Second World War lookout tower, the cries of boisterous seabirds ricochet and echo around steep cliffs as they enjoy the unfettered ocean air in a place known as the 'land of the salty wind'. Gingerly, I approach the edge, peering down the dizzyingly steep drop of hundreds of metres to the treacherous waters below, now a milky turquoise. With acrobatic twists and turns, yabbering seabirds fly sorties, soaring over my head in tumbling aerial turmoil, crisscrossing to their nests on the fifty-metre-high Dún Briste sea stack. Directly across from me, holding centre stage, colonies of kittiwakes are wedged on a staircase of perilously narrow guano-spattered cliff ledges. With their snowy-white heads, happily nesting couples pair off snugly in private crevices, more beak to beak than cheek to cheek. Shunning the company of the crowd, they peck each other, a touching courtship display of how, in one small corner of north Mayo, cliff-hugging love is in the air.

On my way to the Céide Fields, a sooty-faced ewe and her lamb also share a nose-to-nose tête-à-tête, another example of western affection. Liquid sunshine pours down and the day is turning hot. Black cattle chew grass. This stretch of road hugging the coast merits a GCR. On my right, the sea is an all-consuming horizon; inland, smoke rises from cottages with satellite dishes amongst the bogland while a triptych of mountains – Tawnynaboll, Tawnaghmore and Glinsk – stands out in the distance. On the *Late Late Lunchbox* on Mid-West Radio ('Across the region and around the world'), they are playing Status Quo, Rod Stewart, Bob Seger and Hall & Oates.

I am on a return visit to an area I first discovered in 1991. The idea of a centre to interpret this ancient landscape had been bubbling since 1989 and was being masterminded from a small office in Ballycastle by the noted archaeologist and antiquarian Professor Seamus Caulfield. It was another four years before the Céide Fields Centre opened, creating a stir with its dramatic glass-topped pyramidal shape. I did not meet Seamus then but a quarter of a century on I am hoping to talk to him and had phoned in advance to the manager, Gretta Byrne. When I arrive she is being interviewed by Irish TV, so I browse outside where small pink and blue milkworts are starting to bloom. In the foyer, an ancient Scots pine from a local bog provides the centrepiece and, given its age of 4,300 years, attracts much attention. The upstairs viewing area is the ideal place to appreciate the interface of sea and land. The 360-degree panorama takes in the jagged Stags of Broadhaven looking like two pyramids in the distance. The Céide Fields are regarded as one of the most extensive Stone Age monuments in the world and one of the most intact Neolithic settlements in Ireland. Gretta's connection with it stretches back thirty-five years. She first came to the area as a young student in the summer of 1981 when Seamus was excavating the site and the area around Belderg.

'I am from a farming background so the land is in my blood,' she says. 'But the first time I arrived here on my bicycle I pedalled up the hill and all I saw was bare bogland. My impression of the landscape was that there were not even any fields here, as very little was known of the full extent of them. When I came back the following summers to work on my thesis for a postgraduate degree I got to know it better.'

In the early 1990s, part of the thinking, Gretta says, was to use the archaeology of the area as an economic resource to kick-start tourism in north Mayo.

'It was a local initiative with a committee set up to raise funds and stage events. They were supported by public bodies and there was great excitement. Architects from the OPW designed the centre, which opened in 1993 and was marked by a year-long celebration of Mayo 5000. Because the physical remains are not that visual – there is no large upstanding structure – they decided that the centre should be a strong physical focus to the site and the pyramid shape was partly built into the sloping hillside. The vegetation is growing up the outside so when you see it from a distance, emerging out of the bog, it looks like it's part of the landscape rather than being superimposed on it.'

The centre went on to win awards – including the Royal Institute of Architects of Ireland Triennial Gold Medal – for its unique design and it has continued to attract visitors as well as heightening interest in archaeology.

'It took a few years to become established as we are off the beaten track but it has helped put the area on the map. Since it opened, three quarters of a million people have passed through. There's a big interest nowadays in the environment and climate change.'

Moves are afoot to update the centre and they have just been given word that money will be available to refresh the exhibits with new interpretation to reflect changing historic perspectives.

'The work we do now concentrates on dating as well as establishing the prehistoric environment, and the picture is changing all the time. What we thought twenty or thirty years ago is totally different to what we think now and research is continuing. When I was in college the Neolithic sites were thought to be around five thousand two hundred years old but now it is believed to have started six thousand years ago. New discoveries are constantly being made and dating techniques are become more refined, which makes it all so fascinating.'

Eight kilometres west of Céide, at Belderg, Seamus Caulfield greets me warmly, opening a door on to the past. Under a glaring sun, we crunch our way across dry bogland, looking out over stone walls and the largest blanket bog valley in Western Europe.

'Belderg is made up of sixty or seventy scattered houses but if you stop on the high ground and look back, you will see an oasis in a valley of bog. There is nothing for miles around other than the modern farms. If you drive on to Porturlin there is another oasis. And think about this: it is twenty miles by twenty miles which equals four hundred square miles, that's a thousand square kilometres of bog from here through Erris and when you drive on down to Mulranny you're still in it.'

More than eighty years ago, the importance of this area was brought to the attention of the archaeological heavyweights. Seamus' father, a local schoolteacher, sent a letter in 1934 to the museum in Dublin about the significance of the stone walls.

'One hundred yards from us are the walls about which my father wrote to the museum. He wasn't an archaeologist, but in the letter he said that these walls were very ancient because they come to light only when the bogs above them are cut away. Belderg has both Stone Age farming and Bronze Age farming where we are now. We now know that these are Stone Age in date and that these are dairy farmers. We thought at one time that we had cultivation in Belderg – big fields and cattle at Céide – but the new knowledge coming out suggests that they are not cultivating here, but dairying. These are dairy farmers spreading all over Ireland and Britain from mainland Europe. That's why we are rethinking the Céide site and I'm delighted it's getting a revamp.'

Regarded as a unique ecosystem, the area is being rebranded by Seamus who organises guided tours. His company offers 'The Belderrig Experience', a three-day immersion in this historic landscape, which he believes will appeal to the general visitor. He also lectures and leads field trips from the Belderrig Research and Study Centre into what he calls 'the outdoor laboratory'.

'I give a twelve-week course of lectures on this valley but when Seamus Heaney stood here he looked across and was able to capture it in four lines: "A landscape fossilized / Its stone wall patternings / Repeated before our eyes / In the stone walls of Mayo." But the more we look into it now and the more we find out about the Bronze Age, we realise it isn't a landscape fossilised, so it's poetic licence.'

We pause at small cultivation ridges on which barley was grown. Sunlight picks its way across them. With a fifty-year hinterland of research, Seamus wears his knowledge lightly and patiently. We hunker down and I discover he has a zest for triple groupings.

'Look at those ridges: they don't come more minute than that, just a couple of inches high, three feet wide, and yet they were of an extraordinary antiquity. In Ireland it is said that three times the life of a horse is the life of a person, and three times the life of a person is the life of a whale, and three times the lifespan of a whale is the life of a ridge, and the lifespan of three ridges is the life of the world. Everything happens in threes. Isn't that an amazing and acute observation?'

Across the bog we come to an area with tree stumps. Seamus stops to explain their significance.

'This was a five-thousand-year-old forest where there is evidence of ancient storms and forest fires. So we have fields that date to the Neolithic since the trees have given us the absolute certainty that we are dealing with Neolithic field boundaries. All the roots of that tree are in the bog itself. You are looking at something that is around 3300 BC – note those threes again. We have examined the ring patterns of the tree for knowledge of its age when it died, whether it was blown down, burnt, or if it died of natural causes. The most recent views are that trees had retreated from west of here and had gone by the time the first farmers came in. There was a break-up of the pine forest that allowed the farmers in, but if there was no forest there then they had nothing to create boundaries with.'

Seamus is planning to erect permanent engraved quotations to help illuminate the landscape. Irish poets and writers have long cherished a fascination with archaeology and geology, and when he completes his job, short quotations will be unveiled from both 'famous Seamus' and the not-so-famous Seamus.

'When sheep got lost from an area like this farmers would have spent days looking for them, enquiring from the neighbours. They had an expression for that which I believe is a motto for students about not reinventing the wheel: "One day asking questions is better than three days walking." We're using that as a quotation here on a wall, so never mind flitting around trying to do everything in one go, we suggest visitors stop and ask questions and then ask more questions. It's a bit like yourself – you are not trying to do the whole Wild Atlantic Way in one go – you are stopping and asking questions and that is important as this is the most intensely researched thirty kilometres of the entire route of the Way.'

The time for questions is over and I must make progress. Beyond Belderg the Barony of Erris begins in earnest. If anywhere along the western seaboard can be classified as *terra nullis,* the Erris Peninsula qualifies. The coastline is fretted with cliffs, small harbours and vast peatlands. It is a curious barony, a realm with its own unique imprint. There can be little doubt that this area ticks all the Way's best attributes: mountainous waves, raucous gulls, the sea billowing geyser-like through blowholes and a chill wind even on a pleasant sunny day. It was no surprise when in 2013 *The Irish Times* voted it as the best place to Go Wild in Ireland, helping Erris emerge from its shroud of secrecy and tourism afterthought.

The road to Porturlin degenerates into a track, too narrow to be included on the Way. I drive through a treeless, houseless oasis as Seamus had called it, free of electricity poles, habitation or other traffic, apart from a few road-roaming sheep. I am on my way, via the scenic route, to Belmullet. Emptiness and silence, it is said, are the new luxuries. There is an emptiness here that quietens the soul with a spiritual calm, which allows for reflective thoughts about the depth and length of history. It is best appreciated in the mirage-like half-light slowly enveloping a landscape saturated in a muted glow. The whole effect allows my mind to indulge in fanciful thinking about the lifespan of those ridges, of the memory of lives lived and forgotten in whose footsteps we have trodden, where digging turf represents a metaphor for the past.

Twenty-five years ago a more desolate and remote Irish town than Belmullet would have been hard to find. But the place has reinvented itself and is now bucking the trend and thriving. Homogenised Ireland, in the form of corporate anonymity, has not yet arrived. Shop names reach back decades, reflecting a sense of local identity. The town is barely touched by the twenty-first century, let alone the ostentation of the Tiger years. Along the main street, shops sell hardware, clothes, fruit and meat, newspapers and books; there is a dentist, pharmacy and health-food store, hair salon and barber's, a bustling café, a takeaway, bookmaker's, off-licence, pubs and hotel. The Two Euro shop offers fast shoe repairs while queues form at the post office and citizen information office. At Reilly's hardware store, owner A. J. Reilly sells everything from clocks, kettles and galvanised buckets to gloss paint, photo frames and statues of the Child of Prague. He keeps alive the friendly shopkeeper spirit, introducing himself as A. J.

'I like to tell people that it stands for Antonio José which sounds a bit more exotic than Anthony Joseph,' he grins. 'In the early days I was a decorator and wore white overalls. People laughed at me and thought I was a surgeon but I've been in this business for more than forty years.'

He talks about how Belmullet has changed since the early 1990s. 'It was a dilapidated town in those days. My brother said they were going to build thirty-six new houses at the waterfront and I thought he was away with the fairies, but he was right. It has cleaned up well and there are very few derelict sites. We're a bit out in the sticks but we don't have any of the big superstores on the outskirts and that has helped.'

As we survey the well-stocked shelves, he highlights two products that were not available in 1991. 'Organic Chicken Manure is an example. Everything is organic these days: animals, farming and food, drink, textiles, beauty products – you name it. Even manure, because it's healthier. And take a look at this: Peek Premium Polish – that's a metal cleaner that'll give you the best shine you've ever had on your gold, silver, brass or copper, whereas twenty-five years ago I'da been selling you Brasso or Duraglit. A man once came in here and asked me for a pot-mender to fix a hole in his bath. I didn't have one but I got one for him the very next day.'

A few doors away in McAndrew's drapery shop, a family-run business founded in 1948, Liam McAndrew is wrapping up a cotton shirt for a farmer. By far the biggest change he has noticed is in the upsurge of interest in wool and haberdashery, with customers doing their own darning and stitching.

'People are repairing their clothes these days,' he says. 'A few years ago during the boom they'd have thrown out shirts but now they're sewing on buttons, making do and mending, reusing old clothes the way their grandparents did. I spend every Saturday evening emailing orders for balls of wool, spools, zips, needles and thread.'

The setting up of the Way has, he says, been a huge boost to the town. 'This place is heaving with people for six weeks from mid-July to the end of August. Lots of second-generation emigrants are coming home and they are spending money.'

Belmullet is a place where they still eat their 'dinner' in the middle of the day and the offers are wide-ranging. In Fun Bobby's Bistro, which styles itself as 'one of Europe's most westerly restaurants', the latte is served skinny while the Unislim menu offers French toast with berries, pasta, and chicken and lentil broth. As my concession to the slimming world, I opt for a half portion of pork fillet with potatoes and vegetables. The bistro looks out on a phallic-like structure in the middle of a roundabout. I enquire as to its purpose.

'I don't know what it's for,' says the waitress, 'but it cost ninety grand and they stick the Christmas tree on top of it. You're supposed to be able to look through the slits in it to see all four approach roads.' I ask about the best of the bars and she directs me to McDonnells in Barrack Street. 'It's known as a B&B,' she says, 'a Blether and Blarney pub. You'll meet all sorts and all ages in there.'

As I push my way through the crowded bar, a quavery a cappella voice singing 'Stand By Me' crackles through the speakers. McDonnells' customers are indeed a cross section of Belmulletites. Weatherbeaten farmers, fresh from turf-cutting or milking, brush shoulders with wrinkle-elbowed grandmothers, while young girl-band types in tight-fitting minidresses and teetering heels swill tall glasses of Malibu – advance preparation for nightclubbing in the Anchor. Not for nothing is Erris known as the best place to Go Wild in Ireland. Small knots of people at the bar discuss football, boxing and golf. A hen party compares dark spray tans, flashing ankle artwork. Two women give me the third degree on my journey but their interrogation is interrupted by a short man with a paunch, nursing a pint of stout. He asks if I am enjoying Erris and tells me how it is known to some. 'We do call it MAMBB – Miles and Miles of Bloody Bog.'

Five musicians, led by a singer, start a set with 'Deportees', followed by standards such as 'Catch Me If You Can', 'On Raglan Road' and 'The Night Visiting Song'. On a wall, under the words 'Raise your glass to absent friends', a poignant montage of photographs portrays a who's who of Erris characters from 1942. Two framed pictures recall local football teams in 1974 when moustaches and bouffant hairstyles were de rigueur for the players. The owner, Padraig Conroy, both publican and undertaker, is dressed in a cormorant-black suit, having just come from a funeral. The building's origins, he says, date to 1710. During the eighteenth and nineteenth centuries it was a tenement house. He talks about how his dual roles sometimes coalesce.

'I had an unruly customer one night and I said to him: "John, you'd better behave yourself and you'd better heed me 'cos I'll be the last man to comb your hair."'

Our chat is drowned by the musicians. An accordionist heaves his shoulders, raises bushy eyebrows and adds some elbow oompah to the 'Tarbolton Reel', popularised by the Sligo fiddler Michael Coleman. Seamlessly he segues into 'The Sailor and the Lock', 'Galway Ramble' and 'Katie's Cottage'. At the bar a self-appointed 'conductor' called Tom has taken up position. Belmullet's Herbert von Karajan carries out his own unique signals to the music makers. Gesticulating with much arm-flapping and finger work, he adds his voice to the chorus. Wrapping up the entertainment, and reflecting triplism, the singer says there is only time for one more song. 'We'll sing three verses of "The Auld Triangle", although we might sing it three times and you can all join in.' Beer dribbling down his chin, Tom, now taking on the role of ringmaster, lurches from side to side, arms flailing, integrating himself into the singing, tossing his head like a dog baying at the moon and chirruping with a lengthy flourish: '... along the baaaanks of theee Roy-aaalll Cannn-aaaalll'. By the end, like a baby in a high chair, he collapses asleep over the counter. A woman has captured it on her phone and threatens to place it on You Tube with the title: Oul' Tom Foolery – Three Sheets to the Wind.

During my time in Erris, there have been more twists and turns in Manannán's story. The announcement came that his statue was so badly damaged that it was beyond repair. Limavady Borough Council voted to commission a replacement and erect a theft-proof one with stronger materials to ensure its indestructibility. It could take six months to create a new one but it is seen as a legacy for future generations. Councillors argued over whether it should be an exact replica or if a new, bigger version, up to three times the size of the original, should be erected. Some saw it as a valuable tourist asset; others felt it would promote paganism and false gods. One councillor said it was an anti-Christian act, another that it was paganistic, while a third was quoted as saying that as a piece of art, he believed 'it was on a par with Michelangelo's work.'

Several connections link this area with the story of the Children of Lir where they are said to have spent 300 years. According to legend, Inishglora, an island north of the Inishkeas off the west coast of the Mullet Peninsula, is thought to be their final resting place. A spell was cast on the four children whereby they were turned into enchanted singing swans and forced to accept their fate until they regained their human form 900 years later. The Clann Lir bar on the main street keeps the name alive but when I enquire about Manannán, no one knows much about him, and the barman said he would not be in again for some time. Carne Golf Club, three miles outside town, celebrates the link by collectively naming holes 11, 12, 13 and 14 Inishglora, and individually naming them after Clann Lir: Conn, Fiachra, Aodh and Fionnuala. At Carrowteige near Benwee Head, the inevitable Children of Lir loop walk, complete with modern sculpture, has been created. While in Belmullet I had come across information advertising sea adventures on a boat called *Wavesweeper*, the name Manannán gave to his chariot. I tracked down the boat's owner, David Tyrrell, and he explained how his interest in the sea god had come about.

'I always liked watersports and when I came to live in this area from Offaly I discovered the two bays of Broadhaven and Blacksod so I bought my first boat. Then I achieved commercial endorsement, became a qualified skipper and got plenty of experience. I bought a Rigid-hulled Inflatable Boat (RIB) from a man who wanted to license it and name it *Wavesweeper*. When I formed my company I wanted a good name for it and a link with the water so, given the history of the Clann Lir in this area, I thought that *Wavesweeper* would be appropriate. He explained the symbolism of Manannán in terms of the special relationship that exists between the mythical and historical significance of the sea, and I was intrigued by the fact that his boat needed neither sailor nor oar, and obeyed the thoughts of those who commanded it. In 2012 I upgraded to a bigger boat, which I licensed and called *Wavesweeper II* and that's when Wavesweeper Sea Adventures was born.

'Every child growing up in Ireland knows about the Children of Lir and the link to Inishglora. I organised boat trips to it but it is a very hard island to land on as you have to know where to anchor. There are only one or two spots and you must be au fait with the weather and the tides. Very few people want to do it. I have now stopped doing the tours because it didn't make financial sense and the books didn't balance.'

David still offers boat trips but outsources them, hiring someone else to do them in bigger boats, which hold more people. He is an experienced sailor and has had some memorable days at sea.

'There've been one or two wild days in the water when I was certainly hoping Manannán would come along beside me for protection as those seas can be extremely choppy. We did a run once from Blacksod down to Fenit in Kerry. There is no doubt Manannán was angry that day as we came around Slyne Head in Connemara on our way back up again.'

I explain about the theft of the statue, which astounds him. He says he would classify that as 'a hate crime'.

'Manannán must have had great energy as a trickster and shape-shifter. Mind you, every Saturday night without a doubt you'll find those same sort of people in Belmullet. If you visit the pubs you will discover the "cute hoor" syndrome is alive and well. It's very much a part of the Irish culture to have a trick or three up your sleeve and Mayo is no different.'

The Mullet coastline weaves in and out of inlets and bays with villages such as Aghleam, Fallmore, Binghamstown and Frenchport that few people outside Mayo have ever heard of.

From its top at Erris Head, the peninsula is a mere twenty-five kilometres long and narrows to a thin north/south, one-road in/one-road-out finger of land to its tip at Blacksod Point. Its population is 1,800. During my visit a mini-heatwave hits the Mullet. Bright sunlight skitters across the waters of its three bays, Elly, Feorinyeeo and Blacksod, producing a soothing rhythm. But the only sun-worshipper is a chestnut horse dozing in a field. Dormer-windowed houses stand on elevated sites overlooking harbours. A road sign warns: 'Slow – Livestock Crossing.'

The air fizzes with the energy of spring. An exultation of skylarks, crests half-raised, plunders a field for seeds at Cross Lough. Two hover lengthily overhead, singing ecstatically their clear warbling song, the sun striking their wing feathers and white outer feathers while the others skulk or hurtle away on an undulating flight. Succulent pastureland is starred with daisies and dandelions. A farmer returning to his tractor tells me he spread fertiliser on the field two weeks earlier to kick-start growth. Clumps of primroses line the roadside, and at Elly Bay where a golden strand bites into the Mullet at its narrowest point, a woman strides purposefully, leaving the only footprints.

In the Ionad Deirbhile centre at Aghleam, framed black-and-white snapshots evoke the harsh lifestyle of the nineteenth and early twentieth centuries, reflecting the intermingling of the physical and cultural landscape. Exhibitions document the life of the surrounding islands and tragedies at sea, as well as archaeology, geology, folklore and emigration. A three-metre-high iridescent stained-glass window tells the story of the sixth-century Saint Deirbhile in an eye-catching lapis lazuli-coloured dress. She is believed to have travelled to the area on a donkey after fleeing from an unrequited love with a prince in her native County Meath. The window is a replica of one found in the pre-Norman church at Fallmore. Máire Ruain, who has retired from working in the centre but still calls in, tells me the story.

'The prince followed Deirbhile, finally catching up with her and proposing marriage,' she says. 'She questioned him as to

Saint Deirbhile window, Mullet Peninsula, County Mayo.

why he wished to marry her or what attracted him to her and he replied it was her beautiful eyes. She then plucked out her eyes and threw them from her. The prince, of course, was heartbroken and left the area. Water started to spring up from where her eyes had fallen and she washed her sockets in it, restoring her eyesight once more. St Deirbhile's Well, *Tobar Naomh Deirbhile*, marks the spot and the water from it is thought to have curative properties for eye complaints.'

The story of the saint continues outdoors at Fallmore, at the far end of the peninsula, with a newly designed touring loop in her honour. Deirbhile's Twist is a sculpture of twenty-two stones, ranging from one to four metres in height, based on a local legend associated with the saint. Known locally as the 'Mullet erections', they complement the erratics in a field sloping down to Fallmore. A sleepy settlement, it looks out on Duvillaun Island and smaller wave-washed rocks. The sculpture, by Michael Bulfin, was made by raising the existing granite boulders on the site and placing them in an ascending spiral. It resembles a mini-Stonehenge, without the circle dance of tourists. In my thirty-minute contemplation, one car passes.

Blacksod Point, when I reach it, has an end-of-world feel. A few boats are tied up, and three men squat about an engine. A memorial garden, opened in 2013, recounts the moving story of 3,300 people who left these shores on a wave of emigration over a two-year period in spring and early summer 1883 and 1884. They were supported on what was known as 'assisted passage', leaving for Boston and Quebec on fifteen steamships from Blacksod Bay to start a new life in North America. A granite boat sculpture divided into fifteen sections lists the names of all those who boarded the ships. The emigrants were assisted by the Tuke Fund, named after James Hack Tuke, a Quaker from York who worked tirelessly for over sixty years to help those in the west who had suffered. The fund covered their fare and helped them settle with 'landing money' once they reached their destination.

It is estimated that a staggering two million people have since descended from this group of north-west Mayo emigrants making up the Erris diaspora. One hundred and thirty years on, this story is recalled through careful detailed research of the original ships' passenger manifests. In one case, when the SS *Nestorian*, a full-rigged three-masted schooner, was unable

Deirbhile's Twist stone circle, Mullet Peninsula, County Mayo.

to approach land because of her draught of water, a gunboat, the *Seahorse*, was used as a tender vessel to bring the emigrants out to the ocean steamer for the start of their long sea journey. It was a heart-rending sight for those left behind to see loved ones departing in what was the first great mass exodus from the remote western district. The *Nestorian*'s decks were crowded with more than 350 men, women and children, along with their baggage. On the journey, which took up to fourteen days, they slept on straw beds. Nearly forty years after the desperate time of the Great Famine, they had their reasons for leaving. The potato crop had failed in 1879–80 so 'land hunger', poverty and destitution all played a major part. Another factor was eviction by local landlords. Reading through the list of recurring family names brings home the detail: Reilly, Keane, Gilboy, Lavelle, Mangan, Moran, McCabe, McManaman and O'Malley crop up with regularity. Most were not sad to leave Mayo's shores.

Contemporary newspaper accounts of their departure report that 'many were quite happy at the prospects before them compared with their circumstances at home'. They felt that whatever happened in the New World, it could not be any worse than conditions they were leaving behind. The future may have been uncertain, but as they set off on their transatlantic adventure, it must have seemed both exciting and inviting.

A few yards from the memorial garden, Blacksod Point lighthouse stands adjacent to the pier. A sketch of this building appeared at the start of the Mayo chapter in my original travel book of 1993. Its quirky architectural features include a square lantern with a polygonal glazed section facing out across the bay and today offering a viewing point for hungry gulls. Unlike many other lighthouses that have been whitewashed, this one is built of high-quality locally cut granite and looks as solid as the day it opened on 30 June 1866, just seven years before the first exodus. Since then it has remained in use, helping safe entry into a dangerous harbour. It has borne witness to tragedy, but its claim to fame, as recorded by a wall plaque, is about the role it played in the Normandy D-Day landings. The lighthouse supplied Britain with meteorological reports under an agreement dating back to the 1921 Anglo-Irish Treaty. On 4 June 1944, the light keeper, Ted Sweeney, filed a crucially important weather forecast warning of bad conditions, which delayed the landings scheduled for 5 June. The next day, 6 June, a break came in the weather as indicated by Ted, and Operation Overlord proceeded.

The north Mayo coast likes to package its past as heritage. The distance I have travelled from Ballina to Blacksod over five days is no more than 130 kilometres (allowing for scenic diversions) yet history lies thick along it, jumping around many different time zones through a long geologic gaze. Returning to Belmullet in early evening, I divert a few miles north to Erris Head to live in the present. I was aware that it is one of the best places in Ireland to find twites, which are members of the finch family and a bird I have never seen. A desolate road through empty fields via Tonmore and Clooneen leads to farmhouses and falls down to a car park where I pull over a discreet distance from the cliffs. Apart from two gulls paired with their shadows, few birds are visible so I sit still in the car, turn off the radio, and indulge in quiet observation. Within ten minutes my luck is in: two twites appear and are immediately active on the grass, busily moving along a path searching without drama for seeds, dandelions or insects. One moment – camouflaged on grey rocks – they are invisible, the next they twitter with a nasal call and fly across a narrow chasm from one side of the cliffs to the other. The evening light brings them out in sharp focus; their yellow bill and brown underparts is confirmation of identification. One goes so far as to land by me on the wall where for five brief seconds I am able appreciate its heavy dark brown streak and long forked tail. The American writer Terry Tempest Williams says 'there are birds you gauge your life by.' I cherish the privilege of an encounter with *Carduelis flavirostris*, curious flyers, and a small Erris cameo of nature that will live long in my own personal history.

6
Powerful on land and sea

ON THE SOUTH-WEST COAST OF Achill Island the petulant sea is churning up marauding waves when I check into the Bervie beachside guesthouse in Keel. Although it is mid-May, the evening air has turned cold. Black-headed gulls wheel in the wind through a sandstorm. Squirrelled away in a far corner of the island, hidden down a cul-de-sac, the Bervie is a 200-year-old, single-storey, long white building that in another life was a coastguard station. From my big-bedroomed window, Keel Strand starts at the garden gate with the might of the ocean a mere twenty paces away. Distant views reach across to Clare Island and round the coast to the impressive Minaun Cliffs and Dooega Head. Even from this single location, Achill seems perfectly arranged for a painter's canvas. Little wonder that it has attracted illustrious names over the years such as Alexander Williams, Paul Henry, Mabel Young, Evie Hone, Mainie Jellet, Derek Hill, Robert Henri and Camille Souter.

The visitors who come to the west today are classified by the tourist board as 'culturally curious', a 21st-century term coined by marketeers. But there is nothing new about the curiosity of artists and writers. For more than 200 years they have been drawn to the area for inspiration. Along with their palettes and easels, the artists brought with them a curiosity about what art historians refer to as 'genre subject matter': the people who live here and their tough lifestyle. They had a genuine interest in people and were fascinated by the lives they led. Many too were captivated by the western sunsets and subtle effects of its light, developing an abiding love of the landscape.

That artistic tradition and rich heritage is depicted on the Bervie's walls, a mini Achill art gallery. Run by John and Elizabeth Barrett since the mid-1980s, it is a serene house. Bedrooms and corridors are adorned with calming watercolours, sketches, poems, letters and photographs. A small monochromatic framed print of Elizabeth's grand-aunt and grand-uncle, John and Eliza, painted by Paul Henry, commemorates them in the entrance hall. Called 'My Host and Hostess', it brings out their character, and was produced circa 1910–13. Henry came to Achill to paint in 1910 and was mesmerised by it. He stayed nine years, famously tearing up his return train ticket.

'He arrived at the post office in Keel,' John says, 'which was then owned by John and Eliza. The sketch of them was something he just threw off, so to speak, and it was made as a present to them. Even though they had a houseful of it, Eliza did not like his work. If somebody came and praised one of Henry's paintings she would say "take it with you". But they gave him a room in their house and kept him for years. John built up a good relationship with him but I don't know if Eliza really liked him very much. Henry hadn't two farthings to rub together and John got him a job with the Congested Districts Board as Paymaster. His wife, Grace, debunked back to Dublin and Belfast. She had had enough of the countryside and by 1919 he left and started to travel, although always returned to Achill.'

Henry walked and cycled around the island and on occasion travelled in a horse-drawn oil van with a driver who delivered paraffin. The iconography of the west, its blue skies, thatched cottages, stone walls, the cliffs and sea were part of the attraction for him but John says there were other reasons why he stayed.

'Henry found an original canvas here for his work and something unique that he thought he could make his own, looking at it from his point of view, apart from the artistic point of view. People say he was colour-blind but that is very debatable. He had a tendency to find a different angle on painting and worked hard at his craft, producing a wide range of subjects on

Achill and Killary Harbour. What I find disconcerting is that the garish ones seem to be more popular than some of his pastel paintings which have beautiful themes and give a much better feel for the area than his bright reds and browns.'

The last time Henry came back to Achill was in the early 1950s when he stayed with John and Eliza for a night. They had built up business at the Amethyst Hotel where he lodged and a plaque on it records the fact. Some of Henry's work is much sought after. His 'Early Morning in Donegal' sold in 2014 for €160,000.

Henry firmly cemented the status of Achill. John attributes this connection to the fact that there are now 150 artists, living either part- or full-time on the island. Later in the evening over a dessert of bread-and-butter pudding served with the Bervie's home-made ice cream, our discussion turns to the weather that they experience at the North Atlantic's front door. Achill may not be a hotbed of political discontent but the plight of places warring the elements along the coast has become an increasing concern for locals who fear they are being left behind. 'Resilient' is an overused cliché to describe people who have survived the pummelling of fierce storms. But there is something that keeps them here, even though 'extreme' dates have been written into history.

'The winters are fantastic as long as you are in here and looking out at it,' John says cheerfully. 'You take the storms as they come and just live with them. Nobody twisted our arm to live here – it was our choice. The one that did all the damage was on 3 January 2014 – on the very same date that the previous worst one had hit in 1992. It flooded the garden and destroyed the wall but we were saved by the fact that I had put in rock armour. Before that I couldn't get insurance for the place because all the companies refused to insure us and said it would cost us too much. One said that a ship can run for safe harbour but you are stuck where you are. The icehouse was flooded up to three feet as well as the art studio. The waves came into the main house, three guest rooms were flooded and we had just put new carpets in them the previous year.

'For twenty-three years the county council had been hood-winking me because they should have put in the rock-armour protection in 1992 and they just said that wasn't their job but clearly it was their responsibility. We are quite rebellious here on the west coast and badger them to get things done but it can take a long time. The voices of coastal communities are not heard. There is no consultation, and no information is given out by the authorities – it has to be dragged out and you have to fight for it; in fact, the county councils don't have any marine engineers with the experience of knowing what to do when the sea comes in so they spend an absolute fortune on consultants who come in and out on a fine day. Often you don't know that they're doing something until they turn up on your doorstep and then there's nobody to be seen, only the local foreman.'

From his back garden, John has witnessed thousands of high tides and seen fierce storms but the good days outweigh the bad and there are many positive sides to running a guesthouse on Achill.

'Even doing the remedial work after a storm you have a blank canvas. Every penny you made the previous summer is going into paying for that as we have a short but intense season and we put the money back into the house in the winter. You can look out and you know what weather you're going to have in four or five hours so it's constantly changing. Our business is great for meeting a different crowd of people; everybody has a story and we meet all kinds of characters.'

Take hold of the Ordnance Survey *Discovery Series* sheet 30 of Achill Island, turn it around, and you will find it looks like an inverted letter 'L'. It also bears a remarkable similarity to the shape of Britain, an appropriate image since over the years many Achill Islanders went off to the north of England and Scotland to work on farms picking potatoes, or 'tatie hokin'. Almost amputated from the rest of Mayo and Ireland, it covers an area of 130 square kilometres while its total length of indented coastline is 128 kilometres. Its population is 2,500. Seaside settlements, such as Keel and Dooagh, sprawl out in clusters of white bungalows and farmhouses. On a clear day, I circuit the squiggly coastline from Dooagh along a high-level GCR with sheer drops to the sea. In its multiple shades of blue, turquoise and ultramarine, the curve of Keem Bay could be stolen from the Aegean. The beach is dazzlingly bright. Waves roll in rhythmically. Only one other vehicle is parked overlooking the beach – a German camper van whose owner displays their names on the windscreen: Helmut and Beatte.

One hundred years on from his visit, it is not hard to see how Paul Henry was captivated by Achill, even though he once described it as 'a windswept island at the back of beyond'. Reaching any speed is difficult as sheep freely roam the roads. In one case a woman wearing a long, grey coat waves a blackthorn stick at my car as she escorts a gaggle of geese across the road at Bunnacurry, an example of the island's special karma. In the north of the island the road to Slievemore Mountain runs out at the deserted village. Standing at 672 metres, the mountain represents Achill's trademark skyline and is one of the west's most painted, sketched and photographed peaks. On its south-west side, the boundary walls and ruins of about eighty roofless stone houses are all that remains of a village from the mid-nineteenth century. Lazy beds slope down the hill. A grassed-over street, lined with round granite slabs and pillars, is still visible between the houses. Built along the sixty-metre contour of the mountain, they were single-storey cottages with well-cut corner stones and south-facing gables. There is a jigsaw pattern to the walls. I squelch my way along the muddy street and make out the worn doorsteps and storage wall niches that held lamps, cooking pots or pans. In some cases, the floors are a jumble of lichen-mottled stones heavily colonised by clumps of nettles and weeds.

Deserted village, Slievemore, Achill, County Mayo.

Two wagtails, with snow-white faces and throats, join me on a wall, breaking the silence with their warbles. From the road a shepherd whistles at his flock to try and enclose them in one area. The grey stone is cold, although the sun is increasing in strength. I feel the presence of the people who once lived here and wonder how they eked out an existence. Thinking about the hardship, disadvantage and starvation within this barren landscape, and about the generations long gone, it is hard not to be moved by these stones and of the dramas of many winters past, and the people who were evicted and endured the Famine.

The Achill of today is a world removed from that of the mid-nineteenth century. The images of the past may be from a century and a half ago but they are never far away on this haunting hillside, which in 1837 was the largest human settlement on the island. There is a tremendous presence here and a numinous atmosphere. A walk through the ruins is a walk into history. It was here also that the custom of booleying was carried out during the spring when people in coastal villages closed their homes and drove their herds up the hill where there was pasture for the cattle and fertile ground for crops. When the German Nobel Prize-winning writer Heinrich Böll, who owned a cottage on Achill, visited the deserted village, he described it as being 'like an amateurish set for a ghost film'.

Beyond Böll's cottage at Dugort, Atlantic rollers approach from different directions, breaking on the silver strand. Between each wave cresting and dispersing, I count to fifteen. Beside the strand, small, brightly patterned ringed plovers worm-snack in the goalmouth at either end of a football pitch. I watch their curious feeding habits as they slowly cross the grass, pecking the ground. They pause, stare and dip their bills in stop-start movements. In a sudden piece of goalmouth action, one runs to a grassy hump and dips in a thick orange bill with a black tip while another quickly joins in. Stately cumulus clouds move slowly, banking over Slievemore. A short, sharp hailstorm calls to mind the old rhyme: 'Farmers fear unkindly May / Frost by night and hail by day.'

With its secluded bays, inaccessible ragged cliffs and beaches, Achill offers an opportunity to escape from the realities of life. The island is a microcosm of Ireland: a self-contained world with its own smorgasbord of mountains, lakes, bogs, beaches, cliffs and … holiday homes. The 21st-century face of Achill consists of small sites of eight or ten houses that sprang up in the years when the Celtic Tiger mauled the country. Two Australians I had met at breakfast in the Bervie were shocked at the number of holiday homes on the island. Few parts remain untouched by the hand of the builders. Many single bungalows or detached houses, most used only in the summer, pepper patches of the russet-coloured bogland. A man with a black beret and goatee beard, walking his Labrador past the football pitch, pauses to talk about the developments and the people who holiday on Achill.

'Trouble is, you never get to know any of them,' he says. 'The houses are empty for ten months of the year so it's only a seasonal business in the high summer. Money is all very well and brings in more money, but I'm not sure how good a thing that is in the long term. Although I suppose if they come here to retire, then that will bring in some elderly business – but there is an awful sameness about the houses.'

Hoping for the prospect of dry weather, I had brought my Claude Butler bicycle to Achill, and for a couple of days give up four wheels in exchange for two. It is still within the spirit of my journey as the Great Western Greenway, an off-road route, is part of the Wild Atlantic Cycle Trail. At my starting point near the Michael Davitt Bridge, which connects Achill to the mainland, seabirds skirmish and joust with one another in a five-minute squall. The forecast predicts sunshine and showers. The sky is a mix of white cloud blobs with blue patches breaking through. Minutes later a rainbow arcs across it. The Greenway follows the track of a railway that ran for forty-two years from 1895 until the autumn of 1937. For decades the track was left to nature but in 2010 it was re-puffed with cyclists and walkers, and the 43-kilometre route from Achill to Westport is active once again. Cars splash past me on the main road until I find the turn-off to join the Way, a gritstone track along the largely treeless northern side of the remote Corraun Peninsula. It has been a slow-burning, late-flowering spring, but May in Mayo is working its magic. Pink cuckoo flowers, also known as lady's smock, creeping buttercup and the sheen of silverweed line the verges, while every few metres bird's-foot trefoil and knapweed provide colour. Bramble is intertwined with other wayside blooms and the air is perfumed with the coconut scent of yellow gorse now at its peak. As the sun breaks through, views take in Blacksod Bay and the islands of Inishbiggle and Annagh; south of me the hills of Corraun, Srahmore and Mweewillin, as well as Claggan Mountain remain stubbornly covered in mist.

John Barrett had correctly suggested the wind would be in my favour. On several stretches, buoyed by a breeze behind me, I freewheel along the flat path with gentle gradients, accompanied by the whirring of wheels, the clatter over sheep and cattle grids, birdsong and bark of a distant dog. Appropriately, the townland of Tonragee translates as 'backside to the wind'. The pathway is broken up with staggered timber navigation gates. Two Germans pass me shouting a 'Hallo'. Bird sightings include what I classify as the Holy Ornithological Trinity of robin, magpie and blackbird. A quarrelsome party of greenfinches and siskins raids birdfeeders. At bicycle speed, the western world takes on a different perspective, leading to an appreciation of the avian presence, and the registers of the soundscape. Other birds proclaim their presence through whistles, wheezes and song: two chaffinches release a metallic *chwink-chwink* call; a young coal tit, hiding in the branches of an oak tree, repeats its *seechoo-seechoo-seechoo*; meadow pipits, sometimes called 'mipits', produce thin, tinkling *tseep-tseep* piping notes. An ochre-chested bullfinch serenades me along the path beside the indent of the still waters of Bellacragher Bay, which is billeted with mussel rafts. When I reach Mulranny a panorama of land, beach, salt marsh and sea unfolds within the island-studded Clew Bay. Some smaller islands look like upturned currachs while others resemble sleeping whales.

Achill Sound to Mulranny is largely free of walkers and cyclists with no sign of what George Orwell referred to as 'old maids bicycling to holy communion through the morning mist'. I stretch my walking legs by calling into the village tourist office trapped in the middle of a major programme of roadworks. Traffic is reduced to one lane while heavy plant thunders around. Squads of hard-hatted, yellow-coated workmen skim walls and reverse lorries. At the back doors of a van, four men with mugs of builders' tea study plans. The woman running the office says although it may not look like much, the work is part of a village enhancement scheme to extend the promenade and walkway. She suggests I keep an eye out for some of the old Irish goats that can be seen in the area. My best bet is to call at the house of a woman on the other side of the village as she is a goat keeper.

Along the main road I pass the pungent cocktail of newly laid tarmac mixed with three-cornered leek growing on verges. Early buds of fuchsia are struggling to burst into bloom.

Cheryl Cobern Browne has just returned from beach-walking her dog. Originally from South Africa, she met her Mulranny-born husband in America. She now runs an arts retreat centre, Essence of Mulranny. Aside from this, she is the mainstay of the Old Irish Goat Society. In the garden of her house she feeds a goat answering to the name of Naomi. It sports majestic horns that could pass for the handlebars of a racing bike.

'These goats have been roaming the mountains for a long time,' Cheryl tells me. 'They are old Irish goats, which were the original landrace breed for thousands of years. They're almost gone now because of the improved breeds that were brought over in the last ten years but they have started to inter-breed.'

There is no mistaking their distinct characteristics: huge horns, a cashmere coat of long hair and, on the males, an extravagant quiff. Naomi pokes around the garden, foraging and chewing on leaves. The goats are historically significant because they kept many people alive during the Famine.

'They were known in those days as the poor man's cow. When we heard that they had gone extinct, we were curious about the ones we had on our mountain because they look very much like the old ones and it was confirmed that we had them. There's a handful left on the outreaches of the west and they have adapted to the climate.'

Cheryl says the society has tried to raise awareness of their plight in an attempt to preserve them and start them breeding.

'We have had to scientifically get DNA from old specimens that we got out of museums and old country houses which had the original goats so we've got baseline DNA and now we've taken the DNA from our wild animals to compare that. The Department of Agriculture has been supportive of this project since this is Ireland's original heritage goat and is worth saving. The original breed survived very well on their own. Swiss goats have also interbred with them. If you drive through Mulranny you often seen the male herds on the road sticking together, not hanging around with the females until it's time to start rutting in the summer. They are browsers as opposed to grazers like sheep. They love heather and leaves of plants, as well as people's gardens and bits of light wood.'

But not everyone is a goat lover. Cheryl points out that they stir up mixed feelings.

'Some people love them, some hate them because they ravage gardens, some people want us to leave them alone, some are very supportive of what we are trying to do so we've had to be very careful. If they walk past your car they can scratch it with their horns so that is a problem. Our society is working with a researcher who comes over here every three months from London. We are looking at the DNA to understand more about these goats and to make sure that they are definitely associated with this part of the country. We have about twenty in captivity, with many more feral goats on the mountain with the old Irish mixed in. Every year they interbreed with the domestic goats and every year their characteristics are diminishing so it's a fight against time. People get excited about megalithic tombs and dead people from five thousand years ago but we have real, living animals who are critically endangered and have adapted well to Ireland. They are curious about everything and, for me, having reared two orphans, that's the most fascinating thing about them. They always want to know what's in there, what's up there, what's around the corner and what you are doing. They don't show expression like dogs, but you can read them and they're always exploring, which is something you wouldn't see sheep doing.'

Cheryl leads foraging walks on the shoreline, encouraging and inspiring a range of activities. In her creative studio women are busy sewing, knitting and bead-making as well as painting. One puts the finishing touches to a boat that reminds me of Manannán's chariot which, when I mention this *en passant* to

Mrs Man statue and Cheryl Browne, goat keeper, Mulranny, County Mayo.

Cheryl, sparks a connection. She brings me to a corner of her garden to see a statue in the middle of a rockery.

'That,' she proudly points to a striking tall steel-and-copper statue, 'is Mrs Man – Manannán's wife – made by a sculptress friend of mine in 2006. She is wearing a knitted shawl made out of beads and steel wire, and holds an oyster shell lamp, which is a light. Down her back she is covered in seaweed and she looks after the place for me as she is facing the sea. You can also see she is wearing a fish necklace and shells which is why we call her Mrs Man.'

I explain the details of the theft of Manannán's statue, the subsequent search and its discovery, and suggest that Cheryl has a choice of his wife's names if she wishes to use one of them, either Fand or Aífe. She is intrigued at the connection but adamant about keeping Mrs Man which she feels has an evocative ring.

'It's simple, handy and easy to remember, and people love the story of her and Manannán. This *is* the sea god's wife and now you can say you have seen her to add to your collection of information. The female energy that it helps to create is part of the Essence of Mulranny and Mrs Man exudes that energy. We see her from every room of the house and she sees us because we fused her eye in a kiln and she watches us closely.'

Back on the Greenway the path to Newport is a mixture of compacted limestone dust, asphalt and tarmac. The insistent two-note call of a cuckoo rings across pastureland and coastal meadows. A pheasant flies off the path into a field. The guttural drone of a chainsaw rises and rumbles through the air. Most cyclists are pedalling in the opposite direction to me. Groups of schoolchildren ride in a crocodile line, some puffing, others pushing. Another group stops for a break, asking me how far the next town is, complaining that it has been uphill from Westport. Blissfully I dream-doze my way along an elevated stretch, thinking about how healthy, environmentally friendly and unstressful it is. But I am shaken out of my afternoon trance when a group of Spanish students, rounding a corner on what looks like their debut bike ride, forces me off the path, resulting in expletives mingling with birdsong and the warbling Owengrave River. I escape with a few scratches, but ruefully reflect that I have fallen for Mayo.

The clouds lift and the day turns warm. North of me, the Ben Gorm horseshoe in the Nephin Beg range is visible. A short on-road uphill climb takes me to Newport where Clew Bay has morphed into Newport Bay. A tightly bunched pack of hard-core MAMILs (Middle-Aged Men in Lycra) with lavender leggings thrums past me on a high-intensity session. Newport lives in the shadow of Westport, and, as a much smaller town, accepts that it will always be second best in tourism gloss to its glamorous neighbour thirteen kilometres south. With its railway viaduct gleaming in Red Sandstone over the tidal Black Oak River, it looks an agreeable place. A team of gardeners is busy strimming, grass-cutting, sweeping and tidying up in preparation for the An Post *Rás*. Ireland's major cycling event, established in 1953, is due the next week with one of the gruelling stages ending in the main street. The waitress in Kelly's Kitchen says the area has gone 'cycle mad' while the Greenway has been 'the making' of Newport. An old-style tea room, its wall space is devoted to Princess Grace Kelly whose paternal grandfather came from Drimurla near Newport. He emigrated to Philadelphia in 1887 where he founded a construction company. A film festival is now held in Newport to honour the connection.

Beside me, four men argue over mammals (as opposed to MAMILs) and the difference between stoats and weasels. With perfect comic timing, a man chips in from another table, 'It's easy to tell the difference,' he says, 'a weasel is weasly recognised while a stoat is stotally different.' Rather than retrace my route by cycling all the way back to Achill Sound, I leave my pedalling to Westport until the next day and enquire about a lift back to my car. A white-van man called Seamus, sitting by the window, is heading as far as Mulranny and when he offers to run me back to Achill, I leave my bike at the café until the morning. Seamus is in sales and is checking email traffic on his sleek paper-thin MacBook.

'The café for me is the third place,' he says. 'My job involves a large amount of driving, so apart from work and home, cafés are where I spend a lot of time, thankfully most have Wi-Fi so I can work remotely. I often think of how things have changed. My father was a travelling salesman in drapery and millinery and this was something he didn't need to worry about in his line of work.'

On a cloud-free morning the next day, I drive back to Newport and embark on the final portion of the Greenway. Just over a mile out of town where it runs parallel with the busy main road, I stop to chat to John O'Donnell, who introduces himself as the Greenway's caretaker. He is active with his litter-picker, on a mission to keep the route clean. John agrees to cycle with me for part of the way to Westport, explaining what his job entails. Along with a group of ten who help look after it, his multifunctional role is to maintain the Greenway, liaise with landowners, fix any problems that arise, and promote the area and small businesses along it. We cycle up an incline where on a bend of the road an entire hedgebank is smothered in the drooping heads of thousands of bluebells on tall stalks, many buzzing with hoverflies. We glide through a tranquil, lush tree corridor where tightly packed willow, beech and alder flank the path. Butterflies are out of hibernation. Like outriders, a common white and a brown admiral weave alongside us. The margins are decorated with herb Robert, speedwell, wild garlic, violets and trefoil. John is a knowledgeable companion, illuminating wildlife, geography and history. Taking a breather, we climb off our machines to inspect a statuesque fifteen-centimetre-tall hairy plant which he identifies as blue bugle. Large-lipped blue flowers run all the way up its stalk and its dark green leaves bring out a smoky elegance, savoured by bumblebees.

Mayo's love affair with the bike is flourishing. A new section of track recently opened between Castlebar and the Museum of Country Life with the aim being a 200-kilometre Greenway covering the whole county. John talks about the resurgence of interest and the popularity of on-yer-bikism.

'It has grown so much in the past five years,' he says. 'A couple of years ago nationally in Ireland more bikes than cars were sold and these routes were one of the main reasons for that. People are more health conscious and it's not overly expensive, unless you want to spend a lot on a very good bike. Since it opened, the Greenway has been a lifeline to the local economy. It has created at least a hundred jobs with six or seven bike-hire companies, and spinoffs for cafés, restaurants and hotels. In summer our daily average is between 700 and 900 people and we can break the 1,000 figure some days so inevitably we will have litter. The biggest problem is the tag-alongs. Parents give children a bottle of water and they throw it away and the parents can't see it happening. If you get fifty of those a day then that's your bag of rubbish. We had litterbins at the start but that just encourages it more. In the beginning we had a 70 : 30 ratio of local to foreign visitors but now it is 50 : 50 and in some cases maybe 40 : 60. The Greenway has become a spine and complements other activities such as kayaking, hillwalking or golfing.'

John talks about the fact that many people had connections with the railway. His great-great-uncle was employed on it in the early twentieth century.

'He worked on the railway line before emigrating to the US in 1911, later settling in Cleveland. At one time there were 3,000 men working on the line, and some women. Up to 800 worked on one part of it with the Newport-to-Achill section being the busiest.'

We snake past farmland and a fenced-off derelict railway cottage, which is to be restored. Charolais bask behind a barbed-wire fence. In the distance Croagh Patrick – known as nature's greatest cathedral of the west – is a commanding pyramidal presence, having shrugged off yesterday's 'cloak of concealment' (one of the three gifts given by Manannán to the Tuatha Dé Danann through which they could make themselves invisible.) A 'No Entry' sign at a farm with a picture of an Alsatian says: 'I can reach the gate in seconds. Can you?' Verges are adorned with escallonia, olearia, honeysuckle and the sweet-scented white flowers of dog rose, rich in nectar for bees. John laughs when I ask about the distance he cycles during the course of a year.

'I've never thought of that but on the average day I might cycle twenty miles, so it would work out at a hundred miles a week and at least four hundred a month. In the winter it would obviously be much less. The job has its challenges; it just doesn't stop at five o'clock as people may phone you with queries any time. But it's enjoyable and you have to be fit. I don't drink or smoke and it's good to know that you can help somebody if they need assistance.'

John's car is parked a few miles from Westport where we go our separate ways. Around the next corner I come upon a surprising convergence of a hat-trick of signposted townlands: Creggaunnahorna, Slaughar and Aittireesh. The owner of a driveway has built a red-and-black wooden shelter station with a bell and string. I pause to drink water pumped from a freshwater mountain stream via a tap where a mug and chain are attached. Three men, who have walked from Westport, arrive at the junction and are alarmed to see me drinking the water. A boil-water notice is in force and there are concerns about the parasitic bug cryptosporidium. They offer me bottled water to 'wash away my sins'. They call themselves 'The Three Stooges' and ask me to take a photograph of them in the shelter. Like young children, one rings the bell and shouts 'All Aboard', another 'Tickets Please', and the third 'Welcome to Cathair na Mart'.

Of all the towns along the coast that I have passed through, Westport has been rehabilitated beyond all recognition since 1991. In those days its haphazard appearance consisted of a hotchpotch of plastic signage, chaotic parking and what architects classify as 'visual disorder'. Its streets were choked with caravanettes, motor homes and camper vans, and its bars smoke-filled and steamy. I wrote after my visit then that 'it has the feel of an Irish country town injected with a honeypot of tourism'. In 2014, it was named by *The Irish Times* as the Best Place to Live in Ireland. Tourism is now an even bigger money-spinner. In between brightly coloured café, bar, bakery, deli and restaurant facades, the mercantile tapestry is dominated by fashion and chocolate boutiques, giftware, craft and jewellery stores. 'I nearly climbed Croagh Patrick,' proclaims a shop window T-shirt.

Beside the Clock Tower, the Willow Café tea room is well placed for surveying Bridge Street. A sign draws in customers: 'Come let us have tea and continue to talk about happy things.'

A velvet cappuccino with textured milk, conjured out of the Nairobi bean, a high-grade espresso, caresses my throat. Having just burnt off several hundred calories, I justify complementing it with a chocolate-frosted cupcake. Down the street, a funeral cortège throws a mournful silence over the town as a hearse is followed slowly uphill to the Octagon. Most of the businesses have retained their hand-painted signs on timber fascia boards and restored their shopfronts, resulting in a town free of bland corporate identity. Some have pulled down blinds as a mark of respect. The café's shelves hold delicately patterned china teapots and tea cosies alongside an array of large glass jars of Pearls of Africa gourmet coffee, Happy Hazelnut roast and a variety of French blends. Teas from around the world include camomile, spice and the organic Japanese green matcha.

My quest in Westport is not so much for the alchemy of tea or coffee but for a 'wild Atlantic woman' although not in the town's night-time fleshpots. The notorious sixteenth-century chieftain, Grace O'Malley (Granuaile), the 'Pirate Queen of Connacht', is now being marketed as the original 'wild Atlantic woman'. As the chief of the O'Malley clan, she fearlessly ruled the seas from Scotland to Spain and is intrinsically linked to the west of Ireland where she had several castles. It was on the foundations of one of these that Westport House was built in 1730. Her descendants, the Browne family, run the house today as a visitor attraction. I had arranged to meet the pirate queen's fourteenth great-granddaughter, Lady Sheelyn Browne, who in the family's long history of ownership of the house has become – with her sisters – the first generation of women to inherit the title.

The road passes through the estate parkland, farm buildings and over a bridge where twenty giant swans sit on the water; these ones are not moving because they are swan-shaped pedaloes for children. Bold and assertive, the tall bronze statue of Grace O'Malley, erected in 2003 on the 400th anniversary of her death, is sheltered by trees. Just as the doors are opening, I park in front of the grey grandeur of a rectangular two-storey

Georgian house. The mansion is one of Ireland's last remaining historic houses with its original contents still intact. While waiting for Lady Sheelyn to arrive, I browse the palatial front hall, studying the blunderbusses on either side of the mantelpiece. In the days when coaches travelled from Westport to Dublin these were used against highwaymen. The parquet floor reflects light from a glitzy George IV cut-glass chandelier hanging from a richly decorated barrel-vaulted ceiling. On the half-landing of the marble staircase, a statue, The Angel of Welcome, spreads celestial harmony, her hand outstretched to greet visitors. It feels as though I have wandered on to the set of a television period drama recreating a scene from 150 years ago, filled with engravings and curios. In the Long Gallery a score of aristocratic portraits commemorate family members and salute countesses, marchionesses and ladies who could have stepped straight out of a P. G. Wodehouse novel. I am not sure how to address my interviewee and what to expect. The woman at the reception desk selling tickets to visitors reassures me that she is 'very down-to-earth.'

When she arrives, Lady Sheelyn Browne does not strike me as someone who has walked out of the pages of *Debrett's*. She is late for our appointment and is apologetic. Her mobile vibrates in her trouser pocket and she steps outside briefly to deal with the call. On her return, the library alarm is disabled and we sit at a low table in front of a grandiose black stone fireplace by the German architect Richard Cassels (who Anglicised his surname to Castle) with bellows and logs. George III mahogany bookcases are filled from floor to ceiling with several thousand leather-bound volumes. The library is part of the first phase of the 1730 house and was originally known as the 'Waiting Room'. A secret passage behind one of the main walls was used to hide arms. Most of the antiquarian books are from the nineteenth century with an emphasis on Irish subjects and theology. Lady Sheelyn is one of five sisters and was educated in Dublin. She studied graphic design and worked in printmaking in San Francisco.

Grace O'Malley statue by sculptor Michael Cooper, courtesy Westport House.

'I went to the US for a year and ended up living there for seven,' she says. 'Then I came back here in 2003 and always knew I would return. Even when I was in college here, I was involved during the summer or at weekends when we were all put to work, talking about this place and its problems.'

There are some American cadences in her accent but not a trace of Anglo-Irishry. Her veins, though, run thick with the blood of a warrior queen. She talks me through the lineage to Grace O'Malley, an important part of the history of the house.

'We go back as far as 1530 with Grace when her great-great-granddaughter Maud Burke, whose portrait is in the front hall by the fireplace, married Colonel John Browne of Westport. He was a lawyer who owned land in Mayo, and as a Jacobite he fought in the Williamite War. That is the bloodline connection, so Grace is my fourteenth great-grandmother. Miraculously we are still here, and it is indeed a miracle because a lot of these houses disappeared in the 1960s and we've been on a knife-edge since then. During her time here in the original castle, the sea came right up to the walls and it fell into ruin, so it was on this site that her great-great-granddaughter, who inherited the land, built the house. The men were good at picking rich women because a lot of the money came from them along the way.'

The O'Malley family motto, *Terra Marique Potens,* translates as 'Powerful on Land and Sea'. But while piracy and plundering were her stock-in-trade, Grace is regarded also as a shrewd and pragmatic trailblazer. When I ask about how it feels to be part of such an illustrious pedigree, and if she has inherited any common traits or defining characteristics, she pauses, reflecting quietly on the ancestral piratical link.

'It feels great. She was a very strong, determined woman who decided what she wanted to do with her life and went and got it. According to legend, she cut off her hair and pretended to be a boy, stealing on to her father's ship as he set sail and he didn't even recognise her. She was the one who pulled out the sword and killed one of the enemies, which started her career at sea. So I have inherited that determination and probably a bit of the stubbornness too. The very fact that she was leading battles then was amazing, given the all-male Gaelic supremacy of the time. She had guts and even cruised up the Thames to see Queen Elizabeth. She actually gave birth on a ship surrounded by men, then simply got up and continued with the battle. Some of this is colourful but I imagine there was a lot of truth in it.'

'Do you feel any empathy towards her?'

'I do, and the older you get the more you appreciate being able to trace your family. For me there is something phenomenally exciting about going back to the mid-1500s and being able to trace your blood connection. You can see that all the generations had some of her strengths and they all obviously had their own interests. But I don't go with the hares, I definitely do my own thing and stick to what I believe in. If I think this is the way something needs to be done, or this is the way I need to react to something, then that will come out and nothing will stop me from doing what I need to do to try to make it work. Of course, we all make mistakes and I'm sure Grace O'Malley did too, but you learn by your mistakes and I probably have some of her wilfulness and passion.'

In the summer of 2014, Lady Sheelyn's father, Jeremy, the 11th Marquess of Sligo, died. Known throughout his life by the courtesy title Earl of Altamont, he was responsible for reinvigorating the family seat, taking the house in a new entrepreneurial direction. Famously he amended the Deed of Trust to allow the inheritance to be passed on to his daughters.

'We are the first generation of women now to own it and who knows how long it will be because there are five of us. I don't know what the future of the house is – it could be anything, but it has been a challenge. It was all set up in favour of the male heir but dad broke the Trust because by the time he had three daughters, he realised he mightn't be having a son. Then he had two more daughters so what would have happened if he hadn't broken the Trust is that on his death his first cousin, a property salesman in Australia, would have inherited everything. The estate and the title would have gone straight to him, so that wouldn't have made any sense. With a place like this it's very important that you are born into it.'

In 2009 Westport House was rebranded and the grounds have given way to the experiential demands of 21st-century family fun to bring in much-needed revenue. An activity centre and pirate adventure park offer zip rides, laser combat games and a slippery-dip cannonball run. In the basement of the house, beside the dungeons, a permanent exhibition of Grace O'Malley's maritime life is on display. A food festival, as well as the Hooley at the House, are also held in the grounds, while caravan and camping operates from March to September. But the stately home business is a tough world.

'It has always been difficult to maintain the house. In the last six years business has increased by about 100 per cent but it's still a struggle. We now have 140,000 visitors each year, a jump from 2,500 in the 1960s, so we are doing something right. My dad used to be told by accountants to get out of this place. Some wouldn't be able to make it work but somehow we have survived.'

Two statues of Grace O'Malley are on display. The one in the grounds that I passed on the way in stands just over two metres; another made of alabaster stone and weighing two tons is in an alcove off the oak staircase passage. Both were made in 2003 by Lady Sheelyn's uncle, Michael Cooper, specially commissioned for the 400th anniversary of the pirate queen's death.

'There are no photographs of her so they are the only statues of her in the world and Michael is an amazing artist. An awful lot is artist's impression but we know the sixteenth-century dress and I think they are both very strong. I prefer the tall bronze one in which she looks out at the Atlantic surveying her territory. It's on a plinth lifted off the ground so you can look at her from further away and it weathers well. She had a presence about her. When she got on a boat, everyone bloody well knew that she was on that boat, and he has captured that well.

'We have named the park after her and I think she would be seriously proud that her memory lives on and that people are talking about her today. She would also be proud that we are still here and, no matter what happens in the future, the fact that we have survived thus far and that this family has been attached to the house for nearly five hundred years is an achievement.'

From Westport, the Way takes me past Croagh Patrick to Louisburgh, over the Bunowen River and the Doo Lough Pass to Killary Harbour. Roadside spring-cleaning is in evidence with newly shorn hedges and trees. A tractor, with a sticker saying 'Proud Supporter of Mhaigh Eo', holds up ten cars but no one is in a hurry. The landscape shifts into a new ruggedness. At every compass point along this bumpy road, mountains surround me. The afternoon sun lights up the long, wavy ridge of the Sheeffry Hills while the bottom half remains in shadow. On the other side of the Pass, Ben Lugmore and Ben Bury, part of the powerful horseshoe of the bulgy spine of Mweelrea Mountains with its corries and shale scree slopes, reign supreme.

A low wall made up of horizontal stones skirts one side of Doo Lough. At a memorial to victims of the Famine who walked this way to seek relief at Delphi House, the silence is broken only by tumbling mountain streams and the occasional passing vehicle. A couple step out of their car to embrace in the middle of the road, with the atmospheric twin summits of Ben Creggan and Ben Gorm as a rocky backdrop. I pull over beside the thunderous Aasleagh Falls. On the Erriff River the mayfly is up and they are dancing on the water's surface. Two trout pass under the bridge. Bobbing on a boulder, a barrel-chested dipper with gleaming white bib fishes the river with its eyes for the aquatic larvae of flying insects. On a mission towards the bridge, it flies low across the water with fast-beating wings, jinking with a meandering trajectory, plunging in, resurfacing and returning triumphantly to the same rock with caddis fly and a mayfly. With its liquid and warbling *zik-zik-zik* it continues to scout the river from its watch post, its protective white eyelid constantly blinking. In Mayo the bird used to be called the 'water crake' and is sometimes still referred to as the 'wee water hen'. A natural fjord, the dramatically sited Killary Harbour separates Mayo from Galway, where Leenaun snuggles at the foot of mountains.

It is time to return to Belfast but I have a final stop on the way home in Castlebar. The tree-lined Mall with its eighteenth-century houses was once a cricket pitch owned by Lord Lucan and is now the town park. Elegant buildings, including a nineteenth-century courthouse in Classical style with a Greek Doric portico, line the surrounding streets. Crows peck on the manicured grass where a father and son kick a football. Young couples push buggies while gossiping schoolgirls scurry homeward. The Mall bears a memorial honouring the French soldiers who died in the 1798 Rebellion when Castlebar was briefly the capital of the Provisional Republic of Connacht.

But it is another memorial that I have come here to see. Along a path with ornate green lamp standards and chestnut trees of huge girth stands a small, bronze stylised statue depicting Manannán mac Lir. Wearing a cloak and with a confident theatrical stance, looking every inch the god of his realm, he is being pulled over the waves in his chariot by two galloping horses. In terms of scale, at a mere seventy-six centimetres, the statue is a complete contrast to the stolen one. Largely unnoticed, it sits on a plinth on an oval-shaped grassy mound surrounded by stones. It was the work of the sculptor Peter Grant who made it in 1940. An inscription on a plaque records that in 1980 it was: 'Presented to Castlebar by the family of Ernie O'Malley, Author and Freedom Fighter, 1897–1957.'

I climb up to inspect it and notice that someone has Tippexed three letters – 'Frc' – on one of the horses. A man passing by talks about Ernie O'Malley who was born in Castlebar, pointing out the house where he lived on the far side of the Mall. He tells me that I would not have been able to stand on the grass ten years ago because it was a small lake. When the statue was erected, jets of water spurted from it.

Manannán mac Lir statue and horses, Castlebar, County Mayo.

'Originally there was a fountain with water representing the sea,' he says. 'But a few local yobbos and yahoos enjoyed putting shaving foam into it and making a gawdawful mess. The powers that be decided to turn off the taps and the water was removed. So that's what happened but I wouldn't think too many people know very much about Manannán today. He doesn't penetrate the Castlebar consciousness, but if nothing else at least the statue commemorates the name of O'Malley who went on to be an acclaimed writer.'

I think about the relevance of the shaving foam. Who knows, perhaps the 'yahoos' were trying to recreate seahorses? That would have been appropriate since they were reflecting Manannán's horse Enbarr and the translation of the name 'water-foam'. This final inland 'port' of call brings to a close another phase of my journey. I head home to the far end of the road that will soon take me tripping west again.

7
The road to Mannin Bay

TOURISTS ARE SHIVERING THROUGH a June bank holiday downpour, laughing at the 'rainy charm' that is clearing Clifden's streets. Storms have been driven by a strong jet stream speeding across the Atlantic at more than 270 km/h, while on-land winds are gusting up to 110 km/h. The Glorious First of June (from the name of a battle between Britain and France), traditionally known as the first day of summer, has shed its glory. At a supermarket entrance a slippery-surface sign warns 'Wet Floor', underneath which someone has added the words 'Wet Country'. Met Éireann figures show that the west of Ireland differs from the east in one pervasive way: rainfall. In an average year, the east of the country experiences 150 days when rain may fall, while the west has up to 225 days, making it a place beloved of pluviophiles.

In Walsh's bakery and café customers arrive at lunchtime sheathed in yellow waterproof capes, red ponchos and dripping anoraks. The Mazzer machine grinds dark brown beans screaming on their journey from berry to cup, creating a sensory synthesis. Those with a sweet tooth drool over enticing displays of sacher cake, buttercream slices, flapjacks and the emblem of Connemara, rock buns. At my window table, sheets of rain slam against the large panes. Two Danish women shrug shoulders. One says to me, 'Everything is just so grey but we are used to that.' A curly-haired toddler hits the button on his rage machine while his mother, oblivious to his cries, continues to text and scroll. 'Hello, grumpy head,' his sister says. I wrap both hands around a large mug of extra strong coffee, unhurriedly savouring its aroma and warm fragrance, living in a wet mindfulness moment.

Lobster pots, Cleggan, County Galway.

Down the street O'Dalaigh's jewellers are promoting the driving route with their new sterling silver Wild Atlantic Way collection. It consists of druzy agate, offering protection and harmony, larimar that calms excess energies and topaz which releases tension, balances emotions and brings joy. Their shelves also promote the Power of Three through Triquetra, a Celtic symbol representing body, mind and spirit; air, water and earth; Father, Son and Holy Spirit.

The colour pulse of the landscape has changed from yellow to white. May blossom is in full tilt. Hedges flaunt confetti colours of elderflowers, wild garlic and cow parsley billowing on roadsides. Using Renvyle (pronounced to rhyme with 'vile') as a base, I set off to drive the peninsulas of this part of west Galway.

Resembling the shape of a flat right hand, their fingers thrust into the Atlantic in looped roads. They are made up of small settlements and granite islands, many no bigger than an isolated rock, scattered willy-nilly around the coastal fringe. The smallest – which equates to a thumb – is the Sky Road, taking in the three bays of Clifden, Kingstown and Streamstown. The rain has abated and a weak sun emerges as I climb out of Clifden. Early evening views embrace the low-lying Errislannan, or Flannan's Peninsula, with islands and rocks out to sea. Cattle stand on sheer slopes gawping at passing walkers and traffic. A short circular route through Kingstown brings me north to the much bigger Cleggan Peninsula – the forefinger in the hand analogy – which leads to the departure point for boats to Inishbofin. But I am on my way to another island – Omey, accessible only twice a day, being joined to the mainland by a causeway that floods at high tide. I have come in search of the island's last inhabitant, Pascal Whelan.

When I arrive at the car park at Claddaghduff quay to drive across to Omey, the sand is submerged in two metres of water, which is slowly draining. Two granite erratics encrusted in yellow lichen stand at either side of the slipway. A sign warns prosaically: 'At high tide the water is deep enough to cover a car.' A couple in a camper van prepare to bed down for the night. At the top of the road, in Sweeney's Strand Bar, where a picture window looks out over the causeway, one drinker tells me that by 9 p.m. the water will have cleared. 'If you're looking for Pascal,' he says, 'you might be out of luck. He goes to bed early but it's worth a go. There's a full moon; it'll be an exceptional tide so you'd need to take it easy.'

Just after 9 p.m., apart from the fact that there is still a four-inch sheen of water on the strand, it appears suitable to venture over. Blue-arrowed signs point the way across a causeway corrugated with parallel rows of firm, ribbed sand. I bump my way along in first gear, arriving on Omey with water dripping from clean wheels, and join the only road to Gooreenatinny at

Pascal Whelan's mobile home on Omey Island, County Galway.

the far south-west tip. The track turns past unoccupied houses and Fahy Lough before running out of tarmac, signifying that I have reached Pascal's beige mobile home. It stands in a field alongside another mobile surrounded by barbed-wire fencing. My knock on the door interrupts his evening snooze. A dishevelled figure, wearing a striped jumper, and trousers held up by brown braces, says, 'Don't worry, you've just woke me up. You better come in.'

A crumpled brown blanket and dark red towel lie on a seat. Pascal invites me to sit at a table. It is strewn with two plates holding the remains of a chicken dinner, wine glasses, a Bic lighter, a dog-eared pack of cards, shells, toilet roll, binoculars and papers. More than forty DVDs are piled beside a large black battery. Curtains fall off the windows; one window has blown out and is boarded up. A newly opened bottle of Baron Saint Jean Rouge, a vin de pays from Gers in south-west France, sits on the table. He pours two generous glasses into a red goblet, thrusting one at me. It tastes like weak cordial but is quaffable. A green recycling bag overflows with empty bottles, testifying that it is his tipple of choice.

Pascal stubs the remains of a cigarette into a brown oval seashell ashtray filled with butts. Carefully he hand-rolls an Amber Leaf from a flat yellow-and-green tobacco packet that says: 'Smoking Kills' and 'Hand-crafted moments'. He talks about his early days on the island where he was born in 1942.

'During and after the Second World War, I spent the first five years of my life on Omey,' he says in a granular voice. 'It was a place of two-roomed thatched cottages, everything was cooked on the fire and we had no electricity. There was one radio on the whole island. Omey had big families and there were forty children living here. Ours was the second smallest family and the island was fantastic in those years. Europe was in ruins, bombs had fallen all over, and people were starving. Although we knew about it and heard people returning from England talking about it, it didn't affect our childhood one little bit. I can't remember any hunger on the island. We had cattle, chickens, geese and ducks, we had hay and butter, we threshed our own corn and grew our own vegetables. And there was a lot of fishing, mainly wrasse and pollock. It was a great community. Even if people did not like each other they had to cooperate to survive.'

A black-and-white dog curls up at Pascal's feet. He describes Rex as a cross between a Labrador and collie and refers to him as the King of Omey.

'He's like myself, getting on a bit. When I first got him I said it'll be a toss-up as to who is going to go first and he's fourteen now. He's well trained and well mannered. As a young boy I moved away to north Wales with my dad who was an engineer. Between there and here was my life till I was fifteen. When I was twenty I went off to Australia and spent twenty-odd years in Melbourne. I came back to Omey in 1974 and stayed here off and on since then.'

In the intervening years Pascal has led a peripatetic life in Dublin, London, Paris and Strasbourg. He rolls another Amber

Leaf and recharges his wine glass. His lips flick around the paper. He keeps fixed on the shell ashtray as if it holds the memories of the years spent as a successful film stuntman and professional wrestler.

'I worked in films, on stage and on live TV shows, and did so much stuff, including a lot in every theatre in Dublin. Some of the stunts were common rubbish that stuntmen do. There were high falls, car and motorbike crashes, fight scenes. They were all dangerous, of course, and a lot of the time I felt for my life and often got hurt. I enjoyed it but my career ended when a colleague of mine died while we were performing a live show in Waterford. It was then that I decided to give it up. Another stunt partner of mine is here at the moment for a month on a summer visit and is in the next mobile. We recently caught up with each other after forty years and look back on good times.'

Amongst the films that Pascal worked on are *Live and Let Die* and *Butch Cassidy and the Sundance Kid*. In *Crocodile Dundee* he doubled several times for Paul Hogan. He also taught Peter O'Toole how to sword fight on the set of *Macbeth*, and enjoyed successful roles in *Strumpet City*. We gaze out through a window repaired with duct tape. The townland in which he lives, Gooreenatinny, means 'the field of the fox'. It was an area that saw huge changes in the nineteenth century. After the Famine, it was repopulated with ninety-one people living in it by 1871, compared with seven in 1851. On three sides Pascal is surrounded by water. The far end of his field drops down to the sandy curve of his local beach, Trá Rabhach, 'the fruitful strand'. Omey is just under three square kilometres. Resembling the shape of a wild boar, its mouth faces west to the sea and the tiny island of Illaunakeegher. He points out the jagged profile of Cruagh, and the bulky High and Friar Islands.

'I love it here. I live in the peace and magic of a world that I didn't think existed any more. I don't have any bills. I could never handle bills. I've been in show business all my life and one thing you can't have is bills. Living here can be wild and magnificent but you've got to be prepared to move at any minute, to get out of the mobile and into the car. The mobile is tied down but last year someone knocked on the door and, when I opened it, a window ended up in the sea and that was only a breeze. Two years ago we got eight hurricanes in a row. We had boulders thrown into the middle of the field. The island got a cleansing but not to my liking. The only thing to compare with that was the big wind of 1839. You don't mess with the sea. Respect it.'

When I ask if he gets bored, Pascal releases a deep-throated sigh-chuckle, signifying that I am not the first person to enquire about this condition.

'I would get bored living in a housing estate. How many people do you know in an estate? I know everyone within a thirty-mile radius and in the summer there are a few people staying here. We still have the corncrake in my back garden. We get choughs – there was a stack of them outside my door a few weeks ago. I haven't seen any oystercatchers since the storm and we lost our plover, although there are plenty of them on 'Bofin. So far, this summer I haven't seen any boats at sea at all – I lost mine in a storm. The waves don't come up this far but I'd say in another ten or fifteen years I'm gone, but of course I may not be alive then anyway.

'Many people's lives are governed by bus timetables, train timetables or an aeroplane timetable. My life is ruled by the timetable of the tides. People get caught in the sand – my best record is that I lost three cars in one week. Omey can eat cars. You have to be careful if a big tide is coming in, it would have you in five minutes. It depends on the storm as there are parts of it you couldn't drive on. I go over to the mainland nearly every day but I've gone off Clifden. I just go in to do my shopping once a week. I'm a big cook. I love cooking and I'd be starving to death if I didn't.'

In between his harsh smoker's cough, he pauses often, speaking slowly, taking another sip of Baron Saint Jean, which acts as a memory-trigger. I wonder about his social isolation. At my final question, 'Are you ever lonely?', he exhales an irritated hiss.

'Look, this is a stock question and I'll give you a stock answer. There's a helluva difference between being alone and being lonely ... a helluva difference. I do happen to like my own company. I never go without a conversation with people. I have friends regularly coming to visit. I watch DVDs like *The Pianist*, *The Shawshank Redemption* or *Mission Impossible* and enjoy them. I don't need a telly because I'm not in the business any more. Don't read so much because of my eyes but I used to go through two or three novels a week. I'm recovering from cancer and am pretty limited as to what I can do. But when I was fitter I used to fish, dive, walk the island, and picked winkles, oysters and scallops.'

The peace of Pascal's life is determined by the island's oceanic tidal rhythms. I thank him for his time and his wine. Under a strawberry moon, I drive back across the darkening sands musing on the fact that in just a few hours this vast tract of beach will once again be submerged. In the nineteenth century, 400 people lived on this island; now there is just one who comes and goes as he pleases and enjoys an evening pint in his mainland local, the Strand Bar. The story is told of Pascal returning late one night from the pub just as the tide was flowing in. Legend has it that he splashed his way across the water, right arm outstretched, firmly holding a pint of stout.

North of Cleggan, Tully Peninsula – the third or long finger – guards its secrets closely with subdued lakes, beaches and a wobbly line of four hills comprising Tully Mountain. Mweelrea, crowned with its cloud hat, looms across Killary Harbour. Along country lanes at Renvyle on the northern tip, pyramids of fresh hay with black plastic tops are drying in fields, replicating the shape of some hills. Daffodils have withered and the gorse is past its best. They have been replaced by mats of tiny yellow tormentil starring the grass. The floral diversity of one small patch of seafront and hedgebank includes lesser celandine, white clover and red clover, sea mayweed, goldenrod, oxeye daisies, honeysuckle, purple common knapweed and herb Robert. A woman passes me on a morning stroll with a Bernese Oberland mountain dog called Ted. She pauses to discuss the views and the fact that although she has lived here for ten years, she has rarely seen the top of Mweelrea.

For many years I have been drawn to historic buildings and have based myself for several days at Renvyle House Hotel, marketed as a 'stress-free' zone. Its long passages and public rooms with books on Irish cultural heritage, framed poems, landscape paintings and statuettes produce an ambience redolent of an earlier era; bakelite switches with a satisfying click, and the special smell that only a Connemara turf fire can bring, evoke a sense of the past.

The Dublin writer, statesman and surgeon Oliver St John Gogarty bought the house as a summer residence in 1917 for £3,095 'out of the proceeds of my teetotalism'. Gogarty was the inspiration for Buck Mulligan in *Ulysses* (after which his friendship with Joyce is said to have cooled). He wrote that Renvyle was 'where the water lilies meet the golden seaweed at the sea-grey house in the faery land of Connemara at the extreme end of Europe ... In the evening the lake will send the westering sun dancing on the dining-room panels, the oak of which sun and age have reddened until it looks like the mahogany of a later day.' The hotel with its oak panelling was burnt down in the civil war and Gogarty's extensive library of books was also destroyed. The present hotel was built in the Arts and Crafts style and today corridor walls showcase letters, telegrams and pictures. An uncashed cheque from 1942 is made out to Gogarty from *Reader's Digest* for the sum of £7 for quoting seven words from his work. I have always loved the Gogarty poem 'Connemara': 'There's something sleeping in my breast / That wakens only in the West; / There's something in the core of me / That needs the West to set it free.'

Renvyle coast, County Galway, with Mweelrea in the background.

The house became the focus for the Irish literary renaissance of the early twentieth century and a place for literary travellers, many of whom, such as J. M. Synge, left their impressions. Synge's play *Riders to the Sea* was filmed in Renvyle, with many locals hired as extras. W. B. Yeats brought players from the Abbey Theatre to stage his play *The Hawk's Well*. During his stay at the hotel, Augustus John painted a portrait of Yeats.

The gregarious chief executive Ronnie Counihan enjoys explaining the building's history to guests. The hotel dates from 1883 but since at least the seventeenth century a house of some sort has stood on the site, while nearby are the remains of Renvyle Castle, which was inhabited by the O'Flaherty family from the fourteenth century. Ronnie is an ambassador for the Way. His territory commands an 'Islands View' as Crump Island stands in front of the larger Inishturk, while Shanvallybeg and Carrickabullog Rocks are offshore. For him, the Way represents the single most important tourism development ever undertaken on the western seaboard.

'In my opinion it is the most unique tourism product in the world. The land, the sea and, most importantly, the people who live along the Way, represent its very essence. Speaking as a hotelier on the route, I believe the future looks bright, but its success will depend on continued investment in its infra-structure, such as the roads network. And let's not forget the food, which is an important element, too. We have a signature dish, rack of Connemara lamb and fresh Killary scallops, which highlights our belief in supporting and promoting local produce.'

Aside from the eating ethos at Renvyle, my literary nourish-ment includes the second volume of Tim Robinson's magisterial trilogy on Connemara, *The Last Pool of Darkness*. He refers to the area around Mannin Bay, near Ballyconneely as 'The Kingdom of Manannán'. Robinson mentions Manannán's connection with Bran in the eighth-century narrative *The Voyage of Bran*, and the fact that the Galway historian James Hardiman, writing in the 1840s, says that Mannin Bay is named after him. I feel the urge to pay homage so drive back through Clifden, across stone bridges where gigantic purple rhododendron bushes are in full sway, and take a road of hidden dips and sweeping bends to Mannin Bay. High hedges are frothed with fuchsia, hogweed, and purple loosestrife, competing with yellow ragweed, knapweed, and the scrambling pink flowers of dog rose.

This area is classic coastal Connemara: scores of bogs, shimmering lakes mirroring mountains, miles of stone walls, beaches and coves where the tide creeps in over seaweedy black rocks, boreens ending in culs-de-sac or a deserted jetty. Walled remains of abandoned cottages stand in crumbling, weed-strangled silence. Dust-grey ponies, the quintessential feature of the landscape, line up behind walls, whinnying and neighing, and giddy with sunlight. Trees and plants are windblown in one direction and the landscape is dominated by a mass of green and brown. Languid overhanging flag irises with sword-like leaves rise from boggy ground. A bumblebee reverses out of one. In a rocky field, swifts circle repeatedly around a clump of trees beside cream-coloured heifers. With sickle-shaped wings they torpedo through the sky, micro-hunting for small insect prey.

Connemara ponies, Ballyconneely, County Galway.

A signboard informs me that 'Mannin Bay Blueway' offers kayak and snorkel trails. The bay is a Maritime Natura 2000 site and a special place for bottlenose dolphins. Beside the parking area, a turnstone skitters across the road. The shores of the bay are fringed with machair dunes, a rare and fragile coastal heath that grows on wind-blown calcareous sand. The bay coils for nearly five kilometres before opening into the ocean and is enclosed by two arms: one leading out to Errislannan Point, and to the south, Slyne Head lighthouse beyond Knock Hill and the sandy arc of Trá Fhada.

At one side of the soft, shelly beach, brown rocks are splotched with lichen. Some are also covered with masses of limpets clinging tenaciously at impossible angles in sheltered crevices. Tiny colour particles of grain-like shells, the texture of rice, make up the sand. When I pick up a handful, I discover that it is non-stick as I run it through my fingers. My beachcombing produces a triangular piece of lino, a square of green plastic, a Nature Valley crunchy oat wrapper, green nylon, a plastic bottle, a squashed can of sugar-free 7-Up, a tin of pineapple crush, a blue cigarette lighter, a plastic two-litre milk carton, a tangle of blue netting and three plastic bottle tops. At one end of the beach, an upturned wooden currach has been left to soak in a small stream.

The wild flowers of the coast instantly invoke the west for me where the land meets the ocean. Twenty-five years ago, standing at the roadside for lonesome hours, I became familiar with many of these emblematic plants. Mannin Bay is showing off its early summer colours with a galaxy of eyebright, lady's bedstraw, sea campion, bird's-foot trefoil, the thick matting of the ubiquitous bright lipstick-pink of sea thrift, and clumps of silverweed with its yellow saucer-shaped flowers.

I had tried to set up a boat trip around the bay with a local fisherman, Martin O'Malley, who had offered to take me out. But the weather was too rough and he had trouble getting his hands on a suitable boat. He agreed to meet me at the bay as he has spent all his fishing and boating life around it. As I wait for Martin, two black-swimsuit-clad women suddenly emerge from their car and go tittupping across the beach. Performing the front crawl, they swim east to west and back again several times, keeping their bodies close to the surface of the water, legs kicking in the high tide. They swim for fifteen minutes and as they bob around, the wind carries their talk. 'I was nearly going to cancel,' one says. 'I'm glad you didn't,' says the other. They reach a steady rhythm, swim out beyond the breaking waves and the scope of my eavesdropping capacity. When they emerge, they tell me that the water is warm and it gives them a wonderful feeling of being alive. The beach, they say, is not strictly coral but the fragmented remains of calcified seaweed.

'We once had an encounter with a seal and it felt like a whiplash,' one woman tells me. 'The jellyfish are purple stingers, so you have to be careful. There's also a species called compass jellyfish, which is yellowy-white, and we have to look out for that too.'

Martin pulls up just as a south-westerly wind gathers momentum. As well as fishing, he runs sightseeing trips from Bunowen pier and tutors classes in boating skills. He points out features of the beach, the surrounding bay and its underwater life.

'Directly across from here is a salmon farm and in one of the coves at Ballinaboy there is a salt lake with a small ecosystem and a colony of up to eighty harbour seals on rocks. They hunt for crab and eel and have their young in midsummer. There is a rock out there known as the "white lady"' which is a marker or beacon. There's also Mannin Rocks but they are sunken so you can only see them at low tide. The seabed is made up of everything from kelp to zostera, which is a marine eelgrass with bright green ribbon-like leaves. It can be very rocky at low tide. The main thing harvested from this bay is periwinkles exported to France since they love the shellfish.'

Familiar seabirds haunt the shore and sand martins nest in holes on cliff faces. As we cross the beach we scare cormorants and walk over vegetated shingle such as sea lettuce, sea holly and sea beet, an ancestor of beetroot. Martin is used to working in all sorts of weather the whole year round. He speaks about venturing out on bad days.

'I've been fishing fifteen to twenty miles offshore in winter and it gets dangerous so you have to take the nets out. You can misjudge it. It gets totally unmanageable in a boat in the winter. Last Sunday there were storm-force winds. I saw just one boat from the Aran Islands at sea that day and he was trying to get in as fast as possible. Sometimes it's deceptive and can change quite suddenly. A few years ago we had a guy who came into the bay in a rowing boat all the way from Newfoundland. He had recovered from leukaemia and wanted the challenge of crossing the Atlantic in a small boat. He probably drifted more than rowed. One autumn we picked up a bottle here from a school in Newfoundland in which all their names were contained. It came in less than a hundred days, which is amazing. Most of the kids had Irish names. The North Atlantic Drift would have helped it and you get quite a few bits and pieces such as plastic crates washed up. There is sometimes a heavy swell once you go outside the bay – you can see it breaking in the distance since the storm on Sunday.'

We discuss the significance of the name of Mannin and connection to Manannán. He was thought to be an ancestor of the *Conmhaícne Mara*, the people for whom Connemara is named.

'The old people around here would talk about Manannán and it is certainly something that they are aware of. I've also heard about the references to Manannán being angry, and the fact that he is often compared to Neptune. Apart from the mythology, there is evidence of prehistoric and early sites and there would have been settlements here for probably more than a thousand years. There are shell middens all along the shore and people have picked up stone axes and bits of flint, which must have been imported from a long distance because there is none locally.

'It's a fantastic place to live and there is a lot of freedom here. I don't travel much but my last trip was to Istanbul. I went by train from Galway. I don't want to live anywhere that is crowded and most of the world is getting crowded. Here I can walk, cycle or jump in the car and drive to Clifden or Roundstone and I don't ever have to think about traffic. If you're held up five minutes it's a major traffic jam. You can, of course, get a week's rain in winter or summer but I just stock up with books and get used to that life. If it ever gets too crowded, we've plenty of islands such as Inishturk and Inishbofin to spend time on. Many aspects of life haven't changed in the past few hundred years. The sea comes in and out, and although I wouldn't deny global warming, we had serious storms in 2013. But I saw that when I was a kid, it was just as bad, then it died off. You have to remember there was damage to beaches and erosion in the past as well. But we're all aware of global warming now so every time there's a high tide another piece of the ice cap seems to have melted but I don't think the tide has risen to any detectable height yet.'

Connemara's enchantment is best appreciated in June when the colours of the sea, lake, mountain and hillsides range from indigo to brilliant gold, something that Martin has long appreciated.

'The changing light here is exceptional. The special type of sand we have on Mannin beach produces a beautiful turquoise colour in the water. For me, there is great satisfaction and enjoyment working here. I've been to some good places on travels abroad but this is where I want to be, with the mountains behind me and the sea in front of me.'

Back in Clifden, over a fish-finger sandwich and a Galway Hooker pale ale, in Mitchell's restaurant, the owner J. J. Mitchell talks about the area's popularity, especially with visitors from France. The French singer Michel Sardou recorded 'Les Lacs du Connemara' ('The Lakes of Connemara'), which was the title of his album as well as a song. Regarded as a lyrical evocation of the west of Ireland, the song entered the French psyche and is an important part of the recent musical history of the country. It is often sung at the end of French student parties or at weddings.

'It was released many years ago,' says J. J., 'and it is amazing that the song has been responsible for bringing in thousands of French people to Connemara – along with Ryanair – in the past twenty years or more. There is something about it that appeals to them and they just keep coming here because of it.'

On the subject of music, J. J. directs me to Lowry's Whiskey Bar, a few doors up, where he assures me there will be distinctive entertainment. Local knowledge proves correct. A two-man band encourages a virtuoso dancer – who does not seem to need much urging – to take the floor. Slowly at first, hands on hips, his body rigid and tensed with energy, the tall, thin man moves with step-dance precision across the floor. John Dunne is a self-taught dancer, performing with musicians around different bars. His unique freestyle is a mix of Riverdance-meets-flamenco, and involves an element of kick-boxing and leg-stretching. Despite his three score years and ten, he moves nimbly and swiftly in tight-fitting jeans, with small intricate steps, to whoops and screams from his audience.

John's career is a chequered one. He has spent time working in hotels and for an electricity company in England, as a DJ on Connemara Radio and as a taxi-driver. As a serving soldier in the Irish Army, he was involved in peacekeeping duties in the Belgian Congo, Cyprus and Beirut. During a break in his routine, he describes himself as a hybrid, born in Clifden, with a mother from Yorkshire and father from Connemara.

'I was always fast on my feet and had what I call excellent bog legs,' he says. 'As a boy I was used to running and leaping through the bogs and made good speed helping with the turf. When I trained in the army, it was all discipline, marching and timing, so my dancing flowed naturally from that and I quickly became proficient. The slow marches and fast marches are part of it.'

John puts his skill as a dancer of some renown down to the gene pool. He picked it up naturally, he says, inventing his own choreography. He dances to a wide variety of different types of traditional Irish music, with a special fondness for the two-four tempo and the punchy rhythms of the polka. 'Everyone has a performance gene, but in some people it is dominant. I like waltzes as well as the jigs but my favourite music to dance to is the polka, which is popular in many countries. It is honourable and has a lot of history with a strong military background so I enhance that. The session is a game in which you try to keep going faster; that is part of the fun of it to see if I can keep going and it can be strenuous. I do exercises so I am able to keep dancing for ten minutes or longer. The tourists enjoy the dancing and sometimes the Americans put money in my hand. Many Europeans like it, too, since it is free entertainment.

'I use soft shoes, not the ones with the metal tips which produce the clickety-clack sound. There is a great sense of purpose and achievement from dancing. I love Clifden and always wanted to return here – I'm like a salmon returning to the spawning grounds of a river.'

Connemara road sign.

The musicians pick up their instruments and half-a-dozen songs quickly flow: 'Ride On', 'Foggy Dew', 'Lonesome Fugitive', 'Spancil Hill', 'Flight of the Earls', and 'Bang on the Ear'. They introduce John again as 'singer, dancer and late-night stripper.' With good carriage and deportment, Clifden's bar-room exhibitionist par excellence takes the floor again, hands on his side, whirling and cavorting, pirouetting, clapping, and with arms extended, applauding the musicians, the bar staff, the audience and himself.

The sunshine of Roundstone brings out the smell of the sea, permeating the car with a rich aroma. Harnessing the French connection, the village is twinned with Noyelles-sous-Lens in the Pas-de-Calais *département* in the north of the country. Lining the waterfront, a parade of cafés, bars and small hotels would not be out of place in a French commune. The views reach over to Inishnee, a protective straight arm that looks like an island but is linked by road and scattered with squat bungalows, stone walls and rocks. A chorus line of great black-backed gulls keeps an eye on eight boats in the harbour. Just beneath the memorial to the Scottish civil engineer Alexander Nimmo, who designed Roundstone Harbour and founded the village in 1824, three teenage boys, heads hidden under hoods, sit on the wall hunched like the gulls.

For a wider perspective, I pull on my walking boots and make my way uphill, following a paved lane that quickly degenerates into a track. I pick my way across rough boggy ground and ninety minutes later rest on a boulder near the top of Errisbeg. Despite appearances from below, the summit turns out to be a ridge of three rocky hillocks. When I reach a concrete pillar marking the top, a couple smoking a joint nod to me. In the warm calm air, I walk to the edge where, on three sides, the indented coastline has been carved by the sea. Back to back, the perfectly curved white-sand beaches of Gorteen and Dog's Bay are busy with swimmers and sunbathers making the most of a vivid blue sea. Peninsulas are barely distinguishable from a jumble of rocks and islands. Spilling away to the south-west the jutting promontory of Errismore is dominated by the landmark Doon Hill at Bunowen Bay. I embark on a fruitless attempt to count the number of islands. Northwards, the uninterrupted prospect of the remarkably clear, jagged quartzite peaks of the Twelve Bens and Maumturks fills the horizon. Spread beneath me, the sparse, flat Roundstone blanket bog is covered with a glittering crazy-paving of lakes of every conceivable shape, size and sheen. My map names scores of 'Les Lacs du Connemara' but I suspect that not even the French tourists will know that all these lakes are here. The radiant complexity of land and bog-water is bisected by a single road that looks as though it does not see traffic jams. On my descent, with the sun in my face, a lone wheatear accompanies me, rock-hopping, then perching fleetingly, delivering a harsh *chack-chack* call. The words of Praeger spring to mind: 'On such a day the wanderer will thank his lucky star that it has brought him to Connemara.'

My 'lucky star' guides me to one end of Roundstone bog and a historic guesthouse. Run by Lynn Hill, the Anglers' Return is a powder-blue house at Toombeola, a few winding miles from Roundstone. It looks out over the tidal Owenmore River, bordered by tall reeds leading into the bog. From a monster-sized Aga, Lynn produces a plateful of hot scones, served with home-made blackcurrant jam and tea, and outlines the history of the house.

'The building is nearly 200 years old and was originally built by the Martins of Ballynahinch Castle. It used to be part of the castle but by the 1890s it was known as the Anglers' Hotel and the man who owned it was advertising seal shooting – can you believe it? In those days horse carriages met the people at Ballynahinch station. It was a small fishing hotel that became run down. It was later called Derrada Lodge as this area is known as Derrada Hill.'

In 1954 Lynn's parents came on holiday from Cornwall and rented a house in Ballyconneely. 'My mother loved Ireland and was dying to come and live here. In a nearby pub a woman told her that there was an old house down the road that she might like to buy. My mother came to look at it, they bought it and we moved here gradually. She turned it into a small private hotel and called it the Anglers' Return, which was appropriate as it was the Anglers' Hotel now returned. She could barely afford to advertise but did so in *The Irish Times* and *The Lady*. In those days we used to get people coming to stay for two weeks. It's amazing to look back and think that, apart from Foyle's Hotel in Clifden, we were the only other accommodation in Connemara. Bed and breakfasts had not been invented and the other older hotels had all closed.

'We used to have writers, poets, musicians and artists. A group of artists would take over the house and paint for a week. The landscape painter Frank Egginton adored it here. In the 1950s and 1960s, he came every summer and put his little caravan in the yard. He didn't stay in the house but set up in the garden to paint and loved working there. He liked the light and the clouds and the mixed weather, which is so tantalising. There is no continual blue sky, no continual rain, so that is why painters love the cloud effect and ever-changing light. Frank, of all people, really captured the brooding, damp, misty feel of the bogland. There's a great peace; Connemara speaks to people through its silence.'

Lynn embodies the living spirit of the house festooned with wooden floors, runners, antiques, pictures, and atmospheric smell and feel of antiquarian books. Guests pad around in socks, sitting by the fire on comfy settees watching the dancing flames of sycamore logs. As well as looking after the house and garden, Lynn bubbles with thoughts and plans. In between everything else she makes baskets, plays the tin whistle and enjoys step dancing.

'I have lived here, unintentionally, all my life and have had the same home since I was six. It's tough, especially in the winter. The roads are bad, facilities aren't great and you have to drive to get anywhere, but I don't mind the isolation. I jump in that river on a hot summer's day and it is beautiful.'

After her mother died in 1971, Lynn took over the hotel and has run it continuously ever since. The arrival of the Wild Atlantic Way has been a bonus but she feels it is a gimmick.

'Some visitors believe it is being over-exploited with Way cafés, shops and businesses, and that annoys me as I feel we might kill the goose that lays the golden egg because they will overdo the terminology. They should let it sell itself but don't have every single shop and café named after it. It's silly.'

Lynn has a zest for life and for her garden, which she delights in showing visitors. Behind the house a wood leads uphill. Bonnie, her collie, accompanies us, sniffing out badger setts. The garden is south-facing, overflowing with wild flowers, bushes and trees. A charm of goldfinches with their conspicuous three-coloured red, black and white head pattern pop in and out of trees, repeat the same notes with liquid trills, then skip off at speed. Along a path, cornflowers, forget-me-not, heather, buttercups, columbine, lupin and petticoat-pink aquilegia, yellow iris, blue bugle and London pride are in early summer bloom. Rock-covered ferns and wild angelica spreads around another section.

'This used to be the old back yard,' Lynn says. 'At one time it was packed with turf as there was no central heating so all the eight bedrooms in the hotel had a fire and had to be fed all day. There used to be orchards here, now we have copper beech trees, apple and fruit trees, damson tree and a golden acer.'

The Kerry writer, mystic and poet-philosopher John Moriarty spent time working in Lynn's garden, referring to it as 'dilapidated grandeur'. He wrote about it in his autobiographical work *Nostos* in which he described how he set about being a day labourer in Connemara. He had been a live-in gardener at a Carmelite monastery in Oxford and had developed a love of gardening, later moving to Connemara to build his own house.

'John came here in the 1970s to get away from everything', Lynn recalls. 'He re-established my garden and put in young apple trees. He wrote about wrestling with rock and root, and made a vegetable patch, later planting a hazel wood of fifty trees. He had to get out of his own head and do something physical, which is why he enjoyed working in this garden. He gardened for us for years, several days a week, and became very knowledgeable. He liked to say that he walked down three steps, up two steps and down the path where these 150-year-old azaleas are growing. There's still a strong smell off them even today. It's a big job looking after this and it's like continuously fighting a jungle.'

Insistent Connemara raindrops cascade on the windscreen as I prepare to leave the Anglers' Return after breakfast. On the drive around the puddle-filled roads of Cashel Bay, ponies shelter behind bushes, stock-still. Sheep and cattle resemble statues. The only sign of any movement is the bog cotton shivering in the wind while mountains are shrouded in mist. Glinsk is more name than place. I stop for a coffee at the only shop, where Padriac and Mary Cloherty are discussing a front-page headline in that morning's edition of the *Connacht Tribune*. The story suggests that the Connemara Gaeltacht is facing a crisis and could be 'dead' in a decade unless something is done to save the Irish language. It quotes a report by a Gaelic academic,

Professor Conchúr Ó Giollagáin, formerly of NUI Galway and now at the University of the Highlands and Islands on Skye. He suggests that English will become the dominant language of the majority of people by 2025 and calls for decisive action by the government, including setting up an emergency commission to save the Irish language.

'My seven grandchildren are all learning Irish,' says Mary, 'so it is still thriving here. Most of the young couples that I know speak both Irish and English and the children have both languages. But it needs to be kept alive and promoted. We need to make it fun for the children and then they will enjoy it. Here in south-west Connemara we have festivals in Irish and the tourists are very interested in it. I wouldn't believe what the papers are saying anyway and I don't know who's making this up. I might phone them to tell that that it's not true.'

This part of Connemara is solid Gaeltacht country. I follow the Irish-language signs from Glinsce (Glinsk) through Carna around a twisty sixteen-kilometre road beside Mweenish Bay and on to Cill Chiaráin (Kilkieran). Sheds are stacked high with black turf; in the bogs, to help them dry, mini-mounds of triangular-shaped sods are footed against each other, a pyramidal art of exactitude. If any part of the west has a tangy vocabulary attached to its place names, then the small islands and lumps of rock dotted around this part of the coastline reflect some of the most poetic: Illaunnacroagh, Inishbigger, Freaghillaun, Doolick, Skerdmore, Doonguddle and Wild Bellows Rock are a few that jump off the map. But it is a tiny island hidden in Kilkieran Bay that prompts me to find out more about it.

'It's just a lump of rock and grass, there's not much to see,' says Kevin Naughton in Coyne's Bar in Kilkieran. We are studying a maritime map of south-west Connemara showing the islands and isolated lumps of rock in microscopic detail. He is puzzled as to why I want to visit Oileán Mana or Mann Island. I explain that local folklore says that one day the daughter of Manannán was caught in a storm while boating in the bay. She was nearly drowned but when Manannán saw the danger she was in, he conjured up an island to rescue her. All this comes as a surprise to Kevin. His hobbies are diving and fishing so he is familiar with the bays, inlets, islands and rocks, as well as with the vagaries of the weather. He is immediately fascinated by the story and the link to Kilkieran Bay. After some discussion, he agrees to take me out to the island in his small boat.

'It's only about twenty minutes away but it's too late today and is impossible anyway with the conditions at sea, so if the weather is right we'll go in the morning,' he says.

We rendezvous early the next morning, starting with a brief tutorial on riding a motorised crow-black currach: sit tight and hold on to the frames. Kevin revs up the fifteen-horsepower Yamaha engine and we make our way at low tide out of the sheltered Kilkieran Bay at a steady four knots. The sun has come out and the sea appears calm. Workers are arriving at Arramara Teoranta, a seaweed factory that opened in 1947, where Kevin works shifts. Steam rises from large grey sheds. Lorries are laden with brown and yellow seaweed, while Marine Harvesting trucks reverse out of grey sheds with bleeping alarms. Small trawlers, *Golden Adventure*, *Anita Marie*, *Oisin*, *Julie Eleanor* and *Beal Dara* are tied up at the harbour while the *Locator* awaits its cargo of delivery to the Aran Islands.

Kevin's job as factory supervisor involves monitoring various stages of production and checking temperatures. Lorryloads of seaweed arrive daily from all parts of the mid-west, stretching from Belmullet to Kinvarra. The processes include putting it through a wash plant to get rid of any sand, stones or mud, then through a mill and into two store choppers that feed into driers. It is heated by two coal-burning furnaces, broken down, graded, bagged and shipped out in forty-foot containers to various countries, including Japan, China, USA, Australia and New Zealand.

'The Japanese are crazy about it,' he says as he surveys the sea. 'They use it for eating in side salads, feeding to animals, or in medicines, face creams and many other things.'

Herring gulls scavenge around boats, then watch from the shore wall as we slip out quietly. From the water the ridge of Cnoc Mordáin, north of Kilkieran, spreads its long face clear and bright, its sheer rocks paralleling the main road. The sun's shadow glides over the mountain, which shelters the bay. We pass Lettermore and Gorumna islands, linked to the mainland by road, making our smooth way into wider waters. After several thousand kilometres of riding the tarmac and watching the waves from a safe distance, it is a raw, salted experience to ride the ocean in my own black chariot. Kevin, who has entered into the mythological spirit of my endeavour, says I can now imagine how Manannán must have felt; he might even name his currach in honour of the sea god as he has become absorbed by the story. We pass the cages of a salmon farm where thousands of fish are harvested and processed at a local factory for both the export and home market.

Gradually the swells increase with waves rising to more than half a metre. The small boat lurches and heaves. While Kevin keeps a firm grip, I feel exposed to the elements. The sea is getting heavier and I am grateful I had the foresight to skip my honey, banana and Special K. The breeze is turning into a strong, gusting wind as the small island of Mann comes into view. It is a mix of grass and rocks, a few sheep, and a tall marker pillar to help guide boats in the channel from Mackin Rocks. It measures twenty-one by fifteen metres. A cormorant shoots past. In his spare time, Kevin dives off the island and fishes in the area.

'There's a very deep hole just off this side of Mann Island which could nearly be a hundred feet and suddenly drops away. There's a fair bit of activity there with ray, pollock, wrasse and dogfish – it's too rough for anything else. I gear up on Mann if I can get the boat in. Mostly I'm diving in the shallower waters up to thirty feet. It's a different world and a great experience with shoals of fish moving around and you see how they eat, what they eat, how they hunt.'

His experienced eyes sweep the sea as he drinks in the growing scale of the ocean. I detect that he is becoming uncomfortable with the size of the waves farther out, pitted against a small currach.

'This morning it looked grand out there, then it picked up and freshened a bit. But it's deceptive as you don't know how it might develop if the weather turns. When the tide is emptying it might pick up but then calm down.'

As we head towards the island in open waters, Kevin's face begins to show worry lines. What should have been a simple twenty-minute pleasure cruise is now turning into a rougher ride than anticipated as the westerly breeze gathers strength. The smack of the waves hits me full force, splashing my back, soaking trousers, raincoat, socks and boots, and swishing around the floor of the currach. I suggest that we could use some support from Manannán since there is a danger we will replicate the story of his daughter who got into trouble in the bay when a storm erupted. The waves are not so much hostile as mildy peeved but there is a concern that it will turn worse; already they are producing white horses. By the time we get close to the island, Kevin's calm voice has taken on an urgency. He shoots me a look that suggests we abort the journey and beat a hasty retreat. Swiftly, he ratchets up the horsepower and we bounce back across the swells at a good clip to the safety of Kilkieran Harbour, reflecting that the best-laid plans of boatmen and wayfarers do not always run smoothly.

Along the Way, I have rounded many corners and tight bends but for startling seascape diversity, none beats the sharp right-angled turn at the staggered crossroads of the Gaeltacht village of Baile na hAbhann (Ballynahown). Instantly on turning the corner, the immense sweep of Galway Bay opens up ahead of me. I have left behind the rugged nature of inland and lake-dotted Connemara, replaced by the sea on my right. With the elegant grace of a fulmar, a tiny nine-seater plane glides in from the Aran Islands to Connemara Airport at Inverin and idles for a few minutes. Apart from some kinks, the road from here runs in a straight line to Spiddal.

An electronic orchestra of marimba, piano riff and trill ringtones, mixed with the chatter of small groups, illustrates that 'screenitis' – the 21st-century addiction to staring at screens – has arrived in Builín Blasta café in Spiddal craft village. Afternoon light slants across the tables as the Brasilia coffee machine with its steaming froth gushes and cranks into action to meet the needs of Connemara's coffee connoisseurs.

'It's a bit of a dinosaur,' the owner J-me (formerly Jamie) Peaker tells me, 'but it does the job well enough. It processes the Agust espresso-based coffee, a long-established blend of Arabica and Robusta beans roasted in Italy, carefully levelled and tamped.'

J-me, who is from New Zealand, met an Irish woman on his travels in Zimbabwe. They settled in Galway, and in 2007 opened their bakery-style café whose name translates as 'tasty loaf'. I indulge in a cholesterol-charged Connemara high tea consisting of a latte with a leaf-art pattern served with a giant fruit scone, raspberry jam and a dollop of cream. J-me is fascinated by the interest now shown in coffee and brings his knowledge gleaned from travelling to help inform the business.

'Ireland was a bit slow off the blocks when it came to coffee as it was mostly an old tea-drinking nation. But because more people were travelling in the past ten years, it opened their eyes to the scale of different coffees that are available, especially in the US. Our Agust coffee is super consistent and is both a pleasure and a medicine. We call it trendy, cool, funky and a social stimulant, and customer satisfaction is very positive.

'The Way has increased our business. We had a party of French yesterday and they were wearing Way jackets. It's the new Route 66 and is an important development for us.'

I had contemplated making a trip to the Aran Islands as I had done a quarter of a century ago but time is marching on and my deadline to complete my journey is the end of the summer.

Having been back to Aran several times since that visit I have found the tourism stage-managed and formalised with minibus drivers controlling the routes. When I travelled there by boat across Galway Bay in 1991 it was a day of violent seas with the vessel turning into a floating vomitorium. My main memory is of the passengers taking sick, while the cattle below in steerage were also sick. The medicinal whiskey in my hip flask did little to help.

Instead, I settle for a distant view of the islands out to sea. For the moment, after my rocky trip from Kilkieran Bay, I have had enough of boats. By late afternoon the weather has settled down and from Spiddal the sea is an immense widescreen, the water shimmering in an unbroken sheet of oiled-silk smoothness, the whole scene a calming picture. A family is rock-pooling, with children excited about their finds. Two women pull up in a Citroën C3 and lick 99s with large chocolate flakes poking out from the top. An angler casts off, a collie chases a ball, donkeys munch on grass. As I contemplate the empty panorama where sky and sea bleed into each other, an obstreperous party arrives by coach. They are from Louisiana and are on a tour of the west and south of Ireland. Their arrival unleashes a tirade of shrieks from herring gulls. Led by a priest, formerly of this parish, they have come to explore the shoreline. Their accents, from the Deep South, bounce off rocks. Fanning out in ones and twos, they study the flora and whip out cameras, smartphones and tablets. One woman, phone clamped to her ear, decides to put some 'Wow' into the 'Way.'

'George … George … can you hear me in Newalins?' She looks over the expanse of ocean as far as her eye can see. 'I'm standing in Galway Bay on the At-lantic shores and let me tell you this 'lil ole piece of Aaar-lan is beyond beautiful. You would *love* this place.' An ass lifts its head in a field to peer at her over a wall. 'This is *big*-sky country and it's resting on the sea. Awesome would not do justice to it. We're here for ten days' vacation and what a feast for the eyes. I cain't bulieve it – it's wide-open glory. The light here is so different to at home. We've been to see some

Connemara bogs which are truly amazing. I'm eighty-three years and I've never seen them before. You can keep your Louisiana swamps, I want the bogs of Aaar-lan. And hey George, y'know what? They even have their own hookers here but they're not like the ones in the French Quarter that you know, you ole son-of-a-gun. Ciao! Ciao!'

Back in town, the Saturday night foot-tappers flock to An Droithean Donn for a session where six busy-fingered musicians are crowded around three sides of a square at a dimly lit window seat. Two fiddlers, a guitarist, accordionist, concertina player and uilleann piper fuse seamlessly for a series of tunes warming up the room and audience. They start with 'The Blacksmith', then 'The Copperplates' and 'Sweeney's Buttermilk'. The tempo increases with fast and furious hornpipes and polkas.

Ireland being a small country, I discover a long-lost connection to one of the musicians, Máirtín Ó Fátharta, whom I met more than twenty years ago. We were delegates at journalists' trade union conferences on new technology in broadcasting, held in Denmark and Germany. We had kept in touch for a time but with the passage of the years, had lost contact. Máirtín, who answers to the names of Martin Joseph Faherty and Meaití Jó Shéamuis Ó Fáharta, lives nearby in Inverin. For thirty-seven years he worked for Raidió na Gaeltachta, taking early retirement when he was 'released into the community' in 2009. A former teacher, he joined the station when it was set up in 1972. In a distinguished and lengthy broadcasting career, he produced and presented live sports, magazine and music programmes that included the twice-weekly *Ilán a' mhála*. He is a highly regarded authority on Irish singers and musicians. His acclaimed career playing the uilleann pipes and concert flute as well as singing has taken him to festivals and on tour in Europe, North America and fleadhanna all over Ireland.

During a musical interlude we renew our acquaintance, reminisce about our conferences and some of those who attended them. Máirtín talks about his music and interest in the Irish language. He comes from a background with a strong musical pedigree. The thatched cottage in south Connemara where he grew up had a large kitchen suitable for half-sets, musicians and storytellers. His parents loved set dancing and holding céilithe. He learnt songs from his mother, Nan Phaddy Nic Diarmada, who was a well-known sean-nós singer, and picked up others from friends and on the radio, building up a large collection. When he was eight, Máirtín learnt to play tunes on the tin whistle from his uncle, a box player who encouraged him as a teenager to play the pipes. He specialises in the sean-nós way of singing that has been handed down over the generations. As a fluent Irish-language speaker and broadcaster, he is interested in the story in the *Connacht Tribune* forecasting the demise of the Gaeltacht in a decade. He explains his concerns over its decline.

'Forty years ago I used to be having nightmares over the possibility that the Gaeltacht was nearing its end,' he says. 'One of the great Irish language writers, Máirtín Ó Cadhain, was born in An Cnocán Glas just two townlands from here. He wrote the famous novel *Cré na Cille* [*The Dirty Dust*] about gossip, flirting and squabbling between corpses in a Connemara graveyard, and in 1965 he predicted that the Gaeltacht had a lifespan of twenty-five years, so that puts it into perspective.

'Many young people are still learning Irish. The language as a communicative subject is a lot better than it was in 1965 or even 1975. The Irish summer colleges are popular and attract up to three thousand people from many parts of the country, mostly Dublin. The numbers of students in the Gaelscoil have mushroomed within the schools where they are functioning and we have strong areas here such as Carraroe and Lettermore. I think the warning about it being dead in ten years is a little before its time. I will soon have two grandchildren as my second son's wife is expecting twins. Even though she is from the other side of Spiddal, she doesn't speak Irish but she wouldn't stop my son or grandson from speaking it so that will continue for another generation or two.'

Máirtín acknowledges the fact that the numbers speaking Irish have dropped alarmingly over recent years.

'Breandán Ó hEithir carried out research in the early 1980s and reckoned that the number of speakers was down to twenty-five thousand at that time. That was a shock for me then. Fifteen years beforehand it was three times that so the figures were coming down drastically and they are coming down again. I would say that if there are four thousand Irish language speakers nowadays in Connemara that would be a generous figure. Someone told me recently here in Spiddal that they had been to the Aran Islands where more than a hundred children were taking part in a language competition so it seems to be alive there. Although they are learning it in school, in many cases you will not hear one word of Irish being spoken by the kids coming out of school gates and that's a death knell. The political will has to be there to promote all these things – not just language but also the sean-nós style of traditional singing, dancing and other aspects of our culture which is healthy in some areas.'

Máirtín resumes his position, flexes his fingers, reconnecting with his beloved pipes, and relaxes into his signature song: *Bóithríní an locháin* ('The laneway of the pond'). The warm reedy sound of the pipes and the rich timbre of his voice stills the bar. The song is called after the townland where his mother was born, and for which in 2001 he won the sean-nós singing prize and prestigious Corn Uí Riada cup. The musicians rejoin him with a series of finely crafted lilting tunes and waltzes that spin around the room creating an effervescent Connemara musical chemistry. 'The Silver Spear', 'The Merry Harriers', 'The Easy Club Reel', and 'Margaret's Waltz' build up to a resounding finale – a reel called 'Connemara Stockings'.

On Sunday afternoon, I did what you do in Salthill – joined in the nearest the west of Ireland gets to a *passeggiata*, the slow

Connemara laneway, County Galway.

ritual perambulation of genteel social pride involving all ages
from babies in buggies to pensioners on Zimmers. On the face of
it, Salthill prom does not appear to have changed much: people
on benches soak up the view across the bay to the Aran Islands
and south to the Burren hills; the brightly coloured bandstand
is still a prominent landmark; the long-established tradition of

'kicking the wall' (although I have never seen anyone doing this on any of my many visits) keeps alive the legend that kicking the pier-end wall adds years to your life; the annual charity jump into the sea from Blackrock diving tower still takes place each Christmas Day; both the prom and the Long Walk have become even more revered by a passing mention in Steve Earle's classic song 'Galway Girl'.

Along the main road facing the waterfront, hotels, B&Bs, bars and cafés vie for business. The buildings look unchanged since the 1990s, although the new usage of some attests to the changing face of modern Ireland. The former Eglinton Hotel, for example, has been closed for more than ten years. It is now referred to as a 'direct provision centre' for asylum seekers. More than 100 people live in it and run a community garden on reclaimed waste ground. It is one of thirty-seven centres scattered all over the country where people await their fate, evidence of the 21st-century transformation that has taken place. Galway is Ireland's most multicultural city, with the 2011 census recording nearly twenty per cent of its residents as non-Irish. At a recent festival in one of the city's suburbs thirty-three nationalities took part in a community parade.

Salthill is sunning itself on the beaches. Families relax on rugs, and while children paddle and splash, mothers speak into mobiles and beer-bellied red-faced men pull on T-shirts too small for them. Groups sit around in circles, some with blue windbreaks. As children skip the waves, shouts of 'Daddieeee' punctuate the air. Sandcastle builders are recorded on smartphones by parents. Farther along, roistering children smash buckets in a furious temper tantrum. A child refuses to wear a sun hat and throws away his teddy bear. Football and mini tennis occupy a space where a ponytailed teenage girl performs handstands on roller skates, to applause. Women play volleyball on Grattan beach, pumping a plastic football to each other with flair and style. In a piece of colour coordination, Galway GAA's maroon-and-white flags flutter from lamp posts, mirroring the shades of the floral hanging baskets. On the prom, strollers, backpackers, rucksack-laden tourists, ice cream lickers, cyclists, joggers and snoggers are part of the Sunday afternoon milieu of those who want to see and be seen.

A babble of accents shows the diverseness of the place and includes American, Australian, French, Spanish and Portuguese, mingling with a large helping of Dublinese and Galwayese. A young couple sit on rocks holding hands. Two girls are carried piggyback by their parents and handed ice creams. The top T-shirt slogan award goes to a woman with a feminist touch proudly striding alone on the prom. It declares: 'If they can put one man on the moon, why not all of them?' At the Oslo Gastro bar and microbrewery a sign proclaims: 'Don't fill your head with women / Fill it with beer.'

Along Ten Penny Road the seafront is known as Grattan Promenade. A plaque commemorates Louise Grattan who gave her name to the prom which was erected by her in the 1860s to prevent the sea flowing inland. Since the workers were paid ten pence a day the term 'Ten Penny Road' was coined.

Back behind the steering wheel, I round-about my way past industrial and housing estates, numerous sets of traffic lights and distribution roads. The City of Tribes, known since the 1800s for its revered Galway shawl, is now better known for its Galway sprawl. Eventually, the suburbs give way to a clear route past Oranmore, through Clarinbridge and on to Kilcolgan and Kinvarra where I have an appointment tomorrow.

Waist-deep in the pure clean waters of Galway Bay, Diarmuid Kelly and his team are up early to catch the morning tide. This part of the coast is renowned for shellfish, especially the quality of its harvested mussels. Kelly's Blue Mussels – a species native to Ireland – grow wild. They use a filter system to feed on microscopic organisms known as phytoplankton and thrive in cold waters. Each year the company produces 150 tonnes of wild mussels that are high in iron.

Diarmuid has invited me to come along to gain an insight into the working of a shellfish operation. From the tiny pier at the small inlet of Killeenaran, the early morning sun lights up the low Burren hills fifteen kilometres south. Hand-picked off the rocks, the mussels are placed in buckets and net bags for two weeks. The tide softens the barnacles, which are scraped off the shell before the mussels are brought to a factory for washing, hand-grading, purification and the final part of the process, de-bearding. Surveying the sea and landscape, Diarmuid describes his passion for his job and early recollections.

'As a child I enjoyed pots of mussels steamed in their own juices and soaked in bread. Now the area where I grew up has become my office and these eight hundred acres of wild fisheries are where I work for some long days. Although it is physically demanding, I love the open air and the healthy surroundings. The Atlantic flushes in here twice daily, mixing with the rich fresh waters from Clarinbridge and Kilcolgan rivers giving just the right mix of water.'

The natural features play a part in the production of their wild mussels, noted for their texture and strong flavour.

'This part of inner Galway Bay is the ideal location for shellfish as Eddy Island provides shelter from the storms and helps create a microclimate. Plankton feeds off the minerals and mixes with the clear water from the limestone hills of the Burren. Then sandstone from the boggy waters of the Connemara mountains and nutrients from the vast fields of Athenry bring fresh sweet-water. So we are ideally placed for our work.'

Diarmuid's father, Michael, started the business sixty years ago selling Native Oysters from his beds at Killeenaran and it has grown today to be a highly successful export enterprise. Kelly's now supply Native Oysters – also known as the European Flat Oyster – not only to Galway's restaurants and wholesale fishmongers in Dublin, but also export to fourteen countries, from Canada to Malaysia. Their products are found in the oyster bars of Seville and Palma, in fashionable Swiss or Swedish restaurants, and on the shelves of Harrods department store in London. Diarmuid says that Irish people are not renowned as oyster eaters.

'The English, French and Asians love them because of their freshness and the fact that they retain a wonderful juice. They are chewy and full of the life of the ocean. But they've never taken off with locals as it is not what they were brought up with, although of course some Irish people do like them with brown bread and stout. We get very good feedback from our customers abroad and our oysters are regarded as the gourmet's favourite. They're a healthy option and a valuable source of minerals, such as zinc, calcium and copper, as well as being rich in iodine and low in cholesterol. They're also a natural product, not farmed or interfered with in any way. They are sourced from carefully managed wild-oyster fisheries, then in the rich estuarine water of our own oyster beds where they fatten and develop their unique flavour. They filter up to eleven litres of pristine water every hour and if you multiply that by the five years it takes to grow to edible maturity you can see why they are regarded as the essence of the ocean.'

Diarmuid shows me the bright white triangular-shaped Atlantic surf clams, locally known as 'diamond clams', which are bivalve molluscs, also harvested within Galway Bay.

'These clams are a sediment-burrowing filter feeder and, as you can see, they are characterised by the white smooth-shaped shell. They're a small clam species growing no larger than five centimetres across.'

The Kelly shellfish enterprise demonstrates the 21st-century side of making a living on the coast from where historically so many have been forced to emigrate. For centuries the sea has been part of the fabric of Galway. The city, at the mouth of the bay, has been shaped by a colourful past and by its status as a seaport of importance. The menus of its bustling hotels, restaurants and pubs are filled with different types of shellfish dishes, many from the refreshing waters of Killeenaran.

Internationally, the demand for Kelly's oysters is high and the company has built up a loyal and appreciative customer base. It reflects the family's stewardship of their beds and the fact that there is a sustainable supply alongside the need to farm intensively. There is a noble connection in the Kelly family to the sea and the land, which has led to an affinity with this part of the west coast. As a successful mussel and oyster farmer, Diarmuid is proud of his family's lineage, which can be traced back over 1,000 years to the first kings of Connacht and which appears to be secure for the next generation standing by to soak their hands in the same time-burnished tradition.

Via a labyrinth of coastal boreens, I drive from Killeenaran around to the heavily indented and island-dotted west side of Kinvarra Bay for the last stop on my Galway journey. The tranquil Doorus Peninsula, an under-visited tongue of land, which was an island until the eighteenth century, shelters Traught beach and coils around to a full stop at Parkmore pier. Breacan Cottage, a rustic guesthouse hard by the water's edge, named after a holy well in a nearby field, is my destination.

During my journey, I have gained the impression that the Way seems to have put a step in most people's lives. Although this is the case with the Breacan's owner, Geraldine Linnane, she nonetheless admits to having been bamboozled about the route at the start.

'When they put up the blue water signs, I thought it was some sort of gimmick,' she says. 'I was sure they were warning about dangerous waves or floods ahead, because it looks like waves and I said to my husband they must be scared that the cars will drive into the sea. I hadn't a clue what it was all about and on one occasion I turned the car back. I assumed the road was flooded as we get the seaweed coming on to the road in bad weather. Nobody knew what it was about at the start as there was no publicity until later so it was all a mystery. Prior to this many people would not have known about Doorus. I couldn't believe that we were getting it as we are so far off the beaten track. It has made a difference and the signs draw people in. Many people aren't going abroad so much nowadays so the signs are enticing and are encouraging them to spend time here.'

Geraldine has lived in this area for thirty-five years and was an artist before opening a B&B which she has owned for fourteen years. She has produced oil paintings and etchings of the area. She is also a celebrated knitter and, as I discover, is known for her repartee.

'I fell in love with the area, married a local farmer and now I can't get rid of him,' she laughs. 'The landscape and sky are always changing – you're not looking out at a brick wall.

'The tourists who come hold barbecues on the lawn here and then go swimming at the little sandy cove beside us. That was a private beach until my guests started telling other people about it and then it became well known. Most parts of Ireland are accessible now so in a way there are few places like this left. I have a lot of Americans coming to me, and then at different periods we'll have French and Austrians. Sometimes I have an Italian week. The Europeans seem to come in flocks of different geographical groups, depending on the time of year. I don't get many Irish because we're too far away from the nearest pub and as everyone knows they like to be near a good reliable source of drink at night.'

Even though Geraldine has experienced many different nationalities, none can rival one particular group of unusual guests.

'I once had a Saudi Arabian, a small man called Ali, who came here with his wife and daughter. Next morning, lo and behold, I discovered he had six women in the room with him. He told me these were his 'other' wives. I said I only charged you for one, and I challenged him about what he meant. "Who are all these women?" I asked. It turned out they were staying in a nearby hostel but he slipped them in here sometime under cover of darkness when we were all in bed. I asked him where they all slept and he said some of them lay on the floor, some slept in the single bed and some with him. I think they made a hot water bottle out of him. I could just picture him lining up all his wives to shower them – they drenched the place and made it into a pond. I called him Ali Baba and the Forty Wives. This was around the time when I had just started the business and I wondered to myself if this was what running a B&B was going to be like. When I saw them at first I thought they were nuns from the Sisters of Mercy since they had long veils down to their ankles and you could just about see their eyes. Then I saw that they were dripping with big bangles, loads of jewellery and bling. I don't get many like that but it was quite an experience.'

Up until the mid-1950s, the Galway hookers regularly crossed the bay from Connemara laden with turf. With the introduction of bottled gas and better roads, the boats became redundant and many were abandoned. Although there was a revival in the 1970s with old hookers restored and new ones built, nowadays they are seen only occasionally. But in the summer, the annual maritime festival known as *Cruinniú na mBád* ('the gathering of the boats'), held each August, is a much anticipated highlight for Geraldine and her guests.

'All the hookers glide past our window with their original calico brown sails and people love finding out about their history. They used to call them the "workhorses of the sea". Some of the boats would be a hundred and fifty years old but a few are newer than that. There will be a good range here in August that'll include the traditional craft such as *bád mór, leath bhád, gleoiteog* and *púcán*. They're unique, and people enjoy seeing them at close quarters in the harbour. They also race currachs, which are popular as the boats are light and very fast, so we get a great variety. The whole weekend is a magnificent sight. It's dramatic to see so many all gathered together out in the bay on our own doorstep.'

This year the festival will also celebrate the generosity of Canadian people who in the 1880s contributed funds for famine relief, which went towards the construction of piers all along the west coast, including the one at Parkmore. We gaze out through the living-room window where white flecks stream off crested waves, floating through the air on to the ground. The sea is turning volatile.

'It's beautiful living here and when the tide is out you can smell the sea, although today is stormy. I can't believe it when I wake up in the mornings. There is always something new to see and I'd hate to live in a city now. I prefer it here to Kinvarra as it is not as built-up, we're out in the sticks. I tell people that we live in a remote peninsula, because the more remote it is the better the tourists like it – that's what they want these days: total remoteness and to be away from everything. It might sound odd, but tourists like to avoid the tourists, if you know what I mean. They want peace and serenity and we have plenty of that here.'

8
Enjoying Guinness sensibly

THE HAY-BALING AND SILAGE season is under way by the time I reach County Clare. At Bell Harbour, on the coast road from Kinvarra to Ballyvaughan, a combination of farm machinery, Sunday-afternoon drivers, wide tour coaches and cyclists holds up traffic. To escape the crowds and experience true horsepower, I have joined Peter Williams on a sunny morning for a horseback ride. Our plan is to follow the Burren Way, an inland route adjacent to the coastline of this part of north-west Clare. The last time I was on a horse was in the Camargue several years ago, and although keen for a different perspective on the countryside, I have reservations about my equine skills. Peter hands me the reins of a docile-looking cob that he has owned for seven years. I admire its sturdy legs and strong fetlocks.

'It's like sitting on a comfy armchair,' he says reassuringly as he looks me over. He introduces me to Guinness, an Irish gypsy cob with a broad saddle. 'We christened him Guinness because he has a black-and-white ear and he will be good for you. Cobs are quiet, strong and full of kindness. Years ago they used to pull gypsy caravans and are ideal for trail riding.'

Peter gives me some tips. 'When we set off, just loosen the reins. Remember to keep your feet firmly planted in the stirrups. You won't have any problems; just be sensible and follow my tail.'

Our route, south of Ballyvaughan, starts along narrow, flat boreens. With the sun on our backs, we quickly find our rhythm, establishing an ambling gait of short steps, and becoming comfortable with the terrain. Verges are brimful of early summer flowers, including bugle, ragged robin, milkwort and cuckoo spit.

Horse riding along the Burren Way, County Clare.

Getting ready for Guinness, the Burren.

The air is breathlessly still. A young American woman, Loren, who is spending the summer working with Peter, has joined us and follows Guinness's bushy black tail. She is breaking in a new horse called Ozzie. Peter's horse, Oscar, is a four-year-old gypsy cob. Side by side, we talk as we ride, passing a farm with Connemara mares and a field of feral goats moving sluggishly. Peter's interest in horses began as a young boy and his life revolves around them.

'I've had a love of them since I was three,' he says, loosening Oscar's reins. 'I had no interest in school – it was just horses, horses, horses for me. It's a hard job but I love what I do and I've made my living out of buying and selling them, breeding them, breaking them in and training them for other people. As well as running a riding school, we buy and export horses.'

We step up the pace to a free walk with my cob stretching and straining. Soon I fall behind and Peter shouts highlights of the landscape back at me as we go, 'bumper to bumper', which Guinness, with head twisting and minor champing, does not seem to appreciate.

'The bits are left loose in his mouth and not tied up,' Peter says. 'We train them as soft-mouthers and leave the bits in for extra time so inexperienced riders don't pull on them. You can also see that Guinness has one distinctive blue eye. Many cobs have a full or light blue eye. Some people like them, others don't and it doesn't affect his sight, it's just a lighter colour of eye.'

I relax the reins and shift in my saddle. Guinness is sure-footed and easy-going. Peter suggests increasing the tempo to a medium trot and we bounce along a grass-filled track for a few minutes. I am relieved to have such a comfortable seat. My riding hat slips over my eyes which means I am following Oscar's swinging tail. When we ease the pace, a skittish young Shetland pony, which had been giving us frisky glances, comes to a low wall, knocking over stones and following along in a field. Through a repertoire of complex facial movements, he scares Loren's horse, appearing to want to 'stirrup' trouble, looking down his nose at us and causing a minor commotion by the ocean. Guinness keeps an unconcerned blue eye on him as he plods along, before the pony eventually falls by the wayside. In the fields, bog cotton, trefoil and herb Robert all flourish. Brown and white butterflies flicker around flowers in a drunk and disorderly fashion. Could it be, I silently wonder, the influence of the eponymous drink after which my cob is named? We pass through a classic Burren trilogy of rocks, walls and limestone pavement. Clumps of bloody cranesbill – the startling magenta geranium and one of the area's specialities – grows abundantly alongside purple orchids and the wavy-petalled burnet rose.

Our route passes Slieve Elva, site of the legendary battles of Cormac mac Airt, and the forested Knockauns Mountain. Both are nunataks, which means they were higher than the surrounding glacial sea as islands of frozen land above the snowfields. When I had spoken to him by telephone, I told Peter about my interest in Manannán mac Lir and requested a white horse. It turns out there is a connection between Manannán and Cormac mac Airt. In the best-known story about him, 'The Adventure of Cormac', the young king accepts a magical sleep-inducing bough from a mysterious warrior, later revealed to be Manannán. In return for this, he makes demands on Cormac, including the surrender of his wife, which the king cannot accept. Cormac pursues the warrior and finds himself in a castle, where Manannán presents him with a golden cup that can be split apart with lies and put together again only with truths.

'There are many truths and lies in Celtic legends,' Peter says, 'and the Burren is full of ancient stories and tales we learnt as children. As a boy, I used to explore the caves and forts of this area, although most are now inaccessible because they are overgrown with weeds.'

Just as Manannán loved riding across the ocean in his chariot led by Enbarr, so too Guinness loves the flat plains and multi-green valleys of this part of Clare. From our elevated position on a stony path along the Burren Way, we halt to look down on the broad prospect of what is locally called the Green Valley spread out before our feet and hooves. The smell of the ocean mingles with newly cut fields of hay. Coastal views north to south reach from the mountains of Connemara across Galway Bay to Black Head and beyond. At Poll Salach, sunseekers with bandana-ed heads, torsos openly displayed and cool boxes by their sides, bask on deckchairs on the gleaming limestone.

'That's my wraparound office view,' Peter says. 'I don't think there is any office in the world that has a view like this. It's called the Green Valley because it keeps its colour all year, and never gets extreme weather since it is well sheltered. We're about a thousand feet above sea level and higher than the Cliffs of Moher, which you can make out along the coast south of Doolin.'

He shifts our gaze from one point of interest to the next. Out to sea the Aran Islands fill our viewing frame. Inisheer, the smallest of the three, looks touchably close. We make out a beach, airstrip and lake while the small settlements of houses on the island's north side sparkle in the sunshine. 'If you can see them drinking tea,' Peter says, 'it is thought to be a sign of bad weather on the way.'

There is no fear of that this morning. The ocean on this windless and cloudless day is as serene as Guinness who has entered a state of equine-mindfulness. Peter points out the townlands of Ballynahown, Ballyryan and Ballinalacken. He mentions features of the landscape such as the roofless remains of Famine houses standing in quiet abandonment, and St MacDara's Church at Oughtdarra. A clutch of five cuckoos is active in surrounding fields and bushes, an astonishing sight, leading to one of those 'can-I-really-be-seeing-this?' moments. Peter puts the cuckoo-storm down to the fact that there are no people around and to the birds' love of the clip-clop of horses' hooves.

'We see them all the time up here and hear them as well throughout the Burren, although of course it is said that in June they lose their tune.'

On the way downhill, I suffer a minor bout of descendo-phobia, releasing a few 'whoa' interjections to keep Guinness in check. He twitches listlessly and seems keen on a gallop. We embark on a silent trot through Cloghaun and, after nearly three hours in the saddle, arrive in a clatter of hooves at the Mountain View Riding Centre at Poulnagun where Peter keeps more than seventy horses. A sign at the stables says 'Courage is being scared to death but saddling up anyway.'

If there are horses for courses, then my cob is in its natural habitat. Despite the fact that I dismount slightly saddle-sore, I had, as Peter advised, enjoyed Guinness sensibly.

That night I hobble along to the Doolin Folk Festival where one of the main attractions, Stockton's Wing, has just taken the stage at 10 p.m. I had last seen the band performing at the Boys of Ballysadare Folk Festival in 1978 and I was pleased to see that not only do they still have a cult-like devotion but that I was one of the youngest present. Having said that, I was also glad to find a seat to rest from my bumpy horse ride. It is a night of late 1970s nostalgia. Cheers of recognition greet 'Take a Chance', performed with the joyous singalong, clapalong, stampalong support of 1,000 ageing choristers, many – apart from those on walking sticks – with both arms aloft.

Revellers sit at picnic tables in the courtyard or on bales of hay; others huddle around braziers enjoying the aromatic tang of woodsmoke and talking about their vinyl collection. At a makeshift bar of trestle tables, pony-tailed hipsters with Pink Floyd T-shirts that have rarely encountered soapsuds queue to get the attention of staff whose T-shirts say 'Let's get folked up'. I join the crowd standing at the back of the marquee, stealing a sideways glance at a woman beside me. Clutching a plastic pint cup, she starts to boogie, then segues into a swayalong to the anthemic 'Walk Away', resulting in a serious spillage of her Bacardi and Coke on to the wooden floor. 'Not a problem,' she says in a husky voice, steadying herself against a pillar, 'my husband's away to the bar.' When the band breaks into 'The Bucks of Oranmore' and 'The Humours of Tulla', she introduces herself over the reels as Wendy. She has travelled from Wexford with her husband. She smiles with smouldering eyes, describing the energy of the music as life-affirming. 'It's revitalising, uplifting, heart-warming and sexy, in fact my heart's racing,' she purrs. I quietly wonder if she is on steroids or perhaps just old-fashioned cannabis but she disabuses that notion by saying, 'It's like Lucozade: it's energising and gives you a sugar boost and a rush. Some friends of mine have even come out in goosebumps. The biggest thing is that it brings back the sense of being young and not having any cares – but then again, I don't have any cares now either.'

Two of the original band members from forty years ago are missing because of ill health. 'Their wings are a bit clipped, you could say,' Wendy quips. A set of melodic ballads, mazurkas and the slip-jig 'The Drops of Brandy' provoke cheers; other dynamic crowd-pleasers, involving banjo, bodhrán and bouzouki, include 'The Maid Behind the Bar' and 'Queen of the Fair'. Wendy drifts off into a trance as the 'Light in the Western Sky' fades into 'Lonesome Road'. A west-of-Ireland haze descends over her eyes and she slumps deep into a hay bale, blissing in the halcyon days of the 1970s.

My not-so-lonesome road takes me back to Lisdoonvarna where I have come to meet Peter Curtin who runs the Roadside Tavern. He has been a unique presence in the town for more than sixty years. With his bristling moustache, chequered shirt, jeans and easy-going patter, he is every inch the garrulous publican. He has also opened a brewery making lager, ale and stout: Burren Gold, Red and Black. As a folklorist and local historian, he is the fount of knowledge on the Tuatha Dé Danann and their connection to Manannán, purported to be one of their lords. When I arrive in the bar at 10 a.m., Peter breaks off from his perusal of the morning paper and pours two coffees. A single question provokes a torrent of reminiscence.

'My family has been here since the 1800s,' he says with pride. 'I was born upstairs in 1953 when there were two motorcars in the village and one of them was a taxi. The first tractor came a few years later when I was still in short trousers and we didn't even have a bicycle. We used to have a wonderful sign with Connemara marble letters because this business was something for all people – a bakery, a bar and a grocery. My grandfather was a professional baker who came here in the late 1800s, so my family goes back through the aeons of time. We were agents for the butter market and bottled our own stout and racked our own whiskey. The whole shooting match happened here in Curtin's bakery and confectionery. My mother christened it the Roadside

Tavern in the 1960s. She was a matriarchal woman who stuck it out for fifty-seven years.

'The bar is tradition – I don't say that to be lazy about it. My mother – God be good to her – died in 2002, and I was the last person to speak to her. She said "I got as far as eighty; I didn't do too bad." The most important thing was that she said you should always show your goodwill so that's what this bar and my family are about. I don't look upon it as a place where the tills are jingling and we're all rich. The pub in our tradition was born out of a social service.'

Peter is positive about the setting up of the Way and describes it as 'a piece of reality that says there's not much else in the west except tourism'.

'If you want to increase the number of people who come to the west, then in marketing terms it's probably the smartest move that was ever made since the foundation of the state. But my wish is for people to regain their sense of creativity and be leaders and not followers. The people who live here are special and have a strong creative side to the brain and not just a European notion. We desperately need to have that confidence and we want people to engage with us.'

Well read in folklore and mythology, Peter has researched the quasi-historic tales and stories, ranging from mythical times up to the eighteenth century. He acknowledges the work of Thomas Johnson Westropp, the antiquarian who was fascinated by the vividness of the folk tales still being told by country people.

'Education is important in the creative sense,' he says. 'The pen is mightier than the sword, as proved by yourself – Manannán, of course, had a sword, the *Fragarach* which cut through metal. He was the Neptune of Ireland, from what I recall from my schooldays, and there are various references to him in connection with the Tuatha Dé Danann. The important thing is that they have not been forgotten as this is an ancient place where memory lives long. Your man Manannán, if I can call him that, had a crane bag and kept the Tuatha stuff in it.

There were all sorts of treasures and implements, such as knives, shields, shears and even bones, and whoever has these is said to be safe from his enemies. It's still believed that at high tide the treasures can be seen in the sea, but at ebb tide they vanish. For me, the Tuatha really *are* the business with their goddess Danú. Their chief stronghold is up in Oughtdarra and that comes from Westropp's research. He went to investigate the area and met two families who lived close by and they said "you better have your prayers said because the prayers of the Tuatha are there." Westropp also describes how in 1905 he had noted a warning by two locals near Ballinalacken Castle to cross himself as a protection against the Tuatha. Near Lisdoonvarna Castle a green hillock, known as a fairy fort, was a recognised palace of the Tuatha, so all the evidence and scholarship is there.

'A few weeks ago I had a weak philanthropic moment and sponsored two guys to go up that conical hill as it was overgrown with scrub at Oughtdarra. They cleared the scrub so you could see the hill properly. A friend of mine, who is an all-bells-and-whistles archaeologist, then did a preliminary measurement of it, and this place is absolutely off the wall, up the road, off the planet, seriously connecting interest. I take people up there and sit and wait for them to walk around the top of the hill to get the connections and the feel of it by immersing themselves in it. This is a hill fort of military significance; it is not where people lived so it would have been of massive importance, with walls maybe eight or ten feet high, the doorway orientated to the south-east, so narrow that only one person at a time could get through it; otherwise you would have been skewered like a chicken if you tried to get in.

'The Fomorians were the precursors to the Tuatha. But the Tuatha were the most interesting because they were the scientists and the magicians and that was their focus. The Milesians, who came after them, were military and then the other crew who came in, the Fir Bolg, were described as the people of truth. And with the Tuathas, when the Milesians came in, they kicked their ass three times. The three kings said that the way out of this is not to engage with these people, and to go to places in Ireland where we won't be seen, so the idea of the Tuatha going underground is actually real. I spoke with a learned friend a few weeks ago at a gathering and people in the know believe that at least eighty per cent of mythology is factually correct, perhaps even higher than that figure. I love the Tuatha story because of the type of people they were. They were huge into bronze, which denoted a certain amount of stature and it wasn't your common or garden metal. And the Manannán connection is fascinating, especially because he was a trickster. He could make ships disappear and had a boat that didn't need oars, and a certain amount of that is probably true. I can understand why people still talk about him today and why there is such curiosity.'

Visitors used to come to Lisdoonvarna, not so much in search of the Tuatha Dé Danann, but for the medicinal properties of its spas. Today they come in search of a partner at the matchmaking festival held in September when the population of the town explodes for the whole month. In early summer it still retains a quietness about its streets, broken only by musical evenings in hotels. Around the corner from the Roadside Tavern, the haunting and poignant strains of 'Eileen Óg' float down the main street, drawing in music lovers to the Rathbaun Hotel. In days gone by, Rathbawn was an important chalybeate well, noted for helping those with arthritic diseases such as gout and rheumatism. Now in a clever marketing ploy, the eponymous hotel – spelling its name differently – pipes out live evening music through speakers in front downstairs windows, grabbing the attention of passers-by.

In a cavernous back room, musicians under the collective name Ceolan are halfway through one of their nightly marathon performances that will continue to the end of August. There is a long-standing tradition of resident summer music makers spending three months on full board living in the hotel. This musical fixture has been part of the summer scene in

Lisdoonvarna for more than forty years. It is one of the few hotels anywhere in Ireland where musicians enjoy a lengthy residence. Jamie Kirby, a 21-year-old student, is on his third consecutive residential summer, and during a short break he explains how it all started for him.

'At a session one night at Mary Immaculate College in Limerick, a woman who had played here a few years earlier told me about it and said it was great work. The owner of the Rathbaun came to see us play and we were offered the job after an interview so we've never looked back.'

The seven Ceolan musicians are teachers or students who are able to commit to the time required to devote themselves to the music. In most cases they have not met beforehand.

'The musicians don't know each other until they come together on the first night. I've made good friends by playing here but at the start you're not sure what to expect. During the first week we all get to know each other through the music and work out our style. We learn about each other's capabilities and limitations so that is important. Everybody soon becomes friends; it's like being part of a big family. We're given food and board and are kept for the summer, but it is quite strenuous as we play for four hours from eight p.m. to midnight.'

The musicians live in the staff quarters at the back of the hotel. According to Jamie, they do not have any trouble filling their time during the day.

'Lisdoonvarna is an enjoyable place to spend the summer. There's a great feeling about it and it has its own unique character. We also discover different places so the time doesn't drag because you really never get too much of a break. We go for walks, play cards, or perhaps drive over to the beach at Fanore or down to Lahinch. We also continue to practise during the day to make sure we are happy with the sets that we are playing at night. Then at half-five every day, we get a fresh cooked dinner which reminds me of playing in the garden at home as a boy when my mother would call us in for tea.'

Coast road near Lisdoonvarna, County Clare.

Jamie, who was all-Ireland mandolin champion in 2011, comes from a talented musical family. His father and brother are musicians and his two younger sisters play the harp, fiddle and piano. At the evening summer sessions in the Rathbaun he plays five nights a week.

'I started originally with the banjo and it is still my main instrument as I love the power you get out of it. It's brilliant for sessions but I decided to try the mandolin for some of the slower stuff. It's very subtle and there's a beautiful tone to it. The mandolin that I play was made by Dave Shapiro in Doolin who is originally South African. He has a great reputation for making handcrafted instruments. During a typical evening's performance we start with a set of tunes and then reels, which have a good drive to them. Then we vary it with jigs, hornpipes, slides, polkas and waltzes. We get a good reaction from the audiences and there's nothing better than that. Between the tunes we have songs, slower Irish ballads and some country as well.'

Most nights the group plays to packed houses. Tourists enjoy the atmosphere and some shout up requests. Jamie's favourite is 'The Mason's Apron', which he plays on the banjo.

'It is a classic and goes down well – you slide up to the higher octaves. The feedback from the audience is very important to us. They all know the old favourite singalongs such as "The Wild Rover" and "Molly Malone". The Germans have a folksong that is the same as "The Wild Rover" so we try to blend into it, which they like. We have a strong variety of nationalities and when we hear their accents we recognise where they come from. They all have their highlights and some have their lowlights too.'

The group's singer, Maggie, takes the microphone and performs 'The Mountain Dew' and 'The Hunter's Purse'. The audience start clapping with 'Country Roads', while 'The Squeaky Reel' and 'The Kesh Jig' liven the show. The evening ends with a request for 'The Leaving of Liverpool'. It grieves me, says a woman beside me, to hear it sung so beautifully.

The leaving of Lisdoonvarna does not cause me such grief but it is time to follow the coastal road south. A strip of B&Bs runs from Roadford to the pier. It is crammed with craft shops, hotels, caravan and camping parks, and a new row of commerce at Fitz's Cross. I start to count the number of B&Bs but give up after reaching twenty-five. The woman in charge of the community-run tourist information office says the development has annoyed many visitors and, in the opinion of some, is an eyesore.

'It was greed that built a lot of this,' she says, 'but as in many aspects of life there are two sides to everything and you have to take the good with the bad and see the wider picture. In the summer we have thousands passing through for the ferries to the islands or en route to the Cliffs of Moher and there was a serious shortage of accommodation so it is needed in high season. We had a woman from Dublin who hadn't been here for forty years and she was horrified by the scale of what she saw as desecration. She was so upset she said she was never coming back to Doolin. Some people don't like change but they can't expect a place to stand still and to keep the green fields that it had in the 1970s.'

At the pier, Joe Garrihy who works for Doolin2Aran Ferries is having a hard sell since the Aran Islands are not attracting many visitors because of mist. Crab Island, a short distance from the harbour, is just about visible. When I ask how many B&Bs there are in Doolin, he says that he has no idea but lobs the question to a colleague who replies without hesitation or looking up from his screen: sixty-five. I wonder if I should take that figure with a pinch of Wild Atlantic Way salt but further discussion with Joe reveals it to be accurate, especially when they start to reel off the names of the owners.

'People have become materialistic,' he acknowledges, 'but we strive to give a quality experience. We provide the personal touch and there is a great vibrancy because of that. We know we have to get the balance right between commercial viability and creating jobs. The guesthouses are helping in job creation and there is another side to all this development in Doolin: we want our young people to stay here in their own homesteads, the place where they were born and grew up. So all this leads to jobs in the service industry and tourism which means they don't have to head off to Manchester, New York or Sydney to look for work.'

Sealed off behind a fence, a mechanical digger claws at the ground as part of the final stages of work on a new all-tidal 65-metre pier, due to open in a week's time. The existing pier has caused traffic congestion because of inadequate space for parking. Joe says the new one will enhance their business and bring a fresh confidence to their sailing timings because they will now have the proper space and depth.

'The old pier was too small and at low tide the ferries could not get to it. The new one takes tidal issues away from scheduling which in the past has been a nightmare. A currach had to bring the passengers in from the ferries during the summer, and in the rest of the season we couldn't operate for about four hours in the middle of the day. You can imagine the difficulties that posed in terms of restrictions on tour operators, coaches and individual visitors. A further restriction related to space. Only one ferry at a time could tie up along the length of the pier and even this was dictated by tides. This resulted in people coming back from a trip to the islands having to wait an extra hour on the boat as they queued to get into the pier which had a knock-on effect on their travel plans to other areas.'

On the road from Doolin to the Cliffs of Moher the coastline is obliterated by stubborn sea fog that in 1950s London was called a pea-souper. The top of the round castle at Doonagore – one of three round castles in Clare – is shrouded in an impenetrable soporific mist. By 11 a.m. visibility is less than 20 metres. Cars and tour coaches suddenly emerge out of the murk with headlights beaming. Road demons on motorbikes are reduced to an uncharacteristic crawl. At the Cliffs of Moher centre busloads of bemused day trippers stand around, willing the weather to improve. They crowd into the shop, Puffin's Nest café, and Atlantic Edge exhibition, a CGI simulation of a gannet's-eye view of the cliffs, a poor substitute for the real thing. There is no chance this morning of even a walk up to O'Brien's Tower. A small group of Americans pose in front of a wall of photographs showing a blow-up version of the cliffs. A man from Maryland, who asks me to take a photograph for 'the folks back home in Annapolis' says this is the nearest he will get to the cliffs today.

'You take what you get, buddy,' he shrugs. 'We've rechristened them the Cliffs of Nowhere 'cos they ain't nowhere to be seen.'

At the front door the Moher Rangers who guide tourists around are under-employed. A lone ranger says it is extremely disappointing for people who have travelled a long distance because the mist will not be clearing until the afternoon.

'Trouble is, y'see, some of them expect us to have a magic wiper and just clear this in one fell swoop. 'Twas forecast, although not on this scale. But 'tis difficult for them especially when they can't find the right coach to get back to because visibility is so poor.'

I cut and run, driving south to Lahinch where the Way has re-emerged triumphant, and neoprene surfers are contemplating waves. The tide is out and twenty thrill-seekers surf tubular swells on the kilometre-and-a-half-long stretch of beach. Lahinch is a shrine to worshippers of the sport, with a surf shack, surf clinic, surf shop, surf school and lessons, surf café, surf bar and night club. From a white transit van with a sign saying 'Living the dream', two surf-bunnies jump out with yellow boards shouting their couplet: 'When in doubt, paddle out.'

Along the seafront, candyfloss, milkshakes, periwinkles and ice cream cones are in demand. In O'Looney's café, Seattle's Best Coffee is advertised and to test it I order a vanilla chai with cinnamon made from Henry's blend espresso whole bean, which is served in a red cardboard cup with a brown ribbed zarf. Large picture windows look out on the waves now surging higher. O'Looney's likes colourful aphorisms. The quote of the day is lipsticked in red on a square mirror: 'Life is for deep kisses / strange adventures / midnight swims / rambling conversations'.

On the white ceiling beam, triplism is alive and well: 'Live every moment / Love beyond words / Laugh every day.'

A mother and son talk about examinations and further education. It turns into a one-way question-conversation because he is more absorbed in his smartphone than his future. Three customers, lives governed by the tide times, check screens for the details of high tide, which is at 6.34 p.m., and which they reckon they will make. They discuss the prices of boards and lessons, other possible locations to visit and weekend plans for hitting the waves. They look at stand-up paddle-boarders and body-boarders now testing their skills.

Thirty kilometres south, the same ocean is encroaching up to the strandline at Moore Bay in Kilkee. Known as the gateway to Loop Head, it is a resort that since the late 1700s has been perennially popular with people from Limerick enjoying the fresh air and saltwater therapy. The horseshoe-shaped beach has attracted tens of thousands down the centuries. But the swimming did not come without some controversy. In 1833 a debate was held about the problem of men bathing without trunks. To resolve the issue, the beach was divided into three sections, allowing men to swim in the mid-part of the horseshoe-shaped strand until 10 a.m. each day while ladies could swim at either side in the afternoons.

'Prepare to be blown away,' is the sales tagline of the area's promotion. The man behind it, Cillian Murphy, who is chairman of Loop Head Tourism and a restaurateur, is working out a table plan and crockery place settings to seat sixteen hungry geologists arriving for dinner. As an icebreaker, I make a deplorable joke about ensuring the plate tectonics are correct. He had suggested on the telephone to come at 6 p.m., saying he would let me into a few of the area's surprises.

'We have our secrets here,' he tells me, 'and we don't like giving away too many of them all at once. You've probably heard of Hy Brasil, maybe you've even seen it on your travels, but I wonder if you've ever come across Kilstiffin?'

I mumble about an unconfirmed glimpse of Hy Brasil from the Connemara shore but admit to knowing nothing about Kilstiffin.

'It is a small, hidden city in the middle of the Shannon estuary. I can't show you a photo of it because thankfully I've never seen it. If you see it you are supposed to have a lifetime of misfortune. It's one of those quiet little stories that we keep to ourselves. Sometimes when I'm out cycling I remember it as a backstory. It's right off the beach and you might be able to see it from Ballybunion. It's near Horse Island and was swamped by tidal waves, then swallowed by the water and is said to come to the surface every seven years. Some people think it was part of Loop Head Peninsula.'

In 2010 Loop Head won a European Destination of Excellence award, which stirred up interest in the area. According to Cillian this provided a stepping stone and an ethos for working together. He is adamant that they should develop the area as a destination where people spend time in an unhurried manner.

'They need to slow down, embrace the area and spend money. We want to pick and choose how the area develops and we are specific about who we market to and the kind of products we develop. We are squeezed in between Kerry and the Cliffs of Moher. Half a million people coming off the ferry from Kerry pass our front door but don't stop. This is a big challenge. How do you say I only want ten per cent of that? And secondly, to get the ten per cent, how do you go about that? That has been the result of thirty years of marketing the cliffs. It's about going into the marketplace, but tourism is an industry and we've had to look at various things. We sent two local women to the World Travel Market in London and they wowed the German public for a few days. We were adamant from day one that we did not want a procession of fifty-seater coaches and there are very few places you can go on the west coast that don't have that.

'The way in which we manage that is important in terms of promoting our heritage, cultural and natural environment. Heritage trails create an environment for a specific product: some places along the Way have business thrust upon them and they are tearing their hair out because of the levels of traffic. We started from nowhere and are putting in the blocks to build up from the foundation. This means we have a better-than-average chance of making sure that children have schools and facilities, and family businesses to join. We have chosen responsible tourism as the pathway for development in this area and the phrase for Kilkee is "A better place to live in, a better place to visit".

'The main road drives by the entrance to the Way and directs people in so there is a little bit of a filtration system happening by people going to the cliffs and most want to cut corners and skip bits like Loop Head. In a way that's fine because we want people who are culturally curious and want to find what's down this road and perhaps launch a search for Kilstiffin. And Kilkee never ceases to astonish me because it's ever-changing. The six weeks in summer are amazing as I cycle and walk, and no two days are the same. Here's something that will surprise you: we have a stream that flows over the cliffs and it becomes a waterfall like a funnel – reflecting the nature of the contrariness of the west because things will never happen as you think.'

Originally from west Cork and a fisherman-turned-restaurateur, Cillian also has a surprise on the menu. 'Zarzuela stew is a big hitter with us. We have taken a concept from somewhere else and use local ingredients. It is a great dish – it's quirky and people love it. Irish food is probably at the top of its game. We are at a peak and we need to see investment at a lower level for dishes like this.'

There is a comfortable, timeless feel about Kilkee, with its old-school hotels, beaches, bracing walks and cycle rides. One of the most enduring commercial enterprises still plied from blue-and-white stalls along the waterfront is the sale of periwinkles and dillisk. Picked raw, washed and cooked, they are sold in measures.

'It has been going for generations and generations,' Maddy Traynor says from her aproned perch at one end of the strandline. 'People come from all over for them, especially for the periwinkles, which are just little fish in shells and extremely good for you. It's very important for tourism and the visitors love them. People from Limerick, who come here in all weathers, are our best customers. They buy the winkles because they were brought up with them and they have passed that down the line to their children and grandchildren. Apart from them, we have a lot of French and Russians who can't get enough of them. From a health point of view, dillisk is very good for you.'

Maddy has been working here all her life and unsurprisingly is an advocate of the freshness of food from the sea.

'Anything from the sea is good for you, so children of all ages and right up to the elderly enjoy them for their taste and flavour. You have the shell seagrass too and I love them myself. They are moreish and you just want to keep eating them.'

Maddy breaks off from talking to me to serve a French couple who have pulled up on their bicycles. She scoops a pile of periwinkles from an enamel bucket into a blue bag and collects €4 from them. Although Kilkee has changed, she says, it is an old-fashioned seaside resort at heart.

'It's all built-up now with holiday homes, although it's really not a big town: you could walk round it in half an hour. We've got a few caravan parks but it's a beautiful unspoilt bay to look out on. I often think that I've one of the best outdoor jobs of all in Clare or anywhere along this whole coast. I love the sea air, I get a suntan and the wind, and I don't even mind the rain and the hail. There's never a dull moment in this job but it's the people here who help make it. They're very welcoming, and the regulars I've got to know keep coming back to me year after year – sure what else would I be doing?'

The Pantry is Kilkee Central where the Marzocco coffee-making machine hisses and steams like the boiler of a locomotive on the West Clare Railway, immortalised in 1902 by Percy French. Customers indulge in the dying art of conversation with the clatter of cups and clink of cutlery as a soundtrack. It is a meeting place where hard copies of newspapers are turned while tourists scrutinise sheaves of printed maps, tracing the route of their next journey, working out an itinerary for the Loop Head Peninsula. Smart staff in orange-and-black uniforms, some with headscarves, buzz around while matching orange cushions decorate chairs. A sign on the wall reads: 'Lord give me the strength to change the things I can and wine to accept the things I can't.'

The owner, Imelda Bourke, who has all the strength she needs to cope with the expected lunchtime rush, joins me at my table.

Running the café started out as a hobby with a friend and she has been in business for thirty years.

'We've a very high ethos with fresh ingredients and we can't keep the moist carrot cake as it jumps off the shelves,' she says.

She speaks about the Loop Head Food Circle, about how they make 1,000 scones a day, and the popularity of syrups in coffee. Their signature espresso Bewley's blend is made with two shots using beans from estates in Central America, Java, Brazil and Colombia. It has a rich, buttery mouth-feel and a dark chocolate aftertaste. Imelda asks if I have ever seen a mouse's tail in action. I am curious to see how a rodent might be involved in coffee-making so she beckons me to come behind the counter where we watch a waitress conjure a cappuccino. It turns out to be nothing to do with Robert Burns' 'wee, sleekit, cow'rin, tim'rous beastie'. The water is poured through the coffee machine, which with precision produces the exact degree of mouse's tail flowing like golden syrup from two outlets into the cup, ready for steamy milk to be swilled to creamy consistency. Hundreds of times a day the tail flows in this unique roast curve, unseen by customers' eyes. Pouring forth from the machine, it rises like an exquisite soufflé, topped off with delicate foam art in the shape of a Kilkee oak leaf.

I have detected a diminuendo of interest in Manannán the farther south I go along the coast, owing to the fact that he is no longer in the news and has again been forgotten. But reminders of him, and his wider circle, are never far away, and crop up in unlikely places. Take Williams gift shop on Circular Road. A window display features the Celtic Legends Children of Lir sixty-piece jigsaw set for €20. The woman running the shop, which doubles as a tourist information office, tells me that she recalls hearing about Manannán during her schooldays. She laughs, saying 'that wasn't today, yesterday or even the day before.'

But in Kilkee they are more interested in a 1960s revolutionary icon than a mythological sea god. A small plaque, erected by the Kilkee Civic Trust, on the wall outside the Strand Hotel recalls the fact that Ché Guevara (1928–67) stayed in the hotel in

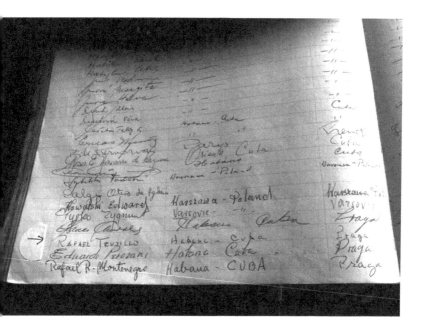

(above) Ché Guevara signature, Kilkee hotel, County Clare, which he signed as Rafael Trujillo.

Ché Guevara mural, Kilkee

1961. Johnny Redmond, who owns the hotel, was not then born, but his family have run it for several generations.

'For years I never knew anything about his visit, then someone mentioned to me about a visitors' book of ours and a friend told me that the signature of Ché Guevara is in it. I didn't take much notice but I began to realise how famous he was. I asked my uncle about the book and he said his wife had given it to someone to use as a prop for a play. I tracked it down to a local house and in the book for 11 September 1961, there is a long list of signatures of Cuban people as well as Czech, French and Polish who came to Kilkee on that date. I found one name signed as Rafael Trujillo. An artist friend had told me that was the pseudonym that Ché used when signing books. Trujillo was a dictator of the Dominican Republic who killed thirty thousand Haitians and was assassinated by the CIA in May 1961. Apparently Guevara used to sign his name as a sort of joke while he was travelling incognito around the world.'

Johnny opens a large red ledger, showing me a two-page spread filled with the scrawling signatures of scores of names from Warsaw, Prague and Cuba. He points to a name near the bottom of the left hand page, written in blue ink: Rafael Trujillo, Habana, Cuba, 12/9/61.

'They were on their way from Czechoslovakia and landed in Shannon for a stopover en route to Cuba. They were being driven by bus to Ennis but there was a *fleadh cheoil* there and the drivers decided to go to Kilkee instead. So they arrived here, and we were still open as it was the second week in September. They took up all the twenty-nine rooms here at the Strand and other lodges on the far side. Ché stayed in Room Two.

'Over the years many people recounted stories about the Cubans' arrival in town and how the word went round. I was told that a local musician turned up with a three-piece band to play for them. None of them drank alcohol: they were all drinking coffee and smoking cigars. In commemoration of his visit we held a Ché festival for a couple of years. The idea was to celebrate fifty years since his coming to Kilkee but it became a bit controversial. We now call it Ché do Bheatha and the theme incorporates wider cultural aspects, with tango dancing, salsa classes, Brazilian music, a masterclass in Argentinian wine, and a rum and cigar presentation. It also reflects other links between Ireland and Latin America. It is more cultural than political, although some Americans do not like the connection. An artist drew an effigy of Ché on the walls for the festival but the county council said we had to take it down as some American tourists had taken serious umbrage at it. The Ché connection attracts a vast amount of interest: for example, a group of twenty Norwegians called in here two weeks ago and wanted to find out all about him. He was fighting for a cause. Michael Collins killed people, so did Cromwell, and Ché had his passions as a revolutionary.'

Johnny talks about his own connection to the town. He bought part of the building that is now the hotel from his uncle in 1991 when he was twenty-three and renovated it, later extending the premises which he now runs as guesthouse and restaurant. In the dining room, black-and-white photographs show his grandmother drying white sheets on the rocks in the 1890s when Kilkee was a small place.

'When Queen Victoria visited the town, she called it the Brighton of Ireland. Historically, part of Kilkee life was to spend time sitting on the strand wall. Percy French is reputed to have had his inspiration for "The Darling Girl of Clare" while indulging in the custom. It is a seaside resort although we don't hang our hat on that as much as we did. Kilkee sat here for years and took what it got, but we are trying to introduce the area to the world outside of Limerick and to show off what our package is. The Pollock Holes, for example, are a phenomenon – four tiny pools with diving boards used for swimming every day. A lot of satellite businesses have also sprung up as a result of recent developments.

'The Wild Atlantic Way passes our front door here right along the strand line. In the past it was a six-week summer season so we've decided to do something about that and have strived to lengthen the shoulder season, to encourage visitors to come outside of the main summer period, but it has been difficult. We ran a big campaign to make sure that the route came through here and that we are now in the spotlight. Prior to this there was no information about the secret snippets – at least it gives it a focus with good signposting that leads people into Loop Head.'

The shape of the Loop Head Peninsula resembles a ballerina's fully extended *en pointe* foot. From Kilkee to the lighthouse at its most south-westerly tip, it is a nineteen-kilometre sliver of flat land with one main road running through it, crisscrossed by short north–south country lanes ideal for meandering, which is what I have come to do. Treeless, but far from tractorless, it is a place where people live close to the land as well as the sea. Shiny machinery, agribusiness lorries and combi trucks are busy in fields, farm stores and yards. Taking up three quarters of the space, monster tractors ply roads that have escaped the attention of the EU grant-aiders.

On Raidió Corca Baiscinn ('Keeping you in the loop') they are celebrating national community radio day. A new presenter has taken the helm for the 10.30 a.m. slot and starts by bursting into song. She croons her way through 'The Fields of Athenry', experiencing difficulty reaching high notes. An attempt to play Foster and Allen's 'Muirsheen Durkin' is defeated when the computer programme lets her down. She has no option but to call on that much-loved DJ figure known as 'Phil Airtime' by unleashing on an unsuspecting driving public all four verses of 'My Lovely Rose of Clare.'

I turn off the radio, put down the car window, and Loop Head yields its agricultural aromas. Friesians with swinging udders plod along the road, depositing their smell signature. Hooded crows peck around circular haystacks and silage heaps wrapped in stretched black plastic. A snatch of birdsong seeps from bushes. Swallows leap from the eaves of a derelict farmhouse. A Massey Ferguson trundles up and down a field, circling around in a wide sweep, while in an adjoining meadow a farmer spreads slurry from a galvanised tank. The pleasanter perfume of flowering hawthorn drifts on the wind beside billows of fading cow parsley. Perhaps the tourist board should make more fuss about the aromatic heritage. At the lighthouse springy tufts of red fescue grasses run to the cliff edge where they are dotted with flashes of purple in the form of statuesque rare Irish marsh orchids. Rock pipits jump in between clumps of sea pinks where the headland plunges to the ocean. Foley's Bar in Cross advertises a 'Silage Ball' on Saturday night with an addendum: 'Rain Ordered'.

Following signs to the northern part of the peninsula, I bowl over to the Bridges of Ross and escape the cocoon of the car with a walk along a boreen where ancient drystone ditches are frilled with a prodigious bouquet of wild flowers: English stonecrop, sheep's bit, navelwort, lesser trefoil, cat's-ear and sticky mouse ear, common dog violet, creeping thistle and plantain. The Bridges of Ross, one of Ireland's most noted autumnal sea-watching migration sites, is a major flyway for birds from North America, Greenland, Iceland and the Arctic heading south for the winter, and attracts hundreds of twitchers. But it should be better known for its flora. On another path near the exposed cliffs, tightly knit clumps of wild thyme, kidney vetch, sea campion, milkwort, eyebright, and centaury bloom within yards of each other.

At first sight, Ross beach looks unprepossessing, featureless and even foreboding on a sunless afternoon. Set within the small north-west facing inlet of Ross Bay, it is layered with grey stones and lacks sand. Across its curved 350-metre surface nothing moves; not a bucket or spade is in sight; it is bereft of birds or, to my untrained eye, any form of sea creature. It does not conjure up coastal romance and will never make 'The Ten Best Beaches in the World'.

I have come here to see a woman who has offered to help uncover the beach's secrets and introduce me to its movers and shakers, hidden from all but the expert eye. Carmel Madigan is an autodidact, a woman who has taught herself to read this beach through five years of detailed study. When we meet, she points out the house where she was born and how important a place it was in her growing up. We don wellingtons and crunch across stones to the tide line, wade out and soon are knee-deep in crystal-clear water. Delicately, we thread our way over slippery rocks of green seaweed. She cautions me to be careful. 'Mind yourself now,' she laughs, 'I don't do ocean rescue,' at which point, to her great amusement, I slither gracelessly on my backside on a rock. When she helps pick me up, the water reflects in her spectacles, which carry the Red or Dead fashion label.

The plan is to seek out marine life such as molluscs, crustaceans and sea anemones. First I am given a mini-masterclass in seaweed. Carmel bends over into the water and, like a magician, hauls from the boulders and out of shallow pools numerous limp fronds. She holds them up for inspection, swaying trophies of the sea, drip-drying them in the breeze as the fresh ocean smells wash over us.

'This is the exquisite and wonderfully textured furbelows kelp with strap-like stipe ... and here we have the robust dillisk found all year, often attached to forest kelp and commercially licensed ... then royal fern weed, quite a large species and now nearly past its time ... that's sea grass which is grey and bare during the winter and starts around St Patrick's Day when the limpets at the edge of the water receive a green coating ... and here is serrated wrack, the well-known *Fucus serratus* ... then sea spaghetti, a distinctive brown seaweed also known as thong weed, which is edible ... over here we have the richly golden punctured ball weed which is another gorgeous beauty ... and then the popular carrageen found in an array of colours depending on the time of year, useful for little creatures, often harvested for commercial purposes and used in cooking.'

Like a flood tide of ribbons of tagliatelle, they blur into each other. I was unfamiliar with most of these seaweeds and

Strawberry anemone, Ross Beach, Clare.

astonished by the sheer scale of what lies in this watery window, a swirling, voluptuous, head-spinning diversity in one tiny tract of shoreline. It is put into context by the fact that Ireland has more than 500 species on its coastline and worldwide there are at least 10,000 types of seaweed. Carmel admits to being mesmerised by them. We splash our way through the quiet shallows. With her gimlet eyes, she knows intuitively, almost to the exact boulder, where to find everything. In the next few minutes she flips over oblong stones and rocks, disturbing briefly the siesta of Ross beach's sea creatures. It reminds me of a childhood treasure hunt. We crouch down to find a dazzling assortment of species that shut themselves away: common dog whelk; limpets grazing the rock; a sea slug with its eggs; green sea urchins gathered in fellowship; tightly packed barnacles galore and one rock adorned with hundreds of white spots. Hogging the limelight is the strawberry anemone, a sea mollusc, sticking to a rock like a shiny, rubbery blob of jelly. With her small underwater digital camera, Carmel captures the moment.

'You can see by the red why it's so called as it looks just like a juicy strawberry – a wonderful sight. They like shaded positions. This is a predator and eats prawns, crabs and small fish. It might move a couple of centimetres but they are not movers, mostly fixed. This is one of the best places on the west coast to see them because they are rare. I am fascinated by anemones, especially the elegant anemone, which you find in middle shore pools and is hidden with carrageen. Then you have the beadlet anemone which lives without the shelter of a hard shell, and the straggly tentacles of snakelocks anemone often attached to sugar kelp.'

In her quest to document the life of this beach, Carmel has not just submerged herself in it, but has interrogated it, taking more than 6,000 photographs, capturing the spirit of it through its marine life, and constant ebb and flow. Her interest in it stemmed from searching for wild flowers with her son some years earlier when it cast a spell on her.

'We got completely sucked in around 2009 and for the next five years. I had zero knowledge of any of it before I started. Now I like to share the knowledge that I've picked up bit by bit because people enjoy it. Every short trip I made I added to my knowledge, studied photographs, read books, kept reports and used different resources to build it up. Each time I came I discovered something new and added to that, so it is completely exciting. You spend ages working on this and it means that you never forget such things as markings on seaweed. Just to read the beach takes a large amount of time.'

We gaze across an expanse of grey sky and sea, ever-changing, now darkening, caressing and collapsing on rocks. For another aspect of her work, Carmel has delved into the life of a small Canadian coastal town at the same northern latitude 5,000 kilometres across the ocean. She has found similarities between the Clare coast and the coastline of Newfoundland and Labrador, and believes that the Atlantic and its moods determines so much of what goes on on either side.

'I have done research on the same latitude link across the ocean to King's Cove on the Bonavista Peninsula on mainland Canada's east coast. I tried to connect with them but they are a small community of a hundred and twenty. Although I haven't been there, I have found that with names such as Murphy, McGrath, Carew and Walsh, they are more Irish than Loop Head itself. It's a much colder environment than here. We are being heated by the Gulf Stream and they are being chilled by the cold Labrador Current coming off the North Pole so they have freezing conditions for six months of the year.'

Full of energy and effervescence, Carmel leads me on to higher rocks of slate, shale and sandstone where Japanese wireweed wound like thick locks of brown hair, and known as the sea version of knotweed, is spreading. Like its sister land plant, it is invasive, clogging up other growth in the mix of a dark, muddy rock pool. Little skulkers are next on Carmel's list as she searches closely for crabs, upending flat boulders without luck, apart from finding wriggling worms. Crabs lodge in cavities and crevices of rocks and she knows their reference points and their rituals. Persistence soon pays off in the form of the mottled-green common shore crab lurking under a rock and, lightning-quick, scurrying sideways for cover from two menacing predators. Then she spots something that I had asked about simply because of its expressive name: the coat-of-mail chiton. Although not as exciting as its name suggests, this mollusc is nothing more than a tiny blob that lives attached to a rock, and which she describes as 'spotless'. It rolls into a ball when disturbed but she carefully replaces the rocks before its equilibrium is upset. Often found in their company are bright yellow flat periwinkles, which are the most colourful gastropod on the shore and whose diet is serrated wrack. They reproduce by laying egg capsules from which young snails hatch. Apart from her biological knowledge, Carmel has also explored social history. This area was once wracked with poverty and she strongly believes that the Famine still has an effect on it.

'Local people do not come here, they do not appreciate this beach and I believe that is because of the Famine. They haven't properly engaged with it since the 1840s, apart of course from removing stones from it for their gardens. They associate the shoreline with extreme poverty but I think it is now time to reconnect with it for its diversity, intrigue, edible offerings and much more. We weren't brought here on school trips or taught about the tidesThe sea for many was regarded as a place of tragedy; in fact, my mother's grandfather was drowned fishing here.'

Like so many other parts of the west coast the savage sea has taken its toll. In February 2014, when it tore along this coast, Storm Brigid caused serious disturbance in the shallow subtidal area. The sea rose to overwhelm the beach, smash the wall and flood surrounding fields; miraculously, it did not annoy the tiny sea creatures, which continued to lead sedentary lives. Aside from her lengthy project recording the life of the beach, which turned into a book produced by herself with photographs, Carmel is also an expressionist artist. She is in tune not just with the texture of the seaweed but also the movement of the water, and in her painting has put her own interpretation on the area and its colours.

She has given me an insight into the glamour of a little-known beach that is furiously alive but which cloisters itself in its own shadows. The tide has come in and covered the area where we explored, leaving the life of the beach to its slumbers. It is not difficult to appreciate how Carmel, a connoisseur of the aquatic world, has been seduced by the inhabitants of the ocean and of what lies beneath. She has provided me with an unforgettable glimpse into a secret life of undersea marvels. In just over an hour, I had stepped into a world that until now I had only stepped on.

As my previous attempt at getting out properly on to the water had to be aborted in Connemara, I have signed up for a dolphin-watching trip next morning from Carrigaholt Harbour. Families with excited children, and a smattering of Europeans and Americans board the *Draíocht,* skippered by Geoff Magee. The pier also serves fishing boats and sea-angling trips and is said to be the home of one of the largest dolphin pods in Europe. Geoff was an inshore lobster and crab fisherman for more than twenty years before setting up a company called Dolphinwatch with his wife Susanne.

We head into a Special Area of Conservation for bottlenose dolphins at the mouth of the Shannon. In small fields on either side of us cattle huddle together. We are urged to keep a sharp lookout as we cross the estuary where the tides are stronger. Geoff provides a commentary, telling us the dolphins face the ocean, working together as cooperative and efficient hunters.

'We might see them along the edge of the sandbank on the shore of Kerry. They also actively forage in the deep-water channel. They grow up to four metres long and are some of the largest in the world weighing up to six hundred lb. They can travel through the water at thirty miles an hour. The boat is obliged to keep a distance and steer a steady course at slow speed so we need patience to see them.'

Alongside us herring gulls argue in the air while razorbills and guillemots ride the waves. A tern with a sprat in its mouth concentrates on a late breakfast. We scan the horizon with binoculars, cameras poised and smartphones at the ready but there is no sign of any plunging or gambolling dolphins.

Then Geoff announces matter-of-factly over the tannoy: 'Fifty metres straight ahead.' A splash in the water and someone catches sight fleetingly of a fin, before it vanishes like a ghost. Our direction takes us on towards the Kerry shoreline where dolphins are often scattered along the edge of the sandbank at Kilcooley Point and the Cliffs of Dooneen. En route, on a tall sea stack we pass the ruins of Leck Castle destroyed in a sixteenth-century battle. This is the first time on my journey that I have had a chance to appreciate the scale of the cliffs, headlands, sea stacks and seabirds from the perspective of the water. A party of thirty shags stands on the edge surrounded by white guano. Close by, a dozen cormorants dry wings, part of their stretch-and-flex exercises.

A dolphin hotspot is said to be off the coast at a beach near Ballybunion. At Culnahisha Bay a rock stands almost vertical. Geoff describes it is a syncline, a rock line that grows progressively younger closer to the centre of its structure. Breeding fulmars hide from us on the cliff ledges. Grey seals bob in the water. This is sea-stack country and near the Cliffs of Bromore we sail past a further two where the rock is painted sulphur-yellow. One is known as the Devil's Castle, accommodating fulmars tucked in on its ledges; the other is the Devil's Footstool where shags congregate in numbers.

Geoff is knowledgeable on both the coastline's nomenclature and its natural architecture. He points out the location of hidden caves and explains the significance of blowholes and 'box folding' that created arches in cliffs. 'The folding and tilting', he says, 'is visible throughout the peninsula and was caused by the pressures of converging continental plates. The folds are aligned in an east–west direction, reflecting the source of pressure which came from the south as the African continental plate pushed northward about three hundred million years ago, long after the sediments had turned into hard rock. This particular fold has allowed Loop Head to resist the battering of coastal erosion.'

In the open sea, my mind wanders to what image Manannán might have seen as he rode the ocean. In his realm, the sea is a *Mag Meall*, a Plain of Delights. My mind-wandering is brought to an abrupt end when suddenly the boat is animated. 'Mackerel!' yells an American. In the distance, more than 100 metres from us, we make out a dolphin killing a mackerel by tossing it into the air, then another, and a third to a ripple of oohs and aahs. All eyes become trained on the water.

'We won't barge towards them,' Geoff says. 'There's also a baby dolphin which is being suckled – a mother and calf – so we'll keep a respectful distance.'

A phalanx of photographers lines up with long lenses and video cameras to capture this natural-world encounter. Children, who had been asleep, jump around, looking down camera lenses and through field glasses, tripping over tripods. Geoff kills the engine and talks to me about his love of dolphins.

'They are smart mammals in the water and like to surf the wave,' he says. 'These days so many people in Europe are urbanised, there are no opportunities for them to see wild animals, even at a distance, so they like their mysterious appeal. Dolphins are warm-blooded and dynamic, and they get activated because they are fishing. They are not doing any tricks but sometimes you will see them leaping which is part of the show they put on. These dolphins know our boat and that we are trustworthy so we stay out of their way, although sometimes they cruise along with us. People love their synchronicity when two or three surface together. Dolphins tend to be curious and look as though they are smiling, but you have to remember these are wild mammals. Bottlenose dolphins could be seen as ambassadors of the Wild Atlantic Way but I see them as ambassadors of the wild ecosystem.'

Exuding slowness, Loop Head is suffused with its own character. If anywhere along this coast epitomises the essence of the Way, then the renaissance of this far-flung part of west Clare sums it up. Like the migrant birds of passage that make their way through here, I feel like a passerine and crank up my own bluebird to head for the Killimer car ferry to cross the Shannon.

When I arrive, the *Shannon Breeze* has just docked from Tarbert in Kerry. A line of cars, transit vans, a motorhome and a couple of cyclists are ahead of me waiting to board. I ask the ferryman about the *Shannon Heather*, a previous vessel that operated on this route and one I travelled on in 1991. His answer makes me feel my age.

'I remember her as a child and have fond memories of being on it,' he says. 'She was decommissioned some years ago and I think may have gone up to Donegal although I'm not sure what became of her after that.'

He talks about the new driving route and its benefits. 'We've been busy enough with tour coaches travelling along it as well as our normal business trade but it's not hectic yet. We've two boats operating and it'll get busier in another few weeks when the schools stop for the summer.'

A bulldog sniffs around my petrol cap as we set off on our twenty-minute crossing. We move off slowly, then soon reach eight knots. The flashing lights of the ESB towers of Moneypoint, Ireland's only coal-fired power station, wink a farewell to County Clare. From the top deck, the views spread over to where west Limerick merges with north Kerry, a countryside enwrapped with woodland. Electricity pylons march across the dark-green forested hills and small fields of cattle. Children shout greetings as we pass the *Shannon Dolphin*, the sister vessel on the route. A washed-out blue sky is streaked with wispy cirrus clouds. No birds have surfaced and there is not a whiff or trace of any hidden city in the estuary. Since Cillian Murphy in Kilkee had mentioned it to me, I had read various theories about the mythical Kilstiffin, one of which says that it is seen on the first full moon in September and is said to be a hidden city of fairies. One man reportedly saw under the water two ghost-like giant towers resembling church steeples. The nearest I can rival that is the lighthouse and two tall, functional beige chimneys of the mini metropolis of Tarbert power station looming in front of me as we slide into our berth.

'*Fáilte go Ciarraí*: Welcome to Kerry: Home and Heartbeat of Tourism', says the road sign where the traffic streams off the ferry. Before tackling County Kerry, I double back along the road through Glin over to Foynes in Limerick to find out about a blend of coffee that is made here. As coffee is a consistent part of my journey, Foynes is a natural place to visit for the story of a special Irish coffee. Nearly eighty years ago Pan Am's luxury flying boat, the *Yankee Clipper,* landed at Foynes, the first commercial passenger flight on a direct route from the US to Europe. As a result, the small town on the Shannon became the focal point for North Atlantic air traffic. Planes no longer land at Foynes but in the twenty-first century Americans still arrive in large numbers – this time on cruise liners. When I reach it, Foynes is heaving with visitors as a large cruise ship, the *Adonia,* has docked for the day with more people on it than the population of the town. In recent years it has been the port of call for international liners touring the Irish and British coastlines, and can now handle the world's largest ships of up to 40,000 tonnes.

Margaret O'Shaughnessy, who runs the Foynes Flying Boat and Maritime Museum, says the cruise ships bring tremendous benefit to the town and other parts of west Limerick. She set up the museum in 1987, immediately recruiting the help of Maureen O'Hara, who was patron for nearly thirty years. For all of that time, Margaret has been at the helm of a place that was created from humble beginnings.

'We started off with four little rooms, renovated them, and it just took over my life,' she says. 'It was set up as a charity and a not-for-profit organisation with a voluntary board of directors. The flying boat has been the highlight as it's the only one in the world. I never for one moment thought that we would have got to where we are today with seventeen staff, forty thousand visitors and increasing every year.

'We get VIPs coming from all over the place. We've had princes, singers and film stars. A few years ago we had Jimmy Buffett, who enjoys flying boats himself, and the Americans who were here at that time started screaming.'

Margaret talks about the Wild Atlantic Way and how it has captured the imagination of tourists, but she feels that Limerick has been short-changed.

'We got the only little bit of it in Limerick so the county has really been left out. It should have gone up the estuary right into Limerick, on to Ennis and back out. They took a short cut by going across the river from Tarbert to Killimer using the ferry. But they don't seem to realise that this part here is still coastal and we have a beautiful vista with the islands and the river. We are a major port as well. Our story is unique and the river played a big part in the Atlantic with the flights coming across it. We call ourselves the calm bit of the Atlantic. We may not have the drama of the Cliffs of Moher but we have a lovely calmness. We have had a spinoff but not enough. They're not doing anything for us, yet Galway and Clare get it all. There's a bit of hassle over it and a lot of campaigning going on to get it redrawn but I can't see it happening. We just have to look at how we can use it. We are Ireland's only aviation museum and don't have any rivals. We also have a new floor that tells the story of the maritime history and personality of the River Shannon.'

The main attraction that I have come to find out about is the history of Irish coffee. Margaret explains the context which goes back much earlier than the opening of the museum.

'The young, enthusiastic Brendan O'Regan had been sent in here to take over the restaurant and set it up. He was very far-sighted and wanted it to be the best restaurant it could possibly be and to make it a place that would attract dignitaries coming through the airport. He brought a lot of staff with him from the Old Ground Hotel in Ennis, advertised for a chef and got a large number of applications. This is the story as Brendan told it to me. A guy from Castlederg in County Tyrone, who was working in Dublin, sent in an application as follows: "Dear Mr O'Regan I am the man for the job. Yours sincerely, Joe Sheridan." Brendan thought: Isn't he a cheeky little bugger? So out of that he said he might as well meet him and Sheridan got the job. But he was older than Brendan and was not too enamoured about taking orders from this dapper little man. Brendan liked using local produce such as Limerick ham and when he noticed that another chef was preparing redcurrants and Labasheeda duck, he said: "That duck is very plain-looking. It needs a little more eye-appeal." That was typical Brendan – everything had to have "eye-appeal". So Sheridan grabbed a fistful of the redcurrants that the woman was using, threw them on the duck and said: "how about that for eye-appeal?" And Brendan said: "Grand".

'In October 1943 a Pan Am flying boat left here for Newfoundland, but turned back because of the weather, and the passengers were asked to come to the restaurant. Joe liked a drop of whiskey and would always have a bottle in the cupboard for medicinal purposes. It was a cold night and as he was making the coffee he just put the whiskey into it to warm them up. They thought that was brilliant; they liked it so much they wanted to know what it was. A few days later he got an ordinary glass and put it into it and topped it off with cream. He brought it down to Brendan and said "Well boys, how about that for eye-appeal?" And Brendan actually said to him "Genius." They asked Waterford Glass to design special Irish coffee glasses so that's how it first began and we still use it today more than sixty years on. It's an Irish story and you can get it all over the world, although some places don't use Irish whiskey.'

The aptly named travel writer Stan Delaplane had his first glass here. Based in San Francisco, he was known as 'the last of the old irreplaceables' by his fellow-columnist Herb Caen. They were on trip to Europe and stopped at Shannon where they were served an Irish coffee.

'Delaplane's friend Jack Koeppler owned the famous Buena Vista Café at Fisherman's Wharf and they decided to try and perfect it there. They made a big story of it and involved the mayor of San Francisco. Sheridan emigrated in 1952 and lived there for the rest of his life. It took them many goes and a long time to get it right. They spent hours perfecting the Irish method of floating the cream on top of the coffee. But they managed to crack it and in November 1952 it became their signature drink. Since then they have made more of it than we have ever done in Ireland. Thousands of tourists go there and queue up for them as it's the end point of the cable car run and a major tourist site.

'Most people have a problem getting the cream to float when they make their own. We do demonstrations here. Full-fat cream is the best although everything over there is fat-free. We like to think that makes the best. They drink the coffee and say they love it. Some people even ask for it without the whiskey but you can't have that as that is a virgin one and not the same. Coffee generally has taken off in Ireland and if you're a coffee drinker you will like this. Our big thing here is convincing people that having whiskey in your coffee is quite different from drinking whiskey. And the whole secret of drinking whiskey is important. I see people stirring it and tell them that is a criminal offence. The secret is the hot liquid through the cold cream and our creams are fabulous in Ireland. We don't put any designs such as shamrocks, ferns or leaves that you get on lattes and cappuccino because that is only dressing it up. We had a world championship here and the guys coloured the cream green but they were destroying the original. We stay with the traditional original design as Sheridan made it – we have to be true to that with the good ingredients and original recipe.'

After watching the five steps involved in making the coffee, a party of Americans sample it, smacking lips and wondering if they should have another stimulant. The consensus is that since they are boarding the liner later in the afternoon and do not have to drive, it would be remiss to pass up the chance of a second helping. 'After all,' says a Texan woman, 'we're on vacation and I think we should live up to my favourite six words in the world: Why don't we have another one?' She buys a Yankee Clipper T-shirt and six-pack of Foynes Irish Coffee glasses, slipping them into her haversack bearing a sticker saying 'Erin go bragh y'all.'

PART III
The South-west
Kerry and Cork

And then I pressed the shell
Close to my ear
And listened well,
And straightway like a bell
Came low and clear
The slow, sad murmur of the distant seas,
Whipped by an icy breeze
Upon a shore
Wind-swept and desolate.

James Stephens, 'The Shell', *Insurrections*

9
The power of the black saucepan

ALONG THE COASTAL ROADS of north Kerry, newly erected notices nailed to trees promote agricultural shows, garden fetes, summer jamborees, half-marathons, regattas, and even a terrier race across the beach at Ballyheigue. The Go Kerry brochure that I picked up in the Ballybunion tourist office describes the town as having 'champagne' air. The woman in charge is puzzled when I mention the mythical island of Kilstiffin that I had been told about in Kilkee. She offers to search the Internet and says the man to speak to is local historian Danny Houlihan, who is away for the weekend. She calls his mobile and puts him on to me. Danny is piping at a wedding in Clare but is happy to talk on the phone. He says that his great-great-aunt saw Kilstiffin.

'My mother used to relate the story all the time about her great-aunt seeing it in the Shannon estuary,' he says. 'It is said to appear every hundred years. Some locals suggest that it appeared with a steeple and with houses so it may have been a sunken church and small city. Older people have told me that during certain weather conditions what was seen in the estuary beyond Kilcredaun was an atmospheric image of a fair day. There was also a belief that in one version when you saw the island, you would die within a year. The best way to sum it up is that it's really a mirage but regardless of the exact truth, it fascinates everyone.'

Danny is in the process of tuning up his pipes before the wedding party arrives as he explains that in the Early Christian period, the monks sought out the sanctuary of secluded islands off the coast. These sheltered locations were well chosen for isolation from the world and provided a peaceful place to pray.

In Coast café ('good food is our business') the waitress says
she has never seen Kilstiffin nor experienced the champagne air
associated with Ballybunion. 'I haven't had a hit yet, but perhaps
one of these days I will. Are you sure you haven't OD-ed on
coffee? I could get you a glass of sparkling water if you like, there'll
be some bubbles in that.' I am certainly seeing stars as my latte art
is sprinkled with them. It is made with Mahers Pure Roast Coffee
from Central America and is described on the packet as a 'refined
blend with an intensive aroma and resolute taste'.

With the school holidays under way, families are thronging
the cafés, ice cream parlours, casinos and amusement arcades.
The town's summer pulse is best felt at the wide beaches, surrounded by a bowl of beige and cream caravans, and suffused
with contentment. The tide is out but an unseasonably cool
breeze does not deter several hundred sunbathers. Adults loaf
on beach towels and tartan rugs behind a line of brightly striped
windbreaks while children indulge in a variety of activities from
paddling, body-boarding and castle-building to kite-flying, beach
camogie and water-pistol shootouts. The pistols are later turned
on two *yark-yark*-ing seagulls. A young boy buries his sister's feet
in the sand, making dumpy boots while other children draw
silhouettes.

As I walk over the beach, long cloud shadows sweep across
the remains of Ballybunion Castle and the multi-hued sea. The
wind whips up the air, and while there may be a certain bubbly
quality to it, it is tinged not so much with champagne as with salt,
sand and suntan lotion. Young children and dogs are let off their
leashes. A springer spaniel circles its mistress and races madly,
finding it energising to be allowed so much beach in which to
romp. With binoculars I scan the horizon, bereft of boats, surfers,
waves or any form of mirageous ghostly island or otherworldly
phantom city. There is nothing to arrest my eye until I swivel
the glasses around to the rust-coloured cliffs where two black-
plumaged choughs with scarlet legs and long, curved bills come
into focus. They hop around short-cropped grass beside the cliff

path, probing into stone cavities in search of insect larvae, slugs or a sniff of the famed Ballybunion Bollinger. In wobbly fashion, with buoyant wingbeats and their unmistakeable melancholy high-pitched *kweeaw* call, they lift off, high on the fizzy air, riding the updraught of the sheer cliff face.

From Ballybunion the road south is through flat countryside and a series of somnolent one-street towns: Ballyduff, Causeway, Ballyheigue and Ardfert. Contractors with flail-saws shave hedges in the interests of rural tidiness while dairy herds of Kerry cattle watch the flaying. Across the calm waters of Tralee Bay, vistas extend over a cloud-filled sky to the Dingle Peninsula. Twenty-five years ago I had spent time with a local horticulturist in Castlegregory searching for natterjack toads and was curious to hear if they have survived. In the intervening years their fortunes appear to have flourished since they are now breeding in large numbers around Lough Gill. In fact, they have become such an accepted part of the north shore of the Dingle Peninsula that a pub has been named after them. Ned Natterjack's is a single-storey whitewashed bar with a red door, matching frames and original signage for 'Player's Navy Cut, Beautifully Cool and Sweet Smoking' and 'Clarke's Plug is the Perfect Plug.' The bar is closed during the day and when I call at lunchtime, the owner Vincent O'Brien is working at the back on a preparation area to meet new health and safety regulations.

He says he is due a break, so we sit on high stools at the bar counter in darkly atmospheric surroundings. Radios from the 1930s and '40s fill shelves alongside enamel jugs while mid-twentieth-century pictures of Castlegregory's traffic-free streets decorate the walls. Vincent took over the bar in 1994, renovating it and changing its name to Ned Natterjack's in honour of the toads. He is involved in marketing the area, sometimes referred to as Kerry's Gold Coast, and has just come up with a new term to promote it: Dingle North Shore, which incorporates Camp, Castlegregory, Stradbally, Cloghane and Brandon. He points out that the peninsula's two coastlines – north and south – are very different.

Ned Natterjack's pub, Castlegregory, County Kerry.

'It's a good description as North Shore is a surfing term and we do a lot of that here,' he says. 'We feel a bit out in the cold about the lack of promotion and yet there is so much going on in this part of the peninsula. Castlegregory is the only true village in west Kerry because it has streets in it – all other villages have just one street. In its heyday it had the same status as Dingle and that's why it's referred to as Castlegregory the Great.'

Far better than any Texan ever could, Vincent eulogises about the area through a series of bests, made up of largest, biggest, highest and longest. We spread the map out on the counter and he fingers a small spit of land running north between two bays.

'That's the Maharees, which has the largest tombolo in Ireland, with seven islands. It's a geographical term for a peninsula that consists of a number of islands joined to the land by sand. Either side you have two bays, Tralee and Brandon, which is a surf beach and at eleven miles is the longest anywhere on the Wild Atlantic Way. It takes in four areas and is part of the Dingle Way. Then at Caherconree Mountain we have the highest promontory fort in the country and of course Brandon is the biggest peak in west Kerry and the second highest in Ireland. People who come to the peninsula have got the name Dingle in their head and go straight to the town, but we are the outdoor playground. We've a short season to make money but we're aligned with the local community council and our aim is to increase business by extending the season beyond the peak months.

'We are right beside Lough Gill and in the early 1990s the ecologists were concerned that building a golf course would damage the toads' habitats but, in fact, the fake ponds they put in have encouraged them to breed more, so it's a positive story. There are hundreds of them croaking at night, crawling all around the place in their Kerry colours of green and yellow. They gather at the edge of the pools and sing to attract a mate. I've held them in my hand and sometimes you might even see one or two on the road late at night. You might come across one in the sand dunes but they are hard to see as they are nocturnal. We can hear them from outside the front door of the bar, croaking in the background; their distinctive song is the loudest of any European amphibian. Most bars in Ireland are named after the owners so we thought we'd do something a bit different. We offer pub grub, stone-baked pizzas, and Chinese dishes from our takeaway, Ned's Wok Inn, but we haven't yet started natterjack soup.'

Shaped like a sausage, the Maharees tombolo, an eight-kilometre peninsula or isthmus, is a narrow oddity and self-contained world. It is one of only a small number of tombolos in Ireland. From its neck at Castlegregory, it runs past the beach at Sandy Bay where water enthusiasts including junior surfers, looking like battered rag dolls, practise falling off their boards. Waist-high in the sea, a group of six plays a wet version of Ring a Ring o'Roses. Sand dunes morph into a wall of rock armour near the pier at Scraggane Bay where half-deckers and pleasure boats are moored. The obligatory school of upturned, glistening, canvas-covered black currachs (known in Kerry as the *naomhóg*) is parked beside maritime paraphernalia of stacked lobster cages, 1,000 used tyres, festoons of looped net, wooden pallets and blue fishing crates stamped with the name Kilmore Quay. Out to sea, seven lumps of rock of varying size constitute the archipelago known as the Seven Hogs or Maharees, one of which contains the ruins of a sixth-century monastic site.

I clamber on to sand dunes for a better view of Magherabeg beach. It is an impressive unbroken honey-blonde curve as far as the eye can see around more than half of Brandon Bay. Surf-surging, from Fahamore in the north, it curls in front of sand dunes, passing small settlements, culminating beyond Fermoyle. In a week's time several hundred athletes will be crossing it for the Brandon Bay half-marathon, Ireland's only running event held entirely on a beach. This afternoon, apart from swimmers, it is deserted for much of its sandy length. The dunes are laced with bladder campion, sand pansies, and the elegant pink trumpet-like flowers of sea bindweed with its white stripes and long-stalked leaves. I train my binoculars to the far shore at Brandon Point where Knockdeelea Mountain is still visible, while the triumvirate of Masatiompan, Brandon Mountain and Brandon Peak are enshrouded in cloud.

A different range of mountains surrounds my route to the Conor Pass, the highest road in Ireland. The pyramidal-shaped Stradbally Mountain stands above Beenbo, Slievenalecka and

Knockmulanane. I pause at boulder-cluttered hillsides where a tumbling waterfall and deep corrie once fed ice to the glaciers. The road climbs up a three-kilometre heart-stopping corkscrew, complete with blind bends and, to my right, sheer drops, till it reaches a viewing point. Dark evening cloud dims the details of the wide U-shaped valley. A rushing mountain brook falls to a lake with stone walls where thick plantations of trees give way to pastureland and an expanse of water leading into the bay. In the evening light, the coarse-grained sandstone rocks are glazed with a purple hue.

My dizzying descent along a six-kilometre serpentine road looks across a patchwork of fields, winding into Dingle where a night of song and verbal shrapnel is under way in the Courthouse Bar. Traditional music singer and accordionist Seamus Begley, accompanied on guitar by Matt Griffin, is delighting a packed pub where six-footers are guaranteed to crick their neck if they stay long in the front room.

After three high-energy Kerry polkas and slides, Seamus's tender voice fills the room with the elegiac '*Óró Mo Bháidín*' ('My Little Boat') and 'Carolan's Concerto'. Not only is he a renowned and unpretentious west Kerry musician, he also engages with his audience, who enjoy his putdowns. Turning the evening into an interactive performance, he pokes fun when he spots a couple trying to stifle a yawn and invokes the Kerry possessive: 'Are we keeping you up?'

'No', replies the woman, 'but my eyebrows are exhausted and my eardrums are sore.'

'Where y'all from?' he enquires. A geographical diversity of answers prompts songs from Liverpool, France, the United States, and 'Oss-tralia'. The packed crowd bob their heads in time, drumming on tables and glasses.

'We'll have a Kiwi one now, "Farewell to the Gold that Never I Found", for this lady from Auckland. Have you any gold out there?' She shakes her head. 'So you don't have any gold and you came to Kerry to find some – did you have any luck?'

'Not so far,' she says.

'Kerrygold!' shouts someone from the bar.

Audience participation leads to a woman from Virginia, who is touring Ireland with a musical group, taking over the microphone and, to rapt silence, singing an impassioned version of 'The Water is Wide'. A friend joins her for a jaunty duet 'Let the Circle be Unbroken'.

Seamus returns to tell a story about his nephew. 'He's training for the business world and trying to become an entre ... enter ... how do you say it in Kerryspeak?'

'A chancer,' roars a red-faced man with a blue-striped shirt.

After a triple helping of 'Waking Ned Devine', 'Saddle Tramp' and 'Safe Home', Seamus asks: 'Have youse no notion of going home – or have they all been repossessed?'

An uplifting and pitch-perfect rendition of 'The Parting Glass' results in couples spontaneously linking arms, turning tightly in circles, and tumbling melodramatically into each other in a small dance area where chairs have been hurriedly cleared. With tumultuous applause and sustained cheers, wine, pint and baby glasses are raised to toast the singer and the song.

To enter the world of Kevin Flannery is to give yourself over to the magical and colourful denizens of the deep. For more than thirty years he has collected and catalogued unusual specimens from the sea, and since the mid-1990s has been involved with the Oceanworld Aquarium of which he was the founder.

'I was dragged up in the Colony in Dingle,' Kevin says, when I meet him in the Oceanworld café. 'My father and mother were involved in the fishing business so I learnt about the sea from them and found it fascinating. In the 1970s I was a fisherman but gave it up as we didn't earn a bob from it. But I saw this stuff from the deck of a boat and my interest developed from that. Later I worked in fish quality with the government. I was poacher-turned-gamekeeper turned back to poacher so I covered all bases and looked at marine life from both sides.'

Kevin was manager of the aquarium, and although retired, still sits on the management committee. It is now a centre of conservation and research, attracting more than 100,000 visitors each year. It all started as a hobby through his friendship with a local publican.

'Mike Long ran a pub in Dingle and for many years collected rare specimens from fishermen. We both had an interest in it and although we weren't academically trained, we were naturalists. Dingle is unique because it is a funnel between the two peninsulas and stretches out in the south-west Atlantic which means we get a lot of weird and wonderful creatures coming in. In the 1940s, '50s and '60s fishermen didn't make much money and most of the time you couldn't give the fish away. Fishermen loved their pint and if they came into the pub in the evening they might bring an unusual specimen. Mike would give them a pint bottle, which cost more than what they would get fishing. All of a sudden they were on the lookout for everything rare they could get their hands on. Mike would analyse it and send it up to the Natural History Museum in Dublin.

'He showed me the symbiosis between certain fish, crabs and anemones. I remember he got a Jacob's biscuit tin and filled it with water. We put in the hammer crab and the anemone and that was my introduction to it all. He had a huge collection and when he died in the 1980s I took on the mantle and questioned why we were sending these up to the "Dead Zoo" in Dublin when we could keep them here and show the people of Ireland what we have in the sea. Around that time there was a big interest in coming to see Fungie the dolphin and from that we developed the idea of an aquarium in a former school. We involved local businesses, the development agency and in 1996 set up the aquarium and convinced people that it would work. Now we are educating tens of thousands of visitors about the sea and showing them that it is not just a place were people dump and pump waste. We have skippers who owned boats who have diversified to running eco-tours and boat trips, angling, diving, kayaking and making a living out of looking at what is there rather than just taking fish from the sea. Of course we can blame the EU and the Common Fisheries Policy, which has been an absolute disaster for the fishing communities along the west coast as we were fooled and negotiated out of it. We are still being annihilated out of it and I don't think anything will change in terms of the Spanish, French and Germans handing back to Paddy and saying: "here you are, we're sorry that we took all your fish." Now we use the indigenous amenities and the sea. People walking the shoreline find things and there isn't a week goes by that someone doesn't come in with something different.

'We've have had poisonous fish, trumpet fish, trigger fish, angler fish, puffer fish, pipe fish and many other types. But on one occasion, in 1997, a woman sent dried-up flesh. Kerry hadn't won an All-Ireland for ten years and this stuff that arrived was called Atlantic football fish. It's a monkfish which swims around like a football and she didn't know what it was and, God bless her, didn't we win the All-Ireland that year. Another time we got an octopus in a net and nobody knew what it was. Each eye was about four inches wide but it took me four years to identify it. The Russians helped me because they had big trawlers and it was a deep-water octopus which had a huge beak, bigger than the largest parrot you can imagine, like something out of *E.T.*'

We walk around the aquarium via an ocean tunnel with arched walls to an Amazon waterfall. Families and small groups stand in awe of menacing creatures, especially those in an enormous purpose-built shark tank. A ferocious-looking steel-grey sand tiger shark, with ragged spike-like teeth, passes the glass wall, eyeing us up. It floats motionlessly, then moves slowly in circles, hypnotising the children. The sharks appear to have respect for unconcerned sea bream with which they intermingle and have tolerance for captivity. In another tank, Molly, a loggerhead turtle with a greenish shell, swim-floats up and down in slow motion, puts its head to the window and peers inquisitively at the people with very smart smartphones. It is said a turtle's bite can be more severe than a shark's. Kevin tells me that the loggerheads are omnivorous and have large, powerful jaws. Along with leatherbacks, they are the two most common turtles.

'The giant leatherback, with its teardrop-shaped body, is one of our biggest of all. They live up to two hundred years and are between two and three tonne weight but we will probably see the demise of them as they can't distinguish between jellyfish and plastic, and jellyfish is what they eat. We're finding forty to fifty pieces of plastic in any one of them each time. Some years ago there was a fascinating turtle washed up on Banna Beach. They hatch in the Gulf of Mexico, move up into the Sargasso Sea, then are carried away by storms and eventually wash on to our shores. Before the aquarium opened, I had three of them at home. We put them into the bath and raised the temperature one degree to try to get the saline solution into them before taking them to a turtle hospital. This meant that nobody in the house could have a bath for a week and we had to go to the neighbours. My mother-in-law used to say she would never eat anything out of our fridge because of all the different creatures I had stored in it.'

We continue our tour, passing an assemblage of penguins, tarantulas, locusts and seahorses who bow to each other every morning in salutation. A fish with a roving eye winks at us. In the touch pool, thornback rays swim with a gentle motion and a graceful beating of their 'wings'. Children dip their hands into the pool to stroke them, giggling at the prickly feel. Kevin has identified at least fifteen new species of marine life in Ireland. Until he started, there had been little documentation of the species and now, along with Declan Quigley, he has published many scholarly papers.

'What happened was that our fishing fleet got bigger and started fishing the deep-water fastness of the Porcupine Bank. All of a sudden we got rare fish. There was no research in Ireland – the Cameroon had more than we had – but we have had a considerable amount in the past fifteen years. I was collecting these creatures for posterity but it was vital that we identified them, and we have so far published more than two hundred and fifty peer-reviewed papers on the species found, which include some incredible-looking animals. I walk the beach often and find all sorts of jellyfish such as by-the-wind sailor. It is a beautiful violet colour and you'll see it washed ashore. We have schools coming here to see what we are doing and to pass the details on is fantastic. The thrill of seeing something different and identifying it is always brilliant; that could take you an hour, a day, a week or longer but for me it is fascinating to pin it down, work out where it comes from and then there's the thrill of explaining it to people.'

In the afternoon I mooch around town, discovering that although the streetscape is the same as in 1991, the town has had a makeover, as well as a name change by lawful decree. The Official Languages Act of 2003 strengthened the rights of Irish-language speakers, leading to all signposts for places where Irish is the official spoken language to be in Irish. For several years, the name Dingle disappeared from road signs and was replaced by An Daingean, since it is part of the Kerry Gaeltacht. Business owners were unhappy about the fact that the cachet of their internationally recognised brand name was lost. After a change of government, dual-language signs were erected to help avoid confusion for tourists – the lifeblood of the town.

Twenty-five years ago, vestiges from the 1970s remained, with tacky plastic signs hanging from shops and bars. A walk around the streets today reveals master goldsmiths at work, artists dabbing on their canvases in light-filled studios, Wild Atlantic Way candle makers, artisan cheese and ice cream makers, boutique coffee roasters, experts in handcrafted gin and more bling than you can shake a dorsal fin at. The kitschification of Fungie with his perpetual smile is replicated in the merchandising on key rings, T-shirts, mugs and other knick-knacks. The years have not been kind to Fungie. Since the early 1990s, he has sprouted grey whiskers, and wrinkles have appeared, but he is now classified as 'the most loyal animal on the planet'. Smells assault me from

Fishing boxes, Dingle, County Kerry.

cafés and slick bistros. The town is a fish-eaters' paradise with upmarket restaurants charging what still reflects the extortionate prices of the Tiger years. Smart shops and mega supermarkets sit cheek by jowl with gastropubs and chic hotels. In the beating commercial heart of Dingle, the summertime tills certainly do jingle. It is a town on the make, which has unashamedly cashed in on the seductive antics of a dolphin.

My cappuccino in Bean in Dingle – somehow Bean in An Daingean does not roll so neatly off the tongue – comes with a fancy tulip design. It leads my competition to find the best-named café and is a top place for quality idling. Michael Bublé croons through speakers, competing with the Nuova Simonelli coffee maker percolating and puffing beside a classic Italian Anfim grinder. Customers, enjoying their half-hour of private magic, browse newspapers; no one is talking, the soothing grey-and-yellow décor encourages lingering. Providing an artistic cornice, chalk art sketches encapsulate the tumbledown synthesis of Dingle's houses and streets. Wall signs read: 'You're my Keeper' and 'Procrastination is my superpower', which reminds me that I need to make some telephone calls but decide to leave it until the next day. The smooth and unctuous coffee, specially blended for the café, is Badger & Dodo from Brazilian, Guatemalan and Ethiopian beans. The owner, Justin Burgess, explains details of the frothing and stretching, and says that takeaways are all the rage.

'Our cups are one hundred per cent biodegradable and compostable,' he says. 'In fact, they are a fashion statement in Dingle. There is no doubt that coffee is the new wine. Ours is full of complex flavours, smooth and rich with a lot going on in it.'

At the pier, clouds hang threateningly over the sea, blotting out most of the Eask navigation tower on Carhoo Hill. This short spit of land wraps the harbour, which is a blind entrance and difficult to navigate, into a sheltered enclosure. Two cobwebbed phone boxes, left as rusting skeletal shells, are useful only as rain shelters or places for advertising forthcoming events. Along the coast these forlorn heritage pieces of the past – now an endangered species since they are used less than once every two days – have been replaced by that most invasive of all species, the mobile phone. In the ten years since 2005, the number of phone boxes has fallen by more than two thirds. In 1991 the kiosks were a refuge from the elements for me, from which I reported on my hitchhiking progress to family and friends. In many ways, keeping in touch from a grubby payphone to a landline was a more efficient method of communication. There were no worries about charging your phone, topping it up, agonising over a ring tone, losing it, sourcing a Wi-Fi signal or being able to access email and social media. Few people, apart from rich businessmen as a must-have accessory, owned mobiles because they were so expensive. Compared to today's pocket phones, they looked like a breeze block. They also cost around £2,000 each and featured a Ferrari-driving businessman with the slogan: 'You can be in when you're out.'

The other street furniture is dominated by three statues. Two thematically linked pieces – a free-standing bronze called 'Undertow' and its small neighbour 'Rope' – capture the maritime history. The Fungie statue is swamped by children of all ages jumping on it, lying across it and under it, hugging it, posing on it and pretending to ride it bucking-bronco style. The woman in the ticket office selling boat trips tells me that it has become a serious hazard. A young girl recently fell off it, injured her head on the cement and was airlifted to hospital. Across from Fungie is an equally illustrious name, albeit for different reasons: Charles Haughey, a former taoiseach later disgraced for tax fraud, is commemorated with a bronze bust on a limestone block. Unveiled in 2005, the sculpted head was commissioned by local fishermen, many of them diehard Haughey fans, in recognition of his contribution to the development of the port. But the most imaginative piece of sculpture is an original currach that has been commandeered, upturned and strapped across the Perspex sides of a bus shelter promoting Tom Crean lager. The Antarctic explorer, who was born in Anascaul in 1877, was nicknamed the 'Irish Giant'. The production of a lager by the Dingle Brewing Company to honour his name capitalises on the interest created in him through books and a one-man stage show. Farther along the waterfront, fishing trawlers nudge each other in still waters; the marina houses forty yachts and cruisers and has quadrupled in size since 1991.

On the other side of Dingle Harbour, black-headed gulls swirl around in the sky, eating flying ants near a two-arch stone bridge. In the midst of the tranquil water, populated mostly

Bust of Charles
Haughey, Dingle,
County Kerry.

by ducks folded and dozing, a rare bird stands in cerebral aloofness. A little egret, with snow-white plumage, long neck and dagger-like black bill, makes precision stabs at the water, sploshing through the shallows in a balletic feeding dance. Then it hunches, motionless, its bill withdrawn into its breast, and rests. Although I had seen their cousins, according to bird books, cattle egrets in France, this is a first Irish sighting for me and it is a delight to watch the exotic creature in close, undisturbed detail. But the encounter is short-lived. A group of walkers emerges from the driveway of a house with an Irish wolfhound, which resembles a small version of a gypsy cob. The bird's circle of tolerance – its distance from danger – has been infiltrated and at the sight of this majestic animal, *Egretta garzetta* swiftly exits stage left.

Back in town where some bars are unchanged in generations, shopping therapy meets alcohol needs. The music-free Foxy John's, an eccentric mix of hardware, ironmongery and beer, is gearing up for a busy night. The proprietor, Donal Neylon, says the bar used to be owned by his uncle, John Moriarty (no relation to the author of *Nostos*).

'He had a great personality and was a real character,' he says. 'He was known to everyone as Foxy John so when I took over the bar in 1990 we decided to remember his name by calling it after him. Visitors love it, especially the Australians and New Zealanders. We used to sell a pile of stuff to farmers but that has slowed down. Tourists enjoy a drink and buy some camping gas at the same time. People are surprised by it and you find a big run on certain things. One of our best sellers in the summer is travel adaptors.'

On the left side, taps dispense stout, the golden-coloured Tom Crean lager and Orchard Thieves cider. Shelves house bottles of beer and spirits. On the opposite side, the contents of stiff brown cardboard boxes are labelled with a black marker. Hanging from the ceiling are a garden hose, a seven-piece screwdriver, Yale locks, a jerrycan, corkscrews, and humble domestic items such as a dustpan set. I browse the shelves where a veritable feast of items would satisfy for months the cravings of home-improvement obsessives: masonry drills, screws, multi-function tools, corner braces, wire nails, hammers, solid drawn brass butt hinges, trimmer line, showerproof slug killer, white spirit, Rattenfalle rat traps, torches, sandpaper, hobby knife, fly catchers, horse clips, Gorilla Tape, netting staples, weedkiller, 13 amp packs, 3-in-one oil, extra-strong louse powder, Kleen-off drain unblocker, and pest and moss control.

Most people, though, come here to get hammered, not to buy hammers. At the bar two greybeards, drinking from long-neck bottles of Guinness, roll cigarettes. In no particular historic order, one rails in short, quick bursts against bad banks, the Black and Tans, and local politicians. The other is indignant at the absence of summer. They shuffle off high stools, retreating for a hunched outdoor puff and a continuation of old and new resentments. In the back room, where the younger resenters assemble, two gaybeards – partners-in-Crean – discuss truth, science and morality, but are drowned out by a boisterous cackle of Munster Hens on Tour: fifteen women, dressed as a cast of Disney characters. These include Pirates of the Caribbean complete with tricorn hats, eyepatches and silver cutlasses. Others pose as Minnie Mouse, Tinkerbell, Peter Pan, Ariel, Pocahontas, and Cinderella, who is engaged in a fruitless search for a lost flip-flop. Before heading to a night club at the bewitching hour, six Disney hens challenge each other to a mothers' ruin gin-drinking competition, clinking ice cubes and toasting Walt.

Word comes from the six-foot-tall doorman that their chariot has arrived. The Disney Queen calls her brood to order. Single file, the Dingle chicks snake their way from their large table past the hardware department in the front bar. One of their number, with a borderline scary cloud of yellow hair, stops to buy a torch battery. 'Always happy to serve a battery hen,' the barman-cum-hardware salesman deadpans. The scene closes as a cachinnation of hens flocks into a swan-white stretch limo where arms flutter from windows like a snakelocks anemone's extended tentacles.

Day breaks slowly over Dingle as I set off for the western end of the peninsula. This area packs in a medley of dramatic mountains, headlands, beaches, caves, coves and islands. It teems with evidence of man's early marks on the face of the land, such as prehistoric beehive huts, monastic ruins, clocháns and promontory forts. On the road to Ventry, the colour is washed out of the hills and coast but the hedgerow flowers are a riotous cascade of crimson, pink, scarlet and purple. Tall spikes of lolloping foxgloves with bell-shaped flowers, clumps of thyme, glimpses of tormentil, sheep's-bit and great willowherb all burst forth. Along a sea wall, gulls peer around enquiringly, on the

The Three Sisters, Smerwick, County Kerry.

lookout for scraps. At Slea Head the GCR curves around a bend, crossing a ford that floods the road, passing a tall statue of Jesus on the Cross with a bleeding left shin. From Dunquin it twists through a steady curtain of drizzle and mist to Clogher Head. Beyond Ferriter's Cove and Sybil Head stands a prominent landmark triptych of rocky tops, known as the Three Sisters, overlooking the ocean where fields slope to Smerwick Harbour. Despite their topographically female nomenclature there is no sisterhood rivalry, since two of them are known under their male names – Diarmada (Dermot) and Hanraí (Henry) – while the central one is called *Binn Mhéanach* (The Middle Peak). A woman in the post office in Murreagh has no idea why they were given male names. 'Some people call them the false sisters,' she says. 'You've probably heard about them – they're known as "perhaps", "maybe" or "I dare say". Along yet more vibrant roadsides, roses are intermingled with miles and miles of nodding fuchsia, bramble, hogweed, hedge parsley, devil's bit and clover.

The travel writer H. V. Morton, who drove these roads in the 1920s for his book *In Search of Ireland,* often referred to the 'ever-changing skies' of Kerry. The western light has provided a fertile stimulus to talented people who have settled in this most inspirational yet easy-going of places. Art galleries, studios and craft shops dominate Dingle's streets. All along the west coast on my journey, the work of artists has drawn me in. I want to find out what drives them creatively and have arranged to call with Maria Simonds-Gooding at her home in Dunquin at the westernmost edge of the peninsula.

Maria's etchings, tapestries, oils on paper, aluminium and plaster works reflect a diverse portfolio of mediums and chart the career of a woman and an artistic journey that has spanned nearly six decades. She has held solo exhibitions in Ireland, Britain, Continental Europe and the United States, and in 2014 a major retrospective was staged at the Royal Hibernian Academy. During her lengthy career she has been much lauded and has won awards for her work. Among her commissions she has illustrated the unexpurgated edition of Tomás Ó Criomhthain's *An tOileánach (The Islandman)* and designed stamps for the Europa Series on Irish folklore. Maria first came to Kerry with her parents in 1947. She recalls vividly her youthful impressions of the countryside that was to have a lasting impact and ultimately inform her art.

'My first memory of Kerry starts just aged seven. Squashed in the back of a small car, I felt like the journey would never end. I was the middle of three children. We were coming from India via our grandmother in Dublin where we stayed some months before leaving for Kerry. On the last stretch of the journey everything changed when the mighty Kerry mountains and the stark, dark bogs on each side of us appeared. The memory of this has never left me. We stayed in a lodge owned by my two grand-aunts in Dooks. Later when my mother had restored a derelict farmhouse enclosed at the back with a cobblestoned courtyard and stables, we moved in. This was an oasis of wildlife, and herons constantly flew in. The front of the house looked out on to a marshy creek and beyond to the MacGillycuddy's Reeks, which my father frequently climbed until his late seventies.'

In that first summer, Maria went with her family to Puck Fair and retains lively memories of the energy and excitement of it.

'We got on the train a couple of miles up the road at Dooks Halt, a small, wooden platform by the side of the road where the train stopped briefly after leaving Glenbeigh, coming from Cahersiveen, travelling at fifteen miles an hour on a single-gauge track, pulling one carriage. The train could be heard blowing its whistle all along the way as it entered the mountain tunnels and over the long viaduct. We all piled into the one carriage like a pack of sardines on top of each other heading for Killorglin. The town was thronged with people, horses and general livestock of every kind. Wads of notes changed hands at the horse fair and the transaction was sealed by spitting on the palm of the hand and good-luck money was handed over to the buyer. The pubs stayed open for three days and nights, celebrating the King Puck goat now crowned above us, his throne erected for the occasion. The Traveller community are so much part of Puck Fair I could not imagine it without them. In the 1950s I met Ella Coffey at Puck, a most remarkable-looking Traveller woman. She was dancing in the middle of the square and I noticed she was wearing a black satin jacket with beautiful stitching on it. When I asked her if she would sell it to me, she replied in a most dignified manner that she would not sell it but she would stitch one for me after going off the drink for six weeks, and this she did. We became good friends after that, and I have many of her dresses, cushions, and aprons she made out of nuns' black veiling cloth which she applied her unique, colourful stitching to. When the first dress was ready, I went to what was known as The Bull Ring in Tralee where she lived when she was not travelling. I was informed the dress was ready when I received a little note from Ella. The envelope was addressed to 'Miss Glenbeigh 8' which was my home phone number at the time, and the letter reached me!'

In 1968 Maria was captivated by the Dingle Peninsula. In the summer of that year she was staying in Kruger's pub in Dunquin and recalls that it never rained. After completing her art studies, she settled in the peninsula when she was in her late twenties. The roof of the fisherman's cottage in which she lives came from the Blasket Islands and is still much as she found it. She lifts a straw place mat on the table and considers it as though it were a mirror holding the narrative of her life.

'I could see across to the Great Blasket where there was a lot of activity, with campers making the most of the hot sunny weather that lasted right through the summer. In Kruger's pub that evening I met the skin divers who were searching for a wreck from the Spanish Armada in the Blasket Sound. They offered to take me to any one of the islands the next day. I chose Inisiciléan since it looked the most remote though I knew nothing about it. When we got out there, we faced a much bigger challenge than expected and we almost abandoned the possibility of landing on the island until we backtracked all along the cliffs and spotted the remains of a plane that must have crashed into the island some previous time. Above the plane a small sheep track wound its way up the cliff. The divers helped pull my provisions up the track to the top before returning. Way down the island was a small dwelling built firmly into the shelter of a small hillock, and when I reached the door there was no sign of the islanders. Nearby was a field enclosed by a stone wall for the protection of one blind sheep from falling off the cliff. At that time there was no communication with the outside world, yet these islanders survived under the harshest of conditions. The isolation of the place gave me an awareness I had never experienced before. There was so much to be inspired by here. I knew I would return to this place but what I did not know then was that later the same summer of 1968, a small Blasket

Islander's cottage on the mainland was to be auctioned and this is where I came to live; it became my home.'

Maria's love of islands has taken her to many places in the world. The regions and countries in which she has worked include India and the Himalaya, the Sahara, Mali, Lanzarote, the Greek islands, and New Mexico. Although she has travelled widely, the place that has shaped her life and work is the Dingle Peninsula, in particular the Blasket Islands. With her gouache and acrylic paints, she has spent weeks alone there working through rain and storms.

'Out here at the westerly tip of the peninsula it is exposed to the full blast off the Atlantic. The landscape and people were steeped in tradition and a whole way of life. This widened my preoccupation with other parts of the world and their struggles, coming from a whole other perspective of extremes and problematical conditions. Like the shipwrecks off the Blaskets, which provided the islanders with wood and other provisions, they saw this as sent from heaven, and so it was with David Lean's *Ryan's Daughter* during the two years they spent here. I was an extra in the wedding sequence for nine nights and was paid three pounds a night. A fortune at the time. Sarah Miles returned several years later for the BBC documentary *On Location,* which gave a good insight into the making and the changes before and after *Ryan's Daughter.* During filming, every house and building was rented in and around Dingle. A whole village was built on the hill just above me, and taken down when the filming finished. Change came and people used to say there was no time now to drop in on your neighbours; we were all so busy with the film. The peninsula prospered greatly with the financial boost it gave when they most needed it.'

In the early days of her stay in Dunquin, Maria found life tough. It was hard to make a living and survive. In the late 1960s, unlike today, there were no restaurants in Dingle, but she handled it instinctively, showing a commitment to self-sufficiency.

'Although there were no restaurants or galleries in the 1960s and we were and still are relatively cut off, it made the peninsula the place it is. With the arrival of *Ryan's Daughter* there was a huge influx of people and interest in the filming. Many people called to my studio. But it was not until later I was given the opportunities of showing my work in New York and elsewhere.'

For most of her adult life Maria has made her home at a remote outpost on the western edge of Europe. When I ask her to define the genius loci of the area, she responds immediately by summing it up through what she calls the *sáspan dubh*: 'the black saucepan'.

'Once the *sáspan dubh* hits you it never leaves you. It is something mysterious, something you can't explain, something which leaves nothing ever the same again. In this area, there is an orchid that is known locally as the *magairlín meidhreach,* ('merry testicle') which gets its name because it is like a bulb with two bulbs at its root. Until the 1960s a woman would put this orchid into a black saucepan and make a potion out of it. For a girl with an eye on a man for marriage, this potion would then be given to the man in question, unbeknownst to him, so that he would fall under its spell. It was never spoken about, but it did happen and still does, for I got the *sáspan dubh*. I don't know if I drank the potion, but I certainly got it when I came to the Dingle Peninsula and I am still under its spell.'

Before I leave, I explain my interest in Manannán mac Lir and Maria insists that I visit Pádraig Ó Fiannachta, an expert on Celtic spirituality in Dingle. She telephones his office and he agrees to see me in an hour's time.

Under a mackerel sky, I drive back to Dingle and along Green Street sidestep a wall of tourists, on my way to the Díseart Centre of Irish Spirituality and Culture. A former convent, it has been turned into an independent third-level institution promoting theology, culture and art. I am sent upstairs, passing a fresco of The Last Supper based on local people in Dingle, and admire the sumptuous colour of Harry Clarke stained-glass windows in the chapel. When I tap and open his door, Monsignor Pádraig Ó Fiannachta's fingers are dashing over the computer keyboard. He beckons me inside to his book-lined study, clearing papers from a chair. With a twinkle behind his glasses, his eyes sparkle with humour in a network of wrinkles. Dressed in a neat suit and a black woollen cardigan, he radiates benignity. His workstation is a cushioned black chair. On his desk lie the *Confessions of Saint Augustine* and other theological works. An affable man, he is glad, he says, at the age of eighty-nine to take a breather from his work. As he explains his current project, he rests his hand gently on my forearm. A PDF document fills his screen. He is engrossed in Pope Francis' encyclical letter on global warming released just a few weeks earlier. But there is a specific purpose behind the Monsignor's close reading: he is translating its entire 184 pages into Irish. He has already completed the first chapter and written eighteen pages in longhand.

The aim of the papal document, called *Laudato Si' (Be Praised) On Care for Our Common Home*, he informs me, is to protect the earth and is not addressed solely at the world's 1.2 billion Catholics but at everyone. The title comes from the Canticle of the Creatures by St Francis, the patron saint of animals and the environment, whose name Jorge Mario Bergoglio took when he became Pope. It is a call to action and adds an ethical dimension to a debate bogged down in economic arguments. Quiet-voiced, Monsignor Ó Fiannachta explains the gist of the pontiff's views on global warming.

'He feels that climate change should be taken seriously but many people are not doing that. He also believes it is a big moral question and that the people who are suffering are the poor. With rising seas, many cities, especially in Africa and India, are affected and these are the people least able to cope with it. You and I produce many more greenhouse gases than an ordinary fellow out in Africa.'

After a long introduction, chapter one deals with pollution and climate change. The Pope warns that the planet is rapidly being turned into 'an immense pile of filth' and refers to 'a collective selfishness'. He calls for an end to consumerism and greed, strongly backing the scientific consensus on global warming. The Pope also demands that fossil fuels be swiftly phased out in favour of renewable energy. The Monsignor scrolls down on the screen and reads a short section from the document that is now officially part of Catholic doctrine.

'Millions of people are dying premature deaths from breathing high levels of smoke. Pollution is caused by transport, industrial fumes, acidification of soil and water, fertilisers, insecticides, herbicides, fungicides and agro-toxins in general. Pope Francis feels that people need to be educated properly about these things so we can all play our part. We have to help the poor and to walk with them, so his first chapter deals with how to do that. Care is central; it is part of the encyclical's title and is repeated many times. I read it through firstly before translating it, although it wasn't his own style – he has experts and consultants working for him – but he did not simplify it enough and I have to find Irish words for things that we would never have used in Irish before, which causes difficulty.'

Translating such a detailed scientific piece of work might seem a formidable task. But it pales in comparison with a project the Monsignor completed in 1982 when he translated and edited an Irish-language version of the Bible – *An Bíobla Naofa*. He is not in the least daunted by his new challenge.

'I started at four o'clock yesterday afternoon and twenty-four hours later I have the first chapter completed. It is quite complicated in places but I find the best way to do it is to write it out in longhand. I hope to finish it in ten days' time. It gives me a great interest. I'm at my desk normally about a quarter past eight most mornings, having said Mass in the chapel here.'

A Gaelic scholar, Monsignor Ó Fiannachta is a former Professor of Irish and was head of the faculty of Celtic Studies at NUI Maynooth for thirty-four years. When he retired from the college, he returned to the west, serving for fifteen years as a parish priest in Dingle where he was born in 1927. Deeply versed in Celtic spirituality, he now helps run the centre and is full of life and talk. We turn from the vexed global warming question to the subject of Manannán which I had come to speak to him about before being diverted. He chuckles to himself as he pauses for thought to outline his views on the sea god.

'I've read about Manannán mostly from literary sources and in relation to the sea, and there are many different aspects to him. As an island nation you would expect Ireland to have a sea god. There are references to him in folklore and in *The Voyage of Bran* and he crops up here and there. Anything I've read about him shows that he enjoyed a joke and was renowned for having women friends. And of course the foam on the waves, or the seahorses, *caiple Mhanannáin*, are named for him, so he is an important figure from that perspective.'

I am interested in how the Catholic Church views the revering of sea gods and ask the Monsignor for an opinion on the Church's stance on it.

'The Church takes all that sort of thing in its stride. The approach has been that we shouldn't destroy the pagan places but baptise them and Christianise them – the people naturally came to these places and had beliefs in gods – St Patrick himself did the same and he is an example of a missionary from the era. When you delve into it, as you know, there is no shortage of fascinating stories in our myths, history, legends and literature.'

I thank him for seeing me at short notice and for his insight into the Pope's thinking on global warming. As I leave him to continue with his work on the papal document, I mention that my next destination in a few weeks' time is Killorglin. He leans back in his chair and, smiling, quietly intones as though in benediction, 'Be careful.'

10
Puckeroos play it their way

THE SKIRL OF PIPES enlivens the town square of Killorglin on the Gathering Day of Puck Fair. It is late afternoon and the Killorglin and District Pipe Band is tuning up. Blue and white streamers across the street provide colour. Crowds throng the square for the *pièce de résistance* of this three-day event: the crowning of a wild mountain goat. Old friends embrace warmly, wishing each other 'Happy Puck'. Yellow-jacketed marshals erect crash barriers while members of the civil defence, search and rescue teams and a large group of gardaí maintain a watchful presence.

The horse fair is already over and the jostling square is at capacity. Young children are raised on to parents' shoulders; a woman swigs from a plastic cup, spilling her lager as she attempts a circular jig in a confined place; teenage boys clutch six-packs of Heineken and bottles of cider. King and Queen Puck parade through the streets, granting residents and visitors alike the 'Freedom of the Town'. Led by bands and floats from rugby and football clubs, and Killorglin Men's Shed, the coronation parade makes its way across the county bridge over the River Laune up through Lower Bridge Street to the square where a specially built twelve-metre stand has been erected. This year's goat is an all-white male, caught near Castlegregory, and he has been acclimatising to his new environment. The goat is transported in his own cage surrounded with ivy and heather. Declan Mangan, who has been on the fair committee since 1963, welcomes the crowds to an age-old tradition – so old, in fact, that no one knows exactly what age it is, although the first written reference is more than 400 years ago.

Puck Fair statue,
Killorglin,
County Kerry.

Seán Ó Sé, the Ceoltóirí Chualann singer from Cork, takes the stage with 'The Boys of Fairhill', 'The Fenians of Cahersiveen' and 'Hello, Patsy Fagan'. The goat is brought up by four men for the official 'crowning' ceremony but a problem emerges – the crown cannot be found. The vehicle in which it was brought has driven off and is now halfway back to Cahersiveen. Minor panic breaks out amongst the officials. Seán is asked to continue singing and manages successfully to stretch out 'Will Ye Go, Lassie, Go', 'The Filemore Draghunt', and 'An Poc ar Buile' ('The Mad Puck Goat') until the crown is recovered and normal service resumes. With a brief drum roll, it is placed on King Puck by twelve-year-old Ciara O'Brien, this year's Queen Puck, who delivers the Puck Proclamation in four languages.

In full ceremonial attire of Celtic-style gown and wearing the traditional tiara, she smiles nervously for press photographs. The winch is attached and within a few seconds His Majesty is raised to his temporary home where he will remain for three days and three nights before being dethroned on Scattering Day and given his freedom again in the mountains. Declan calls for three cheers for puck, 'the only King of the Wild Atlantic Way'. He brings the formal celebrations to an end and concludes, 'I wish you all a Happy Puck, *go raibh maith agat.*'

This year again, as part of what has become a recent ritual, a row has broken out with welfare fears over the goat being caged. In previous years the Animal Rights Action Network (ARAN) had called on Kerry County Council to cancel the raising of the goat, saying the animal would be confined, terrified and confused amongst thousands of partygoers. Another animals rights group, PETA (People for the Ethical Treatment of Animals), also voiced its objections, demanding an end to the practice. They are concerned that the goat is exposed to noise and drunken revelry and believe the use of a live goat breaches the five freedoms safeguarded in the Animal Health and Welfare Act of 2013. These are: freedom from discomfort, pain, fear and distress and freedom to express normal behaviour. ARAN's spokesman, John Carmody, was quoted in the media as saying the goat did not understand the loud noise and being hoisted into the air. 'Tradition,' he said, 'should never be used to justify animal suffering.' The organisers responded to the criticism by outlining a five-point protocol put in place to ensure the goat's safety has been checked by an independent vet. Called 'Freedoms of Goat', it outlines five matters in which it guarantees the animal's freedom: freedom from pain, injury or disease; freedom from hunger and thirst; freedom from discomfort; freedom to express normal behaviour; freedom from fear and distress.

Puck Fair is not only surrounded by controversy but is steeped in history, mythmakers, legends and storytellers.

Killorglin in August has always attracted its share of mytho-maniacs, never mind a few nymphomaniacs. I ask around about Manannán mac Lir since this is a place, whatever the debate about the goats, that he would assuredly have looked on with approval. A wander around the huckster stalls reveals that his 21st-century equivalent, the three-card tricksters, have gone to ground. Tuneless accordionists strike up gypsy music, a lone French singer strums a guitar, and reggae pours from a street corner. Princess gowns, T-shirts, colouring pictures, scented soaps, New Age necklaces, earrings and other showy jewellery, handcrafted boxes and súgán stools are on sale. On special offer, mobile phone accessories include satnavs, a hands-free car kit at €79.99, and a cut-price tool kit. This year's hit is the spinning mop, with demonstrations attracting onlookers, notably twice as many men as women. The magical mop has two heads and sells, claims the patter salesman, for €20 while in the catalogue it is €46. Another trader along the street is offering it for €17. 'The way to a woman's heart,' says the salesman, 'is through a good mop.' Queues form at hot-dog and burger grill vans. The air is scented with an exotic commingling of crêpes, steaming chicken korma, and candyfloss. Tattooists and fortune tellers have set up shop in caravans. The fair has always attracted publicity and has an appeal for journalists and writers. By 7 p.m., Reuters and the Press Association have flashed the news on the national and international wires that Puck has been crowned once again.

In Falvey's Bar, which styles itself 'A Step back in Time', pints of King Puck, a newly brewed India Pale Ale for 2015, is this year's must-have drink. I squeeze past burly, helmeted men kitted out as San Francisco 49ers with their names on the back of their football jerseys: Dwight, Carlos, Ricky, Joe, and the rest of the gang are ensuring they will not forget each others' names if their stag party goes astray. At the counter, the affable owner Declan Falvey, who is on the fair's organising committee, takes time off from bartending for some reminiscing. The winds of change have blown through the fair, and he cites the biggest differences between now and twenty-five, or even fifty, years ago.

'The security, the marshalling, the stewarding and policing has all changed considerably in recent years. We don't want to sanitise Puck Fair but we have to be squeaky clean and there is still a great structure to Puck. It is well organised, with two fairs: the crowning and the dethroning. It has turned into a homecoming festival and if people aren't able to make it they can look it up on the webcam and check the website. It is really the Christmas of Killorglin. People plan their holidays around it and still take three days off to come here.'

Falvey's Bar was built in 1901. Declan talks about its link to the fair. 'My mother hated it but my father loved it. Years ago it was very rough and ready. There would have been a lot of drunks and it was quite difficult running a pub that didn't close for seventy-two hours. They were smoke-filled places unlike today's bars which have a much cleaner atmosphere. I like meeting different people and Puck gives me the chance to do that. We don't dress the fair up to make it anything it isn't. You'll meet buskers and singers, and the greatest and quarest of people coming to it. The important thing is that people want the fair to survive and to thrive for their grandchildren.'

Declan speaks about the controversy over the raising of the goat and says that while he respects the rights of the groups, he thinks their protests are 'over the top'.

'We have a local vet who is very conscious of the welfare of the goat and its freedoms, and if we thought for a moment that he was in any harm, then we wouldn't hold it. Don't forget he is well fed, looked after every day, and returned to the wild in better condition that when he came down.'

The walls of Falvey's feature photographs of the Laune Rangers, the Kerry All-Ireland Gaelic football champions, sketches and cartoons from previous pucks and framed pictures. A dark and distinguished portrait of Charles Stewart

Parnell looks down on the drinkers. No one knows if he came to Puck but Declan says his father and grandfather were admirers of the statesman.

In a back room, the Puckeroos, a group of musicians from Dublin who have been attending the fair for forty-five years, entertain a packed house. A bald man with a lumberjack-style shirt rises from his corner seat, launching into a stirring version of 'The Auld Triangle'. The 'choir' of up to fifteen musicians and singers, several with banjos and guitars, breaks into 'In Dublin's Fair City' and 'On Raglan Road'. A local man in a green-and-gold football jersey with 'Ciarraí' in large letters asks: 'Arra, why don't youse singa Kerra song?'

'We don't know any, that's why,' comes the response. To the Kerryman's chagrin he offers a song for Killorglin: 'Dirty Old Town'. One of the musicians sets up a small portable keyboard, known as an organetta, and joins the others for 'Blanket on the Ground'. As well as Irish ballads, the Puckeroos sing folk and blues. Each afternoon they perform in Falvey's and after a siesta re-emerge in late evening to occupy a long table until the early hours. The bars in town have a special dispensation to stay open until 3 a.m. during the festivities.

'Arra, singa Kerra song,' the man pleads again, to no avail.

In between the non-Kerry songs, some customers talk about the fair's enduring appeal. 'We've had people of seventeen different nationalities here,' one woman tells me, 'and there were Tibetan musicians a couple of years back although I'm not sure if they were able to play any Kerry songs. Years ago south Kerry people would have come but now it is more non-Kerry people and tourists who attend. Many locals who went to England for work come back to Puck, and life in Killorglin is geared to before Puck and after Puck, last year's Puck or next year's Puck. I am of the old stock so I would say there's certainly a much wider stratum of society here now. Mind you, if these activists have their way, it'll probably be a plastic goat they'll be putting up there in a few years.'

A tin whistle and bodhrán are produced by the Puckeroos but still no Kerry songs are forthcoming. Against a roomful of Dubs, the Kerryman is fighting a losing battle. He remonstrates with them but they launch into 'Molly Malone' and 'Down by the Liffeyside'. Then the lead singer asks: 'Is Kildare any use to ye? It's about as far as we go, so here's "The Curragh of Kildare".'

A woman beside me, with a flamboyant wool hat in shocking pink, admires her newly purchased mop and wellingtons. She raises a large Jameson and shows me a freckled arm with a goat tattoo. 'See that? Puck Fair is in my veins and in my bloodstream as much as any whiskey and it'll never be any different.'

A despairing Kerryman tries again. 'For Chrissake, do you not know "The Kerry Dances" or even "The Rose of Tralee"?'

'We can play them but not very well, they'd be outta tune,' says the singer.

The Puckeroos' rabble-rouser finally relents and hollers: 'Here's a Kerry song. It's our very own, specially composed and written for Puck Fair.' From behind the bottle and glass clutter of the long table he rises to belt out 'The Puck Song':

> We're the boys from Dublin Town
> We drank 50 pints on the journey down
> In Falvey's Bar we had a fair sup
> Before we went to see the Puck
> A greater sight I've never seen
> A Puck with a crown that has no Queen.
>
> The following morning we were found
> With a half million people standing around
> Shapes and sizes you've never seen
> All asking why the Puck had no Queen
> It wasn't until the very last day
> The Puck shouted down 'I am gay!'

To escape the crowds and music, I buy a 'King' burger and saunter down to the bridge over the River Laune where swallows are snatching insects spiralling in shafts of light. The birds rise in looping playfulness, zipping and swirling, then undulating, circling and veering at right angles, dipping their bill into the water, skimming under stone arches, readying themselves soon for a long migration to their wintering grounds in southern Africa. Their striking presence goes unnoticed by the thousands crossing the bridge but is monitored closely from on high by a sparrowhawk.

By nightfall the revellers have taken over the square while hundreds of people are traipsing up and down litter-filled streets. With the day's haggling over, and the goat erected, many now follow the Puck pub trail. Groups of young stiletto-shod girls in tight denim shorts and with bare legs cuddle-pose for photographs. They raise tall glasses of the special 'Pucktail' drink, a potent cocktail of vodka, peach schnapps, orange and cranberry juice that has replaced 'Sex on the Beach'. In an entryway, a young rucksack-laden girl pauses and throws up her dinner. Young boys, no older than thirteen, furtively light cigarettes.

Despite the clamour and the opposition, there is a good-natured feel about Puck. Admission to each of the twenty bars in Killorglin is tightly policed by armband-wearing bouncers. Drunks are not allowed in and queues form if there are too many people. At 1.30 a.m., I make my way back to my guesthouse through the still-crowded streets. Before leaving the square, I glance up at His Majesty. He seems unperturbed by the music and frivolity all in his name and the fact that so many people are acting the goat in what is regarded as Ireland's greatest Dionysian festival.

Steaming piles of dung greet visitors on Tuesday, the fair day before Wednesday's scattering. Scores of cows and calves with yellow tags dangling from their ears stand on Langford Street. Tall cloth-capped farmers in corduroy trousers lean on long sticks looking over cattle pens as they discuss business and take stock of their beasts. Old photographs of the cattle fair show the pre-eminence of the black Kerry cow but none is to be seen nowadays. The line-up includes white-head Herefords, Limousin continental bullocks, yearling heifers, fat Charolais and Friesians all hugger-mugger in small groups. Occasionally, one attempts, with a distinct lack of finesse, to mount another. Substantial sums of money appear to be changing hands although exact figures are hard to come by. 'What happens at Puck, stays at Puck', a ruddy-faced farmer tells me firmly, eyeing my notebook suspiciously. A young boy screws up his face at the muddy mess and says to his father: 'I wonder how long it takes to clean up all this.'

High in his cage, King Puck nibbles on his breakfast of leaves and cabbage, and appears content with his fame as he looks down on his subjects. Announcements are made about the day's events, which include bonny baby and fancy dress competitions, storytelling workshops, circus acts and a Euroshow funfair. Street entertainers have taken over the square. Children laugh and point at the Wibbly Wobbly penny-farthing cyclist while stilt walkers hand out balloons twisted into six-legged spiders. Publicans are gearing up for another busy day. Small knots of three or four men sit on high bar stools supping the elixir of Irish life. My departure from Killorglin marks the start of a trip around the scenic Ring of Kerry. The prospects, though, of any dramatic coastal views, or of seeing Ireland's highest mountains are nil for the MacGillycuddy's Reeks are lost in a miasma of mist.

It is a surprise to come across layered, oblong mille-feuille vanilla slices, known as the Napoleon, and eclairs with chantilly fraise in a small café in the far west of the Iveragh Peninsula. Billy Bunter would be drooling at the mouth with the range of pastries, pear tarts, gateaux and brioches on display in the glass cabinets of Cahersiveen's Petit Delice tea room and bakery. The gleaming Conti copper boiler percolating a Costa Rican blend is one of the most glamorous I have seen. It is especially graphic in its range of gurgles and splutters, let alone its whistles and lights flashing in noisy choreography. Steam rises like a reliable swirling Kerry fog; we are talking not just top-of-the-range, state-of-the-art or crème de la crème, but 'fantastique' according to the Frenchwoman from La Rochelle running the café. 'It cost', she says '€7,000 and never lets us down.'

When I enquire about the mechanics of the machine and brewing methods, she does not need prompting. In delightfully accented English, she launches into a description of its innards: thermally isolated and thermally insulated, an internal rotative pump, adjustable temperature, slow pre-infusion system, direct access to the setting of each coffee group, and a cool-touch steam wand with non-stick coating. Before she moves on to the grinder and a history of French aeropressing, I make off with my crumbly croissant and double espresso putting fire into my body. There is something aesthetically appealing about the workings of a coffee machine and a caffeinated paradise that is welcoming, warm and instructive. It may not capture the *mise en scène* of Cahersiveen but it is a seductive place to while away an hour on a wet day when strolling the streets is not an option. There is a feeling of having strayed into south-west France, rather than south-west Kerry, and a place often labelled as the most westerly town in Europe.

To complete the picture, a print of Van Gogh's 'Starry Night' hangs on the wall. I chew over the artist's genius and his opinion of coffee houses: 'The café is a place where one can ruin oneself, go mad or commit a crime.' With his triplism, Van Gogh was ahead of his time. Caffeine is now seen as the most popular psychoactive drug on the planet. According to the *Diagnostic and Statistical Manual of Mental Disorders*, the listed symptoms for this type of disorder includes restlessness, nervousness, excitement, gastrointestinal upset, involuntary muscle twitching, rambling speech, a rapid and irregular heartbeat, and sleeplessness. On the other hand, caffeine withdrawal is now also listed as a disorder. Symptoms are headaches and psychomotor agitation such as bouncing one leg rapidly. Sure enough, a man across from me, glancing through *The Kerryman*, knocks his boot against the table leg alarmingly fast. He is part of the new order of people drinking more coffee than ever and a member of what has come to be known under the term Jitteratti.

From Cahersiveen, the Skellig ring road, a thirty-kilometre circular loop off the main Ring of Kerry, runs beside Portmagee Channel, which separates Valentia Island from the mainland. It is the most westerly promontory on the Iveragh Peninsula. I had made enquiries about a boat trip to the Skelligs but the adverse weather means none will go for several days. Landing on the island is difficult at any time and in bad weather well-nigh impossible. There is a Manannán connection that I am keen to find out about but the nearest I get to it is the Skellig Experience on Valentia. According to legend, the sea god was an early invader of the island before it was re-baptised as Michael.

At the Moorings restaurant in Portmagee I mull over my options. A couple of al fresco diners brave the elements at a clutch of tables, fending off an insurgence of giant squabbling Kerry gulls. A flash mob of fifteen dive-bombs the harbour at a speed of sixty kilometres an hour, scavenging bins and trawlers. Waiting around opportunistically, some stand on car bonnets. Others, with bloodcurdling screams, loop like Messerschmitts, coming to rest on the statue of an anchor as well as a guano-splattered memorial to those lost at sea in these parts during the Second World War: eight German aircrew, eleven US airmen and thirteen Greek sailors. People walking past instinctively duck. When scraps of bread are thrown on to the waterfront, a raucous feeding frenzy breaks out. One gull lopes off and fearlessly plops on to the table beside me, deftly snatching from a plate the crisp skin remains of a fish lunch, gulping it in one go, quicker than you can say 'Take me to the Skelligs.' For good measure, he hops to another plate, greedily adding a side order of chips to his meal. My close-up view enables me to appreciate the size of his huge grey wings – probably up to one and a half metres – the formidable hooked weapon of a bright yellow beak, black tail, dazzlingly white breast and razor-sharp talons. His unblinking yellow-eyed stare is a look that both thrills and chills. I pull up my jacket hood, keep my broadsheet newspaper handy for protection, glad that I have not migrated to reading it on a tablet. I could not imagine fending off a marauding gull with the swat of an electronic device. I gobble my crab sandwich before it, too, is plundered, and ask the barman clearing the table about them.

'They're aggressive some days,' he says, 'and noisy most of the time. We can't do much about them. They're a nuisance although they help clean the plates. But they do put people off sitting outside and they're not exactly toilet-trained.'

If there has been a musically ornithological leitmotif to my coastal journey, then it has been dominated by the unlovely vocalisations of these white-feathered vultures, ranging from cackling manic laughter to a despairing wail. Of all the birds I have seen, they and their trumpeting calls have resonated as my constant companions along the Way. But they are this week's media villain and an outcry about them has erupted in both Ireland and Britain, with many negative stories surfacing in the past few days. Kerry appears to be a hotspot for incidents. Two mature ewes were killed by gulls on a farm at Camp on the Dingle Peninsula and a motorcyclist on the road at Waterville was swooped on, in an attack that he compared to a Second World War Stuka dive-bomb. In another nasty incident, a great black-backed gull attacked a swimmer in the sea at Fenit beach. The gull pecked the man's hand, then returned a second time for another bite, breaking skin and drawing blood. Lifeguards quickly directed him to the emergency department of Kerry General Hospital for tetanus shots.

The situation is even more serious in England where a Yorkshire terrier was killed in a garden in Cornwall by a seagull, leaving what was described as a 'site like a murder scene'; a tortoise was pecked to death, while a racing pigeon and starling were also killed by gulls. Other attacks, not on the same vicious scale, involved ice creams being whisked from hands, and sausages stolen from barbecues. In a pointed form of revenge, a seagull was poisoned and dumped in a police station yard at Bridport in Devon.

Although it has not seemed like it to me, in Ireland herring gulls, which are a protected species, are declining in numbers. The opposite is the case in Portmagee. It is hard to think about the gulls without recourse to metaphors of planes, so to escape the Spitfire summer and *Larus argentatus,* I take refuge from the blitzkrieg in the Cois Cuain gift shop. Wild Atlantic T-shirts and sea salt are for sale. From a wooden sign at the front door, I note down the 'Advice from the Ocean':

> Be Shore of Yourself
> Come out of Your Shell
> Sea Life's Beauty
> Avoid Pier Pressure
> Take Time to Coast
> Don't get Tide Down
> Make Waves

Over the Coomanaspic Pass, the viewing point for the Skelligs is attracting few passers- or drivers-by as both it and Valentia Island are covered in thick mist. Radio Kerry is celebrating twenty-five years since its founding and is playing Irish classics from Dickie Rock, Brendan Shine and Christy Moore. 'The kingdom' news is followed by the weather for 'the kingdom' – long spells of westerly winds driving in heavy rain from the Atlantic, more showers to follow tomorrow. The death some weeks earlier of Val Doonican prompts a trio of songs, 'Delaney's Donkey', 'Paddy McGinty's Goat', and 'O'Rafferty's Motor Car', all of which take me back to the 1960s. Doonican, the presenter reminds us, had a long apprenticeship in the foothills of show business and when his career finally blossomed he quipped: 'It took me seventeen years to be an overnight success.'

When I reach it, I find that the aptly named town of Waterville is positioned on a narrow isthmus between Ballinskelligs Bay and Lough Currane. Water not only surrounds it but floods the streets, rushing down drains and gutters. Raindrops sluice down the panes of houses, pubs and cafés. A conveyor belt of high waves rolls into the bay. Waterville's two most illustrious heroes, memorialised in statues, are soaked. Charlie Chaplin vies for attention in alignment with the 'high priest' of Kerry football Mick O'Dwyer. Both are depicted in classic action poses. Mick is captured with the ball gripped determinedly in his hands and an expression that says 'this is mine and I'm keeping it'. The more relaxed Charlie, with cheeky grin, is wearing his trademark bowler hat, tie, waistcoat and suit, as well as having a walking stick in his left hand. Rain drips steadily from Mick's nose and from the famed short moustache covering Charlie's philtrum.

'Chaplin loved coming here,' Paula Huggard tells me over a pot of tea in front of a blazing log fire in the sitting room of the Butler Arms Hotel where I have come to dry out. 'He was a regular guest with his family in the late 1950s and during the 1960s. He was driving through Waterville one day, decided to call in here and asked about a room. He was told the hotel was full but Billy Huggard gave up his own apartment to him and Chaplin came back every year up until the early 1970s. The locals were shocked because he was very different from his screen character of a tramp and didn't appear the way he looked in the films. He enjoyed going off fishing every day in the lakes around Church Island and the local gillies knew him well. Every evening people lined their fish out on the black-and-white tiles along the corridor and displayed what they had caught. It was a competition to see who caught the most – Chaplin was competitive and walked into the fishmonger's in Cahersiveen, bought a fish and put it out, which got a good laugh. He loved the back bar where the locals drank and was a down-to-earth man. He also liked the fact that everyone left him alone to allow his family to enjoy swimming, horse riding and sand yachting. We're keen to preserve his memory and named our conservatory in his honour. The statue is simple and not on a plinth, reflecting his easy-going nature. There's also a festival held over the summer showing his old films, which is extremely popular.'

Paula, who runs the hotel with her sister Louise, outlines some of its history and its eccentric visitors. Apart from Chaplin, many other notable names have been associated with the Butler Arms. Walt Disney came for a stay after Chaplin told him about the hotel, and, on her visit, the Queen of Tonga got special treatment.

'She was a huge woman and because we didn't have a bed big enough we had to make a special new one for her in the 1960s. When Count John McCormack came, he sang on the stairs standing right beside the newel post.'

Paula goes off to fetch visitors' books from the late nineteenth century. I browse old volumes in mahogany cabinets. Some of the titles are Prescott's *History of the Conquest of Mexico*, *My Autobiography* by Benito Mussolini, *Johnson & Sanderson Stock Exchange Investment Handbooks, 1920–30*, *Game Shooting* by Robert Churchill, and *The Sporting and Athletic Register* from 1908.

A leaf through the visitors' books shows that it was more than just comedians who stayed at the hotel. Many guests were English and it particularly appealed to retired army colonels, clergymen and politicians. One of the biggest names to come here in Victorian times was Arthur J. Balfour, known as 'Bloody Balfour'. When he stayed in June 1894, he had already served as Chief Secretary for Ireland. He became Prime Minister (1902–05) and later foreign secretary. In the visitors' book he summed up his stay in an understated way by drawing a fisherman and signing the book with a single word: 'Moist.'

When Paula's family took over the hotel around 1916, it had already been operating as a coach house since the 1880s and had twenty-four rooms.

'Even then they had a lot of repeat business and families stayed much longer in those days. The same families came at the same time each year and when they were leaving they would book again for the following year. There was a dance hall at the back and a game called 'roll the red', which was played on a billiard table. After dinner, residents would gather around the table to play it. The idea was to keep the white ball moving. People ran around the table and everyone got to know each other, which led to some later matrimonial pairings. It became a popular match-making game – there wasn't much going on and it was a social gathering.'

Many guests enjoyed prolonged stays but none can rival that of one of the most colourful characters, a retired army colonel, Morton Henry Knaggs, who had served in the Boer War. He came for a month in the mid-1920s and loved it so much that he stayed for twenty years, becoming as much a part of the furniture as the tartan Parker Knoll armchairs and glass cabinet bookcases.

'He was an expert rose grower,' Paula says. 'He used to sit at the bachelor table in the restaurant and knew many of the guests and those at the commercial traveller tables. His father had been the colonial administrator of Barbados, and during the First World War he was deputy assistant director of the War Office. His death notice in *The Times* stated that he died in a Dublin nursing home on 4 March 1948. His address was given as the Butler Arms Hotel where he had been a permanent all-year-round guest. He was later buried in Waterville, the place he loved most.

'My granny was Catholic and my great-grandfather Martin Huggard was Protestant. She was very religious and every day in the kitchen she would say the Rosary twice, at noon and six p.m. And it didn't matter who they were or what religion they were, she made everybody kneel down for it – staff, guests, delivery men. She was quite stern and people did what she said, but she was highly regarded as a professional hotelier.'

One hundred years ago, an anonymous guest curiously wrote: 'The Butler Arms, hath many charms, but none for me.' Today, the timeless appeal of the place is summed up by log fires, tub chairs and the fact that, in the lounge, the stopped mantelpiece clock stands at ten minutes past five. I dine at the lone travellers' table in the Chaplin conservatory, surrounded by black-and-white smiling photographs of the man and his family walking the streets of Waterville.

The summer budget for road mending and hedge cutting has run out in the south-west corner of the Ring of Kerry. From Waterville, across the twisty Coomakista Pass the road degenerates. I rattle over potholes, bumps and uneven tarred patches. Considering its reputation as one of Ireland's main high-season tourist routes, extreme care is required to avoid the wide craters. Hedges are choked with bramble and bracken overflowing on to the roads with tour coaches brushing the branches back. The route is awash with commercial attractions such as Derrynane historic park, and fairy and tea gardens. One shop offers 'Ant-teeks,' another states 'Wet cyclists welcome.' A sign outside a café: 'The Kerry Way is the only Way.' Sodden haystacks have turned to mush and have crumpled. Eventually the road improves but the view worsens. To my right, the Kenmare River is barely visible while rain blows through the inland valleys. Views are restricted to rows of bungalows along a sixty-metre contour line, and an occasional isolated farmhouse.

Two Kerry bog ponies stand in the downpour, seemingly as much at home as a dog lying contentedly by the fireside. The small, chestnut ponies with their flaxen tails are part of what is known by the marketing meerkats as the 'Kerry brand', which consists of an unspoilt landscape and clean environment. Some see the region simply as postcard fodder. According to statistics, in 1991 there were few holiday homes in the county, but the situation has changed dramatically since then. In the boom years, between 2002 and 2007, a staggering 17,600 homes were built in Kerry alone, and 7,600 of these were one-off houses in the countryside.

For all the despoliation, grim weather and atrocious roads, it is still possible to detect an older Kerry along this route. From Sneem and on to Kenmare, luxuriant green drapery fills the windscreen. Beyond the Blackwater Bridge at Lackeen Point, full-leafed trees, sturdy with age, carve out lush road tunnels where branches of ash, beech and sycamore touch like Michelangelo's Sistine Chapel fingers. Curling mists mingle with pale ribbons of smoke rising from cottages with red creepers around the door giving the appearance of a 1960s John Hinde postcard. Cackling magpies lift off a freshly asphalted road on the way to Kenmare, which marks the end of my 'Kerrysphere' travels, the penultimate stage before the final leg of my wanderings, which will bring me to west Cork.

11
Whatever you seek is here

AT THE END OF AUGUST, I head west Cork-wards on a mission
to find a rock star in Beara, Munster's most far-flung peninsula.
My detective work takes me across the county border to a
location near Eyeries. I pick up the trail again from Kenmare and
after thirty minutes on Kerry's roads, experience a no-fuss, no-
fanfare entry into Cork. A few miles beyond Lauragh, a bridge
with a sign half-hidden by branches denotes that I have crossed
the county boundary. The telltale colours of red-and-white flags
at farmhouses are also a giveaway of having reached the 'Rebel
County'.

Hillsides are covered with purple heather and dwarf gorse.
Tall-hedged fields and ditches are in their florid prime with chest-
high swathes of orange montbretia decorating mile-long stretches
of uncut grass verges. When I stop to check directions with a
topiary gardener clipping and pruning plants with secateurs, he
explains that deer like to eat the montbretia bulbs. 'They enjoy
the taste of them but they leave the rest. It's a bit like ourselves
drinking beer – we love the taste but we don't eat the glasses.'

Hedge cutting, he says, is officially banned between March
and the end of August to encourage biodiversity, but in some
cases they are cut to help visibility for road safety. 'They're an
important wildlife corridor, not just for insects and birds but
also for bats and other animals. You'll see any amount of foliage
overflowing on these roads especially at this time of year, and
you'll not be short of artefacts either.'

A walk down the road bears out what he says. Hedges glisten
with silvery spiders' webs, quarrelsome birds, and are laden with
shiny blackberries dangling temptingly. Earthy and leafy scents

of holly, wild ferns, blackthorn and whitethorn bushes, rowan, goldenrod and the creamy blossom of meadowsweet spring from roadsides. The air is perfumed with the stillness of late summer. The hay has been cut for a second time and the changing colours of the crops indicate the onset of the harvest. Within a few minutes' drive the countryside turns to grey rock. Whaleback-shaped boulders and craggy outcrops define the landscape of this part of west Cork. The road curls around Ballycrovane Harbour where sea mayweed dances along the wall. It hugs the coast to a remote headland at Kilcatherine Point, a triangular sliver of coast on the northern side of Beara, which casual visitors do not tend to penetrate.

My aim is to locate the Hag of Beara, also known as the *Cailleach Bhéara*, who has a connection to Manannán mac Lir. As in other parts of the west, the sea god is prominent in the mythology of Munster. The Hag – wise woman or witch – has metamorphosed from a human figure and taken the form of a rock waiting for his return. At the top of Kilcatherine Hill a sign beside a gate warns: 'No more butts: Do not throw your cigarette butts on the ground.' Along a path with birdsong and flowers, my quarry lies in the distance. I pick my way over to a large jagged-edged and flaky conglomerate erratic fenced off at a tip of land. It stands, raw and angular, on a grassy mound just over a metre tall, measuring the same in width.

From its commanding position, I gaze out to sea. Barely a ripple breaks the surface of the wide arc of Coulagh Bay which breathes light into the day. It stretches from Cod's Head to where it meets the Kenmare River at Kilcatherine Point. Apart from the small lump of Eyeries Island near Creha Quay, the Hag has an unimpeded waterfront outlook to the west. As I swing around, the vista takes in the wide prospect of the southern section of Beara with its small coves, inlets and bays. In the mid-distance the village of Eyeries huddles under Miskish Mountain, behind which rise the dramatic inland slopes of Maulin, Lackawee, Knocknagree and Hungry Hill.

A close inspection of the rock shows that it is blotched by white lichen and furred with moss on its north-facing side. It has become a shrine, decorated with a variety of eclectic offerings carefully placed along a dip in its surface and on its darkened shelves at either end. These include a stick with a red scarf, a St Brigid's Cross, rusting money (every denomination in many currencies from coppers to fifty cent), shells and small stones, a screw, pen, ring, teaspoon, pencil sharpener, badges, earrings, a bangle and bracelet, a curious tiny plastic cowboy figure, the curved six-inch white jawbone of a sheep complete with its row of molars, and artificial flowers.

Around my feet is a mosaic of real flowers. The grass is spattered with wild angelica, herb Robert, dangling bells of heather, thyme, hawkweed and spikes of rare bog asphodel, all crackling with the static of insect life. Another rarity: it is one of those breezeless coastal days, *sans* fog, *sans* mist, *sans* rain. The sun is not strong enough for butterflies but is sultry enough to induce bees to alight on sheep's bit flower heads. A funnel spider, which emerges from the depths of its long cobweb, darts back into its intriguing tunnel hidden in a grassy bank. Apart from the distant squawk of gulls, surprisingly few seabirds are active.

I have arranged to meet Anne O'Carroll whose background is in tourism and law. She wears many hats as she is also a folklorist, historian, journalist and inter-culturalist, which makes her ideally qualified for helping with my fieldwork. Anne, who lives nearby, arrives shortly after me along with Checker, her black-and-white dog. This is a special place for her, somewhere she has made many visits. We discuss the views, the variety of blessings, and how the Hag's wind-blasted appearance, with the suggestion of a face, has been sculpted by the weather.

'We're up high here so it is a dramatic and exposed place,' she says. 'The Hag is apparently looking out and waiting for her consort Manannán mac Lir to return. People know about Manannán because he is in the pantheon. He would have been a star of his day and was looked up to. You can see that with the

Offerings on the Hag of Beara rock, County Cork.

lichen it looks as if the Hag has white hair streaming out in the wind from her head. There is an energy at this site with fabulous views and good air quality filtered all the way across the Atlantic, which is why there is lichen on the stone. It's traditional to leave an offering but this has only started in recent years. You have to be careful never to leave any of your own hair or a nail clipping because then she will own you, so never leave any part of yourself or you will be in her power.'

Not just in Ireland but in many parts of the Celtic mythological realm, the Hag had a pre-eminent presence and was renowned as an influential fertility and power goddess. In Munster she is known as the 'Shaper of the Land'.

'She was enormously powerful throughout the Celtic world. In Scotland they used to say when it snowed that it was the Hag of Beara plucking her geese, or if there was snow on the mountains then she was said to be hanging out her sheets. There was a huge, natural area where the sea came in and they call it the Hag of Beara's cooking pot. But she represented many other things too. She would have had many consorts and as she had seven lifetimes she had plenty of time to get through them all. So it appears that, in terms of any god, demigod or hero you can mention in Celtic mythology, she had him as a lover. She worked her way through them until she grew to be an old woman, at which stage she turned back into a young woman, started off again and so it continued.'

Checker, who has gone off to sniff fence posts, perks up with the appearance of the sun. Several other 'Hagoraks' arrive to inspect the rock and photograph it. The Hag's domain covered the entire length of the peninsula, and for generations she has been a prevailing part of the oral tradition of south-west Munster.

'She is reputed to have had fifty-five children on Beara alone by all these various gods and warriors so although old friend Manannán was a big dude, he was in fact only one of many. Apparently she married many young husbands and then just worked them to death before moving on to the next one. She had huge boots and could step from one peninsula to the other. It is said that she used to challenge men to scything competitions and they'd all line up to the sound of a trumpet or bugle and start scything. Then she would cut the whole field and scythe the legs out from under the men, so you wouldn't mess with her. She was a tough cookie.

'She was also a goddess of harvest and of plenty, a life-giver with superpowers, and was really *the* goddess before Christianity came. So you have your patriarchal version that she is sitting here waiting for Manannán to come back; and then you have your Christian version that in nearby Kilcatherine church a male saint was sleeping with the Bible under his head as a pillow. She would be annoying him, poking him and throwing rocks at him because she was angry that Christianity was coming in and taking away her power. In the Christian version, he gave chase to her, threw the Bible at her, and this was how she turned to stone. Of course, there are lots of clashing versions, different stories are told and retold.

'Many of the wedge tombs and standing stones which are man-made are in beautiful locations because they had to have access from the sea and were often on an elevated, protected position. So it certainly is a grand site in which to hang out and wait for some fellow to return to you, no matter how long a time that might be. And as far as I'm concerned it's nice to see something with a powerful woman in it. Even though we are still being paid less in 2015, I like to look at the Hag of Beara and think maybe our day will come again.'

We walk back to the road and look down on the Hag, an open-air museum piece with a striking history of many love affairs. There she stands, four-square, an ancient, lonesome figure, waiting and longing. Who knows with any certainty about her longevity, but she looks cheerful enough, slumbering on a sunny day, exuding an air of glacial gravitas, and still with a strong 21st-century pulling power.

The twin villages of Eyeries and Allihies (colloquially known as eyesores and allergies) are full of painterly charm. Eyeries has spilled paintboxes all over itself. Facades of simple and symmetrical two-storey houses in primary colours give them a distinctive individuality. The route to Allihies ranks as one of the Great Coastal Roads of my trip. After a long, straight stretch through Urhan, it twists in short bursts of a kilometre or two in a delectable rollercoaster, paralleling the grassy ridgeline of the Slieve Miskish Mountains, climbing through Knocknagallaun and Cummeen. Sheep on the road stare vacuously. Tall engine houses stand out in the landscape with chimneys sticking up like stark fingers. They are all that remains of a copper-mining industry that was a major business here in the nineteenth century.

At one corner, the mountain ranges of the Ring of Kerry, which had been more imagined than seen on my visit, unfurl in front of me. From Dooneen viewpoint, the Skelligs in the far distance are visible for the first time, and on a day of unusual clarity the MacGillycuddy's Reeks thrust upwards in the afternoon sun. Cyclists pause for breath-catching and view-drinking. A driver from Limerick, who has stopped to gape in awe, tells me he had no idea this road existed. Up and down hill, a tractor and mower perform the seasonal grass-cutting in a sloping field noisy with gulls. Across the water, I follow the flight path of two ravens, listening to their *caw caw* until they disappear from sight. The last blackbirds of the summer are singing; soon their fluting songs will be heard no more.

The buildings that I had seen in the mountains are a reminder of the mining business that thrived here two centuries ago. Its fascinating story is told in Allihies Copper Mine Museum. The mine opened in 1812 and grew to be one of the most important and extensive copper mines in either Ireland or Britain. The parish of Allihies increased rapidly within a few years and it became one of the busiest regions in Ireland. By its height, the Allihies mine had produced 300,000 tons of copper ore, which was transported from Ballydonegan to Dunboy by sloop or over the mountain in horse-drawn carts. It was then loaded on to schooners and shipped to Swansea for smelting. A mix of copper ore, quartz and rock came out of the mine and was broken up by hand and by a steam-driven roller crusher. It was then carried by horse and cart to the 'dressing floors'. Stories of the draining and pumping of steam power, water power, horse power and man power are recounted in the museum. Cabinets contain shining examples of polished ammonites, calcite orange, amethyst stones, rock crystal and tiger's eye, a stone said to possess fierce, dynamic energy and which is especially protective during travel. It was carried as a talisman against curses or bad luck.

Down at the wide man-made beach at Ballydonegan, camper vans are parked for the night. Drying clothes hang on a fence. The sand, made up of 100,000 tons of crushed quartz washed down from the mines, is covered with sea rods, seaweed and

Beach chair, Allihies, County Cork.

kelp. In the centre of the beach, someone has placed a tattered, brown leather armchair with a torn seat, perhaps an early version of a lifeguard station before they acquired their yellow huts.

Catch a clear morning and the Atlantic will live long in your memory. The day begins with dawn light flooding my bedroom in Allihies and casting a delicate hue over the sea. By 10 a.m. when I reach the Bealbarnish Gap, the ocean has a silvery-blue sheen, the influence of the Gulf Stream. The sun stirs an excitement. Tourists pour off a bus to capture the allure of north European light and languid air. Their eyes dance across the sea as they watch, agog, a pod of tumbling dolphins in Garnish Bay. This is the sparkling Atlantic – more meek than wild – that they have come in hope of seeing, and they are unexpectedly rewarded with a summer's day akin to the Bay of Naples. Strips of cirrus plumes are high in the deep blue sky. Like Banba's Crown, where I began my journey many months ago under different climatic conditions, this, too, is a place to contemplate the ocean's majesty. It reminds me again of the limitless scale of the Atlantic, an infinite sheet stretching beyond Dursey Head and its famed hat-trick of islands: the Bull, the Cow and the Calf. Leaning over a five-barred gate, I indulge in the moment and through field glasses track the flight of a glossy shag hurriedly making its way across the water's surface.

Beara's sun-heated roads are choked this morning with SUVs. The heat is also raising temperatures amongst motorists suffering wing-mirror rage. With a loud 'thunk', a camper van clips my driver's side mirror, cracking the glass; a farmer remonstrates with a 4 x 4 owner about the amount of space his mirrors are taking up on a cramped track already swaddled with montbretia, fuchsia and loosestrife. An hour's steady driving through Castletownbere, Adrigole and Glengarriff showcases the south of the peninsula, enclosed by the still waters of Bantry Bay, and on the other by the long chain of the lumpy Caha Mountains straddling Cork and Kerry.

Umpteen pithy tourist-board slogans attempt to sum up west Cork and its towns such as 'A place apart', 'A history book come to life', or 'Not just a place but a state of mind'. It is reputedly home to more artists per capita than either Paris or London. In its bars you are likely to rub shoulders with musicians, poets, painters and potters, and a hotchpotch of dreamers, hippies and philosophers. Such a bar is to be found in Bantry, although since it is lunchtime, it is early for many of these alternative lifestylers to assume their positions at the counter. The owner, Vincent McCarthy, looks around the Anchor Tavern, rubbing his beard and puzzling over how things have changed. I had visited the Anchor in 1991 when the then owner Bill O'Donnell recounted his hitchhiking exploits around the world in 1958. Vague flashes of recall jump out from the walls. The newspaper story of his trip still remains framed alongside maps, pictures and maritime memorabilia. Vincent pours me a Segafredo coffee, telling me that, after Bill retired, his son ran the bar and then leased it to someone else who altered the entire character of it.

'He ripped out everything, completely changed the furnishings and when I took it over in 2009 I returned everything to the way it had been. In terms of changes I varnished the walnut counter, put in a new ceiling after the smoking ban, and re-covered some seats although those settles have the original cushions.'

It is still a dark and dimly lit bar with one light bulb dangling in the centre. The window display has kept its lighthouse (minus its winking light), a hooker, bellows and a sextant, which have been exhibits for many a year. A small wooden sign says 'All those who wander are not lost'. Vincent spent twenty-four years in the United States working as a painting contractor in Boston. In 2007 he returned to Bantry, his birthplace, and took over the bar two years later. He speaks about the changes to two drinkers who might well have been sitting in the same high stools in 1991 but they do not appear interested. One asks me if I could lend him €100.

'The biggest changes have been in the smoking laws and, of course, we now have a beer garden. Things have changed in Bantry too. There's only one man now living in the main street, whereas years ago many people lived on it, either above or behind their shops. There have also been harbour developments and since the height of the Tiger, too, other things have changed. Vickery's was an old Bianconi coaching inn which was sold a few years ago to a development consortium to be turned into apartments. Against that we've new hotels and new businesses opening so the place is still hanging together.'

While Bantry has moved on, the Anchor remains firmly rooted in its historical past. I have been swept back to 1991, which leads me to think on the words of the celebrated New York Yankees baseball player Yogi Berra, who famously quipped: 'It's like déjà vu all over again.' I skirt around the roads of the Sheep's Head and Mizen Peninsulas, pausing briefly in Durrus and Schull before reaching Ballydehob at the inlet of Roaring Water Bay. Twenty-five years ago, the town had eleven shops that sold groceries; now it has one. The amount of choice for shoppers is the biggest commercial transformation to Ballydehob since my last visit. In those thriving times it had ten pubs, most open all day; now there are seven, most open only in the evenings. It also had a bank and a Garda station, both of which have closed. In the case of the bank, Allied Irish Bank has replaced it with a mobile one outside the community hall on Mondays and Fridays.

In many ways, Ballydehob is symptomatic of rural towns along the west coast where there has been a serious depletion of services. But it still has managed to keep its carved timber fronts with architraves, fascia boards and raised lettering.

And the picture is not all despondent. Undaunted by the downturn of the austerity years, Emma and Jamie Budd opened their café in the spring of 2015 to help put the town back on the map. It is based in the legendary Annie's Restaurant, which closed several years ago. Now with their footpath furniture and enticing blackboard menus, the Budds are determined to help the town restore its community spirit. Jamie points to his sparkling Nuova Simonelli espresso coffee machine, equipped with T3 technology to control the temperature; could this be the saviour of Ballydehob?

'This is a world-class machine which takes advantage of scientific research and sets a new standard in terms of precision, reliability and performance,' he says. 'You can have one boiler at seventy per cent and another at ninety per cent, so it's all about timing. With the three-dimensional temperature control it's very accurate and can be adapted to each blend of coffee. It brings out the flavour profile notes to perfection.'

Jamie talks of light, medium and dark roasts, of long unfolding aftertaste, but does not have much time for latte art. 'We don't specialise in it as it's a little bit gimmicky but it's all to do with the wrist and with the little knocks and nicks you can perform. Internationally in the world of coffee, the Australians and the Japanese are the people taking it to a new level. Single-origin is big and the connoisseurs are drinking from filters now. Two-and-a-half minutes is the perfect time to let it filter.'

While exactitude in timing, coffee, teas and their numerous varietals might reign supreme, there is no question about the all-embracing interest created in food in this area. In a few weeks' time the West Cork Food Festival will take place in thirty-two towns and villages, as well as on eight islands. Walter Ryan-Purcell, who runs Lough Beg farm near Schull, has called into Budds and speaks to me about his work in food production, which involves supplying supermarkets and shops all over Cork and Kerry.

'We decided last summer that we must make something that people eat every day, so now we bake gluten-free oat bread and sell it in virtually every supermarket in Cork and Kerry. We're doing two thousand loaves a week and we've just developed a gluten-free oat tea brack and within three weeks we're at seven hundred bracks a week. We're just starting a flapjack next, and then we might do a gluten-free apple tart.'

A champion of farmers' markets found in towns throughout Cork, Walter says they are now in danger and he fears for their future.

'There's a worry that farmers' markets are becoming coffee mornings and the Supervalus are becoming the new markets. Take a city like Cork. They've put a big shopping centre at every entrance junction to the city, so that's where everyone is shopping. I know people living in the middle of Cork city who travel to the suburbs rather than five minutes over to the market because they can put their shopping in the boot of the car.

'Our big thing is goat's-milk ice cream. Goat's milk is so much healthier. It's naturally homogenised. With the milk you buy in the shop, it's not so much the pasteurisation that's the problem, it's the level of homogenisation which is breaking down all the particles to minute sizes, and they're being immediately absorbed into the system. When you eat food, you're meant to digest it slowly so it should keep you going all day. But people are now eating sugary bars and all the rest of it, which gives a short burst of energy but then you're dead again. Don't forget, if you have porridge in the morning, you're fairly good for the rest of the day.'

Fifteen kilometres away, the talk in Skibbereen is of the creation of a new rural digital business scheme with initially seventy-five jobs and the potential for another 500 by 2020. The Old Bakery building is to be renamed 'Ludgate Hub' and will, according to those behind it, create an 'entrepreneurial ecosystem'. The project takes its name from a Skibbereen man, Percy Ludgate, described in *The Southern Star* as being the 'Bill Gates of his time', having invented the prototype for the first laptop computer in 1907.

Mona Best, who runs Bridge House B&B, says it is positive news and just the tonic the town needs. I have checked in to what at first sight I mistake for a Marrakesh souk. With its bohemian décor, classified as 'Victorian boutique accommodation', Mona's house is an extravagant mix of antiques, flower power and karma. Hanging baskets of nasturtiums and petunias welcome guests at the front door. Mannequins stand in the hallway and landing; small Buddhas sit on the floor and on tables; candles flicker in the foyer. A cabinet overflows with cut-glass china and figurines while stark African facemasks are fixed on doors. It is hard to know which way to look.

Mona is recovering from the 'after-effects' of her seventieth birthday party shenanigans the previous night. She was a hairdresser before opening her guesthouse, which she has run for more than twenty-five years. Known as 'Skibbereen's style icon', her sense of fun is illustrated in an epigram in the hall: 'Too bad that all the people who know how to run the country are busy driving taxi cabs and cutting hair.' With her yellow bike, Mona is a free spirit and cuts a distinctive figure.

'I am a bit quirky, a bit of a drama queen,' she admits. 'I do my own thing. In my outlook and thinking, I am a very positive person but as I feel that there is so much negativity around these days, my home has become my stage.'

Upstairs the theatrical flourishes continue unrestrained in the idiosyncratic bedrooms. My wallpaper is adorned with a leopard-skin pattern (calling to mind Oscar Wilde's famous last words, which happened to be on the subject of wallpaper: 'either it goes or I do'). He would have appreciated the thirteen rose petals lying on the bed covers. Stiletto-heeled shoes sit on the mantelpiece and lamps come with red heart-shaped shades. The perfume of potpourri diffuses around the room. Bedside books left for me offer a contrasting reading experience: *Fifty Shades of Grey* and *The Good News Bible* !

Mona shows me her poster birthday card from friends and acquaintances, which echoes her eclecticism. She is variously described as being 'the cat's pyjamas', 'full of natural madness', and 'zany and fun'. One contributor states: 'You are the indisputable, unapologetic, creatively demonstrative manifestation of how life should be lived.'

After breathing in the feminine flamboyance of Bridge House, I turn my mind to a masculine evening that I have arranged to gatecrash. Many months earlier in Donegal, I had visited a women's group at their Afternoon Club in Bundoran. Now I wanted to see what the men had to say. Where better than a Men's Shed, the new phenomenon and worldwide community-based organisation that has swept through Ireland?

When I arrive at their 'shed', which turns out to be a Georgian gate lodge connected to the Liss Ard estate south of Skibbereen, the whiff and sizzle of a charcoal barbecue percolates the night air. Some men are busy chopping spruce logs while others are gardening, reflecting the fact that it prides itself on being a grass-roots organisation. Part of a collective national network of more than 100 set up in Ireland in 2011 and run as a charity, its purpose is to maintain the health and well-being of its members.

Nic Pease offers me a welcoming plateful of tasty pork sausages and fried potatoes. Thin rashers are added to the pan. We sit on hazel chairs made by the men, sip from mugs of strongly brewed tea, and discuss their work. Buster, a stocky Staffordshire bull terrier, pokes around my shoes and legs, peering at my plate with teeth meeting in a scissors bite. Nic, originally from Manchester, was involved in setting up the Skibbereen shed in 2013. He had previously worked with groups in voluntary and personal development and was a therapist.

'Before we started meeting we did a day trip to other sheds around Cork city and west Cork and they were completely different from each other. Someone came along to explain the idea behind them as I was completely new to it. It was the first time I'd heard of them and I thought they were a great idea. I'd worked in community development, so I was asked by the resource centre to get involved. It's one of those ideas that's so obvious that you wonder why they haven't always been there. The ethos for me is that it's not to be set up as a service. It's meant to be run by men, created by men, and for some it has elements of service for other people. Some see it more as voluntary work or just a social get-together, so it's not just one thing and it's important to keep the emphasis on that.'

Buster has returned to see what is on my plate. I cannot help but think of the stories I have read of pit bull terriers mauling young children. He looks up again, black nose twitching, allowing me to appreciate the muscularity and strength of his jaws. Feeling slightly intimidated, I admit to not being a lover of pit bulls.

'He's harmless with people,' says Nic, 'but if another dog appears he's like Mike Tyson.'

In the past two years the men have worked on specific activities. One project involved making a flood barrier gate for the resource centre in Skibbereen where they used to meet. The building had major flooding problems and this helped ignite the men's interest.

'It was really amazing the moment we started doing something concrete. It just completely came alive then. Once we had a focus, people jumped to do it. We had a screwdriver, a pencil and paper and something to work out. If somebody comes up with an idea and if a few other people want to do it, they'll do it. It could be anything. Some are into model trains, some are into photography. We provide a community space where men belong and feel welcome, whether they've come to work on something jointly or an individual project. They enjoy the company of others or a cup of tea. Amongst other activities, we've helped build a slipway and erected bird boxes in trees.'

The motto of the Men's Shed is: 'Men don't talk face to face, they talk shoulder to shoulder.' Nic believes that this simple insight resonates with most people when they hear about their meaningful activities.

'Men will talk more easily when they're doing something,' he says, 'I think that's definitely true. In parenting, the mother and baby are eye to eye, the father and baby face the world together. One of the biggest jobs was a currach that we made which took several weeks. We had a core of retired people and long-term unemployed working on it, as well as people who are getting on with normal life, but want company. There aren't many places where men can meet these days. It's either the pub, or you could join a rowing club, play football, tennis or badminton but others want something more casual. When we were making the currachs, there were five or six lads in their twenties who were building their own boat. It was great to have the mix and age range, which worked well. In the past the sort of environment that the Men's Shed provides happened naturally through creameries, or in garages or workplaces where there was a slower pace of life.'

Nic has lived and worked in west Cork since 1990 and enjoys the blend of nationalities who have settled in the area.

'There are a lot of Germans and English here because it's tolerant. And it's become a normal part of the culture. When we moved here it was an economically depressed area, so having an influx of people was good. The school that my kids went to was only still open because of the influx of blow-ins. A third of the children were international and it was continually threatened by closure. If it hadn't been for those kids, the school would have shut. It was bringing people to a community that was slowly emptying.'

Nic and another Men's Shedder, Ian Osborne, originally from Bristol, show me around the one-storey gate lodge. If an estate agent was offering it on the property market, the sales pitch would describe it as a period house with classic personality and in need of tender loving care.

'When we moved in here the wiring was absolutely chaotic,' Nic says. 'I didn't know if it would pass an inspection, but now it is safe. The estate started renovating it about twenty years ago, ran out of money or changed their minds, stripped it and never finished it. So it looked a lot more derelict than it was. It's actually a fairly sound building and suits us perfectly.'

Ian, a man who enjoys his quotes, likes the company of the others and the fact that they work well as a group.

'Every man's shed is his castle, and here it's like a woodman's country retreat. We've been involved in litter clean-ups in Skibbereen and along parts of the Wild Atlantic Way, especially on the beaches where the litter is deadly. My view on that is that those ruining the earth shall be brought to ruin themselves. I also like to quote the motto in Latin on the town hall in Skibbereen for which I did the sign-writing on a lifebelt, and which for me sums up living here: *Quod petis hic est* – "Whatever you seek is here".'

Bits of this road are memory-filled for me. West Cork is a series of cheerful workaday market towns separated into gossipy groups. The cars have changed from Opel Kadetts, Toyota Coronas and Nissan Sunnies to Land Cruisers, glass-tinted Range Rovers, Freelanders and 'Castletownshend tractors' (the Irish version of the Chelsea variety). A latticework of flowering hedges sprout

Preserved phone box, Castletownshend, County Cork.

honeysuckle, marsh thistle, upright hedge parsley and purple
loosestrife with elegant colonies of oxeye daisies. Many years ago
hedges had offered me protection and shelter, singing to me in
high winds. I recall, in this area, long hours spent standing by
the roadside watching the insect life around the oxeyes. They are
the plant of John the Baptist, whose feast day of midsummer, 24
June, is well passed. In some places the oxeye is still associated
with the thunder god as a 'thunder daisy'. Despite being flailed
by mowers, driven over by white vans, peed on by pit bulls and
lashed by sea storms, they are still in flower – a tall wayside
survivor, each with a golden-eye disc of tiny yellow florets surrounded by a ring of white.

On my way to Glandore, via Castletownshend-of-the-tractors, I am startled by the sight of a concrete *Telefón* box with timber green frames at the top of the sharply sloping main street. Even more startling is the fact that a woman has just emerged from it having made a phone call. It is my first sighting of such a use. Batt Maguire, of Batt's grocery shop, says people passing through the village are stunned when they see it.

'This one is still in good working order and we're very lucky to have it. About twenty years ago Telecom engineers wanted to replace it with a modern aluminium one and came to remove it. But a local man occupied it for a full day and saved it for us. He simply wore them down so they gave up and went away.'

Many summer day-trippers, as well as the sailing and boating fraternity, come to Castletownshend, swelling its population from 100 up to 800 in high season.

'We've been decimated by holiday homes here,' says Batt. 'Forty-three new houses were built during the boom but only five are lived in all year.'

The village is awash with history and promotes its famed literary connection to Edith Somerville, co-author of the *Irish RM* stories. Its buildings portray a unique fashion statement, but, according to Batt, when it comes to historic photogenic attractions, there is only one that matters.

'We have one of the steepest streets of any town in Ireland with a famous sycamore tree in the middle, a castle from the seventeenth century, a church that dates from 1827 with a Harry Clarke stained-glass window, we've quaint houses and a pretty harbour, but despite all that, the only thing that people want to photograph is this phone box. The locals have taken over ownership of it, and we have two community workers who paint it and keep it clean. We got a signwriter to recreate the correct lettering and recently a new door was installed. We look after it well because it's an important part of our architectural heritage that would have disappeared. We don't know for how long, though, because they might come and take the electronics out of it some time. But if I had a euro for every photograph taken …'

A series of S-bends rolls down into Union Hall where I have come to look for a wave. Known by the name of Clíona, it was one of the three great waves of Ireland, according to the ancient Irish topographical system. Legend has it that Clíona was one of the three daughters of Manannán's chief druid, Gebann. Also known as the 'Queen of the Munster Fairies', she fell in love with Ciabhán and he took her back in his currach to Ireland where they landed at Glandore Harbour. One afternoon, he went inland to hunt for deer and as she lay sleeping on the cliffs of Glandore, the sea rose. A huge wave overcame her and swept her away from her lover for ever. Depending on which story you believe, the wave either drowned her or returned her to Manannán's kingdom – or, in a third theory, she was lulled to sleep by the musician Iuchna. Ever since, it is said, she can be heard mourning her lost love in the special wave which echoes and cries through the sea cliffs here.

From the terrace of Shearwater B&B on an elevated site overlooking the harbour, not even a wavelet is in sight in serene Glandore Harbour. The fishing fleet has been out at sea for several days. The only ripple on the phlegmatic surface is caused by the narrow band of a speedboat's wake as the pilot follows the sailing instructions of 'avoiding Adam and hugging Eve', two small islands marking the entry into the harbour. The villages of Union Hall and Glandore eye each other on opposite sides connected by the single-lane steel structure of Poll Gorm Bridge. At the beach children enjoy the last of the summer holidays, digging holes in the sand, while four girls paddle in the shallows. A grey heron lifts off, quickly followed by its partner. Gulls sniffing the air on the harbour wall, hoping for mullet and sprat, seem less aggressive than their Kerry counterparts until a sudden flapping breaks out and they disperse. Shrouded in the distance, hillside haciendas, swanky split-level houses and ivy-clad stone mansions are partly visible through tree cover.

The woman running the Union Hall Coffee Shop, where luxurious florentines are an afternoon delight, contacts her father, Jim, whom she says may be able to help me. Jim Kennedy runs Atlantic Sea Kayaking and is well used to making his own waves. An energetic instructor, he is a former Irish rowing champion and has several times been both an Irish and British kayak champion. He supplies me with a concise CV.

'I won the world's longest non-stop marathon of a hundred and twenty-six miles. After that I worked in music for ten years. Then I retired and came down to west Cork. I now teach around the world and run tours with my wife. I am known as the old man of the sea kayaking world. Steinbeck and Hemingway are my heroes.'

In one of Jim's roles, he is an ambassador for the Way, which he believes has helped focus on people and communities right along the coast.

'It really is an eye-opener for Ireland. Last year we hosted the World Adventure Summit, which was a great thing. I think it's fantastic for the country and has been a great marketing ploy for the west.'

Jim is well versed on the subject of Clíona and her wave, accompanied by its eerie sound, and on the connection to Manannán. Along this coastline of sheltered bays and inlets, seals, dolphins, basking sharks and whales are all found, but in the midst of it, the famed wave is still remembered in the area as 'Tonn Clíodhna'.

'I am aware of Clíona's wave, especially from the older people because they are the ones who are into the romance of it, so it is often mentioned. But what we call the wave here is the tide, the easterly wind. It happens here and it happens on oceans all over the world. If you revert back to the seventeenth century, all the beaches were the result of an earthquake in Portugal that caused a tsunami and hit the southern coast of Ireland. The tsunami deposited vast amounts of sand and shale and many people were washed off islands. We are well used to waves of more than thirty feet in this area. In February last year they reached more than a hundred feet and sometimes you can even be talking about waves of up to a hundred and seventy feet. So, although it might look calm here today, that sea can be treacherous. As regards the eerie noise that you mention, I can say with certainty that that is caused by the seals on the rocks. When the wave is there and when the wind is onshore, that's when you hear the seals.'

The fragrance of newly mown hay is a pleasant aroma on my scenic estuary route to Kinsale through the dark green-and-gold farmland that folds around the bays of Rosscarbery and Clonakilty. C103, 'the station that loves Cork', is playing Rod Stewart, Elton John, Stevie Wonder and Joan Armatrading. At regular intervals tractors towing balers trundle along the crest of stripy hills, over and over, repeating the action in a display of precision manoeuvring. Herds of up to 100 well-fed black-and-white heifers chew ruminatively.

In the bird world, although autumn has arrived and many songsters have stopped singing, I had heard that White's Marsh would yield some avian spectacles. When I stop there, many wading birds are roosting in the early evening high tide while others feed hungrily. Excitable redshank, with their bright orange legs, pick insects from the surface of the water. Known for their vigilance as the 'watchdog of the marshes', they raise the alarm when sensing a threat. Beside them elegant greenshank, their heads and breasts heavily streaked, lunge at prey with their upcurved bill. They repeat their *teu-teu-teu* call before hopping on to the soft, muddy margins for an extended poke around. The marsh is a mix of freshwater and saltwater. Co-habiting amicably beside the shanks are dunlin, lapwing, and what I mistake at first for a TBD (tiny black dot) which, when I refocus my glasses, turns out to be a solitary moorhen in distinctive black plumage. Cocking its tail and with a jerk of its head, it struggles with a tangle of aquatic plants. Suddenly, into this marshy jumble of waders I catch sight of a snipe, then a second one, their extraordinary long bills digging into the water for worms or insects. I had only ever

West Cork signpost.

seen fleeting glimpses of a wisp of them catapulting away when flushed from the undergrowth in hill country. Now the yellow stripe on their mottled brown back shines like gold. At the far side of the marsh, spread open like freshly washed handkerchiefs, a dozen or more white egrets roost in trees.

A few miles away at Inchydoney beach the air is still. The surfers, swimmers and dog walkers have left. On stone walls I come across a strange connection to a sea god – although not the one that has absorbed me on my journey. Sea ivory, which favours rocky shores, spreads over a wall near the beach in a brittle grey-green crinkly lichen and is known as Neptune's beard. I swing north to Timoleague where lesser black-backed gulls fill a section of the mudflats of the estuary of Courtmacsherry Bay where it meets the Argideen River. The highlight is a prayer of two dozen black-tailed godwits probing in their summer plumage at the water's edge. Glinting in a pool of colour in the evening sunlight, they pick worms and search for midge larvae, indulging in a short-lived bill swordfight. Their striking chequerwork black-and-white rump and tail contrast with their huddled chestnut heads. On an apparent whim, with grace and speed, they rise vertically. In a dramatic display flight, their *kruu-wit-tsew* song competes with the noise from the funfair chair-o-planes, part of the harvest festival on the other side of the bridge.

As darkness closes in, I move to a quieter section of the estuary. All along this coast I have eavesdropped in cafés and pubs; now it is the turn of the night-time gossipmongers. The last slither of dusky twilight slips away as I relax into the velvet-dark soundscape of the west Cork earth creaking a chorus of crackles, chirps and tiny whistles. The movers and night-shakers are out. Bush crickets, grasshoppers and unseen birds busily communicate through the cool air. From a distance, a curlew rolls out a *cour-lee* call. Soft clucking sounds, and, from foliage, weird thin squeaks like those of a mouse add to the sound effects amplified by darkness. An owl hoots. For an hour the rich drama of clicks and buzzes plays on. A calm consumes the place, draping a veil over an evening of companionable tranquillity. My searches for traces of Manannán and the sounds accompanying Clíona's wave may have proved fruitless, but in this small enclave, I have discovered an 'Otherworld' with its own fly-by-night creatures.

It is late when I reach Kinsale and the San Antonio guesthouse, owned by Jimmie Conron. With part of it dating from the 1790s, it ranks as one of the oldest houses I have stayed in. After the breakfast rush is out of the way, Jimmie shows me around the rooms, which retain original period features such as cornices, ceiling roses and fireplaces. The elegant mantelpiece in the front lounge came from his father and, since it is from the 1750s, it is even older than the house. Jimmie speaks about the developments since my last visit to Kinsale in 1991 when I wrote about the hanging baskets and flora that still bedeck the streets.

'It's a tourist town as it was then and still is but every place has been upgraded since. The centre has been cleaned up of dilapidated buildings although there are a couple in the main street but I suppose it was a simpler time then as it was pre-boom. I remember 1991 primarily because it was the Rugby World Cup which was hosted by the Five Nations. There was a fever that took over the country with Ireland playing Australia at Lansdowne Road and nearly winning. In terms of housing, the main developments have been on the outskirts of town, especially up Compass Hill.'

Jimmie says that the town has always had a colourful blend of people, which can be traced back to the 1960s.

'Kinsale always had a great mix of people. It was a relaxed place when the hippies came in those days and I remember one bunch who cleaned up the Charles Fort, which had just been designated a national monument. So everything was good until another bunch of hippies came along and left it in a bit of a mess. Aside from the natural harbour, the fort is the biggest feature of Kinsale.

'There's a good group of people that I know going back years and I suppose you look at it a little bit through slightly jaundiced eyes because you are always trying to promote the place. We enjoy the pubs but it's mainly the people at the end of the day. And the older people are great – all the time that I've been here it has been like that. The majority are not judgemental – they'll live and let live. But don't forget when you consider that it's three hundred years before you're regarded as part of what we might term "old Kinsale", then I don't have that pedigree so I don't qualify.'

The population of Kinsale, at around 3,500, may not have grown much since 1991, but it swells to more than 9,000 in summer when it is thronged with myriad nationalities. Curious to find out about the history of World's End, I stroll around the tight streets and alleyways, looking into bookshops for information and cafés for inspiration. Evidence of its historic and architectural past is all around. Pavements are crammed with tourists clutching tablets while a group of fifty join a history walking tour. The coffee revolution has, of course, come to Kinsale. As if by osmosis, I am drawn into the Little Owl Café, tickled by their chalkboard challenge:

> No Hipsters
> Don't be coming in here
> With your hairy faces
> Your vegan diets
> Your tiny feet and your
> Sawdust bedding – no, wait
> Hamsters. No Hamsters

The owner, Karen Garvin, used to run a health food shop and despised coffee until she opened her café. Now she takes the new age of coffee seriously and has unlocked her inner barista. Their ethically sourced Santa Isabel blend, which has been produced for more than 100 years, is an important medium roast from Guatemala, without the use of pesticides, herbicides and fertilisers.

'It's one hundred per cent Arabica and grows at a higher altitude so it is pure and cleaner, and the roast-masters have put a lot of craft and skill into it,' Karen says. 'We also use Colombian and Rwandan coffee. It was roasted by hand in small batches five days ago and the suppliers only sell to a few places. I stopped drinking coffee for years, but ironically, all four staff here, who didn't drink it either, now do so and we allow ourselves one a day.'

Karen has perfected the art of brewing and grinds the coffee to order. My latte packs a satisfying caffeinated punch. She is now aware of the health benefits of coffee in moderation, which can help reduce the risk of certain diseases.

'Many people have stress in their lives and we were dealing with a lot of the side-effects of that. From a nutritional aspect we told people to reduce their coffee intake because of chemical reaction to it but you can still enjoy that beautiful taste of it without the excess.'

A visit to the library a few doors away yields slim pickings. The librarian is not from Kinsale and has no knowledge of World's End, other than that she once heard that the people who live there are known for dropping their aitches in their speech. One reference I find suggests the name came from Viking longship men who wintered in Kinsale. A 1740s map in a local history book shows the early development of the town and its walls. It pinpoints the location of World's End Gate at one end of Main Street beside the Municipal Hall. It was one of a number of metal gates embedded into the walls that enclosed the town; the others were Water Gate, Friars' Gate, Blind Gate and Cork Gate. Beyond World's End Gate lay the harbour and boats, and, I guess, what was then thought to be the end of the known world.

Nothing beats on-the-ground probing, so I head off along the Pier Road, passing a replica Kinsale hooker erected as a memorial to lost seafarers, and the Spanish Galleon mainmast, both attracting photo opportunists. The mast was erected in 2001 to commemorate the 400th anniversary of the Battle of Kinsale when English troops defeated a mixed Irish/Spanish force. More than fifty flashy yachts, halyards clinking, create a forest of white masts in their marina berths. I am intrigued by the name of one vessel, *Enbarr*, the very same moniker of Manannán's horse that so defiantly rode the waves. At Pier Head, just past the Trident Hotel, a large building called World's End House signifies that I have reached the topographical extremity. A First World War memorial, hidden in an entryway, stands beside an old wall, its

THIS PUMP WAS ERECTED BY
VOLUNTARY SUBSCRIPTION
FOR THE USE OF THE GENERAL PUBLIC
IN MEMORY OF THE GALLANT MEN
OF KINSALE AND DISTRICT
WHO FELL IN THE GREAT WAR
1914 — 1919.

First World War memorial, Kinsale, County Cork.

crevices sprouting tufts of shiny wall-rue fern. The memorial commemorates the men of Kinsale who fell in the war and strangely the inscription adds a year to the accepted end date: '1914–1919'.

I leave the traffic behind and walk uphill where the road leads to a cul-de-sac. It passes St John's Terrace, a curved row of pebbledashed houses known as Ferryview Cottages, dating from 1907, with weather-beaten front doors of blue, yellow and terracotta. Weeds shoot up from chimneys' brickwork, and satellite dishes are clamped to roofs. Windows display model ships in bottles or on stands, mirroring the residents' maritime connection. A snarling Alsatian strains fiercely on a tether behind a locked gate. Large bushes of out-of-control lilac buddleia, fuchsia, and masses of red valerian flourish on the wall; a giant beech obscures views of the harbour. There is a raffish air to the place. Several rusted and mouldering cars look as though their engines have not spluttered since well before 1991, although the soft tyres still have a serviceable tread. Two men in vests, arms tattooed with snakes from shoulder to elbow, lead fawn boxers hunting for smells. As I pause to admire the valerian – more ruby than red – an angular figure emerges from one of the cottages to place newspapers into his recycling bin.

Tommy Collins, unshaven and with a mouth of few teeth, has lived in World's End all his life but is uncertain about its toponymic history.

'It was always called World's End,' he says. 'I dunno how it came about but these cottages were built out of saltwater. They useta bring it up here in barrels from down the slip, so my father told me.'

A retired herring fisherman, Tommy, who was born in 1940, at one time operated a ferry across the harbour.

'It was a small rowing boat and in the 1960s I took people over yonder and charged them the grand sum of twopence one way and fourpence return, so I made a few bob out of it. I could take up to six people across and locals liked it. But it wasn't easy as I had to learn to work with the tides especially after two or three days' rain. Y'see the bridge was seven miles up the river. Sunday was a busy day with people going to Mass, but then people got cars and the ferry stopped.'

Over the years members of Tommy's family and his friends left to work abroad. He remained true to the place of his birth, staying in Kinsale all his life. He recalls some tough times.

Fishermen's cottages at World's End, Kinsale, County Cork.

'I shovelled coal in the dockyard and, for three lorries with eight ton of coal, I would get twenty-one shillings. I've done everything for a living but people in this town gets no t'anks at all. Kinsale has changed a vast amount. If I went up the town, I can tell you this now, if I met six locals that I knew I'd get a prize. I told a few Yanks that the streets are so narrow you could shake hands across the road. But we can all keep out of each other's way if we want. Kinsale is run by people who have come in from outside and taken over the place and they dictate to others and I 'ate people doing that.'

Tommy's happiest memories are of growing up in a small town in the 1940s in the pre-television days before tourism. It was a time when everyone knew each other and talked to their neighbours.

'When I look down 'ere at all these new 'ouses, I don't know who they are. But when I was a kid I knew 'em all. We useta run around Joaney's garden, as we called it. I played around 'ere as a boy and ran up these two little 'ills. When we were at school we useta get an awful ribbing 'cos we useta talk different as we didn't pronounce our aitches which the monks did not like and they were always dictating to us too. Some people'd talk about the 'tree trees' in one area, dropping the aitch. The monks useta make up sentences with the letter aitch in it and they'd make us say them to try to get us to pronounce our aitches. One of them was: The women in their 'igh 'eels walkin' up de 'ill. We useta add: we 'ate those 'orrible women who walk up de 'ill.'

Back in town, the restaurants are cooking up a gastronomic Saturday-night storm. Blackboards chalk up 'just-landed' evening specials and by 8 p.m. the streets are laced with fishy and garlicky aromas, while tandoori and balti mix with Italian and Thai cuisine. A staggering array of fishy entrées dominates menus. I muse over how Irish culinary sophistication has changed. In 1991, salads were called just that; now they are 'power' salads accompanied by a 'bouquet garni' of bay leaves and a vast amount of rabbit food. A generation ago the choice (after a starter of orange juice with a paper doily) was breadcrumbs-on-sea with cod or haddock dripping in batter. If the chef was feeling adventurous, scampi could be rustled up. Chilli was used as an adjective before becoming a noun in the cooking pot. The popular roast carvery, known to some as 'lamplight' food, was served up by bearded, white-coated chefs brandishing huge knives like machetes.

With the end of my journey in sight, I choose the Lemon Leaf Café for a last supper, comprising Wild Atlantic Way cod fillet burger and Cute Hoor lager from a Cork brewery.

After dinner, the vapour of e-cigarettes, the new rage, mingles with old-fashioned smoke rings from Player's Navy Cut medium at the doorways of pubs. For all its touristic side, it is not hard to see why Kinsale, with its tight tangle of laneways, steep flights of stone staircases, historic terraces, and bow-fronted windows, has such an irresistible pull, especially for the hanging-basket brigade. The floral virus was equally as strong a quarter of a century ago and sees no sign of letting up. Most west Cork towns have now succumbed to it, leading to what one newspaper commentator refers to as 'Clonakilty Disease'. But it is not just dense thickets of window boxes and baskets: Kinsale appears to be overrun by different types of bars: nail bar, wax bar, health and beauty bar, artisan tapas bars, noodle bars and wine bars. While there is no shortage of pubs – twenty-five at the last count – the traditional music is geared to tourists who desire nothing more demanding than the chance to sing along to 'The Wild Rover' or 'Black Velvet Band'.

I ask around for some guidance and am advised by 'in the know' locals to try the Spaniard, a historic bar a kilometre or two out of town towards Summer Cove, on the bend of a hill. When I turn the corner, I am confronted by twenty rowdy 'hens' in black dresses sitting at outside tables holding pink balloons and flaunting 'L' plate stickers. My heart sinks. So much for advice from knowledgeable locals. I have second thoughts about entering but when I hear taxis being ordered to take the hens back into town, I reckon the bar should be 'poultry' free.

A three-man band, For Folk Sake, on guitar, box and mandolin, entertains a crowd of no more than twelve, half of whom are watching rugby highlights on television. They are midway through a set of classics: 'Living on your Western Shore', 'A Man of Constant Sorrow', and the song of 1798 – 'Boolavogue'. The Spaniard, which dates from 1703, is a spit-and-sawdust bar, now minus the spit. Loose chippings sprinkled over the slate floor prevent accidents. One of the drinkers tells me that when two Americans recently visited the bar, they were told that the chippings were the remains of a furniture fight from the previous night; they hurriedly drank up and left.

Another round of tunes comprises 'Dance a Set for Me and Claire', 'The Ashplant', 'The Mountain Road', and 'The Floating

Crowbar'. The crowd, now swollen to fifteen, joins in for 'The Captains and the Kings' and a recently written song, 'The Old Head of Kinsale', about a controversy over restricting access to golfers and guests at the Old Head. The development triggered a bitter campaign to preserve public access to the headland by a group known as 'Free the Old Head of Kinsale'. It took the form of what were called 'incursions' by locals holding 'People's Picnics' at the Old Head. Hillwalkers and environmentalists staged protests at the site in a crusade that ended up at the Supreme Court.

A series of polkas, the reel 'Madame Bonaparte', named after Bonaparte's wife, the Empress Josephine, and 'The Gravel Walls' draws the music to a close. Before he finishes, Gerry, the box player, is asked for a request.

'Could you play "The Engineer"? 'Tis a well-known song.'

Gerry replies that he is not aware of it but the man insists on its popularity throughout the country. Gerry repeats that he does not know any song of that title and asks the man to sing a line or two from it, to which he immediately obliges: 'And now, the end-ish near …'

My journey's end is indeed near and the summer is over. It is almost a year since I set off to travel around north Donegal at the start of my odyssey last autumn; now the Cork trees are raining leaves. For several thousand kilometres the sea has been on my right-hand side. Long ago, with so many detours and diversions, I lost track of my mileage, but reckon it has topped 6,000 kilometres. My trip has seen some of the warmest, driest and wettest days on record, indicative of the extreme weather experienced throughout Europe. Frequently the rains came down in heavy torrents, playing havoc with outdoor events and leading for the first time in living memory to the cancellation of the annual Croagh Patrick pilgrimage walk on the last Sunday in July. Blame for the diabolical weather has been pinned on the jet stream where cold air from the north clashes with warm air from the south, and a ribbon of high-altitude wind stirs up

End of the Way sign outside Kinsale.

Atlantic depressions across the ocean. The only benefit has been the amount of energy generated by the western wind turbines, which have been working overtime.

All along the coast, I have followed *Mare Atlanticus*, the Great West Sea, watching it thrashing, thundering and roaring, and on tranquil days, witnessing its easy-going currents and tides. Whether from the perspective of a wide beach, headland or tombolo, at the foot of craggy cliffs, from the end of a peninsula or promontory, the experience has ranged from the architectural wizardry of foaming chaos to a composed, even-tempered sea.

Many words sum it up: inscrutable, unpredictable, incomprehensible, immutable, mystifying, salubrious, rejuvenating and, on certain days, imperturbable.

From the comforting embrace of convivial cafés, the sea's frenzy never felt violent. T. S. Eliot said he measured out his life in coffee spoons. Ireland's coastal cafes, where many an hour was spent stirring those spoons, are now places for the mass medication of the population. People are not just addicted to caffeine, they worship it; coffee-fuelled shopping, I discovered, is holding streets of entire towns together and has become the new community focus.

Leaves are fading from green to pale yellow, signalling the departure of summer and my departure from Kinsale. A mile out of town, the final wavy blue-and-white Wild Atlantic Way sign with the word 'End' is shot through with a diagonal red line. On Lyric FM, a favourite piece of music, the divine terzettino, or trio, 'Soave sia il vento' from Mozart's *Così fan tutte* leads me to ponder my year of travel as I contemplate the relevance of the aria's words: 'On your voyage, may the winds be gentle; may the waves be calm.' Three minutes of musical magic signify a deep truth. They sum up the ocean that has been an eternal presence, and which, when its name is rolled slowly around a caffeine-coated tongue, represents a syllabic Power of Three in its hard and sonorous resonance: At-lan-tic.

Valediction
Letter to Manannán

UNCEREMONIOUSLY THEY DUMPED you in a forest, hardly a comfortable love bed for a powerful sea god. To witness a divine lord connected to the Tuatha Dé Danann lying face down was unseemly. For someone so well known who retreated into seclusion, you would have enjoyed being the centre of the newshounds' attention. I am sure you would be flabbergasted to learn that you have 21st-century cheerleaders fighting your corner. When the police euhemerised you by issuing an appeal for information on a missing person, it caused great mirth.

On my coastal journey you were a constant presence. As I stared into the ocean in all kinds of weathers, it occurred to me that you must have been acquainted not just with storms but with a variety of abundant marine life. You were said to be a prosperous farmer but the fish were your calves and lambs. Your otherworldly kingdom, the Land of Promise, was the Tír Tairngiri. Did you party in the palaces and halls of the Happy Otherworld? The sea holds many secrets – danger, threat and uncertainty; you knew the cliffs, bays, headlands, and islands better than anyone.

Food was important to you. Apart from dining at feasts, you owned, I discovered, birds, hounds and magical pigs that could be eaten one day but would be alive the next so they could be slaughtered and eaten again. You will be pleased to know that your spirit still roams the west. Those sparkling seahorses – *caiple Mhanannáin*, Manannán's horses in Irish folklore and a leitmotif on my journey – are widespread. The sea was your domain, and you cut a dashing figure, a swashbuckling charioteer, reposing as you crossed the surface with your fleet-footed stallion Enbarr riding the Three Great Waves of Ireland: the Wave of Thoth, the Wave of Rury, and the long, slow, white-foaming Wave of Clíona.

The might, energy and symbolism of the Power of Three was familiar to you. Mythology bristles with triple imagery and rambling stories feature your dynamism. One depicts you finely clad and carrying on your shoulder a branch with three golden apples. It is said the apples touched each other, making delightful music that would soothe to sleep the sick or wounded. Another tale claims you presented three great gifts to the nobles of the Tuatha. The first was the enchantment known as the *féth fiadha*, 'art of semblance', believed to be a cloak of concealment through which the nobles rendered themselves invisible. The second gift was the feast of Goibhniu, the celebration of which warded off age and death from their kings, and the third was 'the pigs of Manannán'.

As a multipurpose god, you crossed many boundaries, becoming both trickster and magician. Your tricks exemplified the mischievous, not to say cunning side of your nature. Your shape-shifting, like the Homeric Proteus, causes much interest, heightening your inscrutability.

There are innumerable colourful accounts of your life. Sometimes you had the persona of an old man in a grey cloak that changed colours; at other times you were riding and ruling the waves, borrowing iconography from Neptune. As a supernatural being, a sea trader and navigator, you could travel where you wished, appearing and disappearing at will. Countless different guises have produced a dramatis personae: rogue, charlatan, conniver, cunning opportunist, clown, beggar, wizard, celebrated merchant, mythical mariner, necromancer, mighty warlord and, rather unkindly, fake and imposter.

By all accounts, you enjoyed philandering and, if we are to believe the centuries-old gossip, had many wives and numerous affairs, not to mention a wide and complicated fan base. They must have scratched out each other's eyes to ride with you in your

chariot, to sit side by side with you and enjoy your enigmatic presence. You had many paramours, including Fand, a wife and deity of water, who was also the lover of Cúchulainn, to whom you once gave a visor to protect his face; Áine, the sun-goddess, became a fairy patroness of love; Caíntigern, with whom you had an affair and who was the mother of the hero Mongán. It is said your passion for the beautiful young Tuag, who was guarded by a company of women, was unrequited; and lest we forget, another wife of yours, Aífe, was transformed into a crane by a jealous rival Iuchra. Ménage à trois? Just speculating.

Your legendary crane bag – a veritable Aladdin's Cave – was one of your most important possessions, containing treasures of the Tuatha. After Aífe died, you used her skin to hoard things precious to you. Amongst these were a magical knife that could cut through stone, an invincible shield that no weapon could pierce, a shirt that protected you from weaponry, the King of Scotland's shears, a smith's hook, the King of Lochlainn's helmet, the bones of Assal's swine, and the girdle of the great whale's back. Whoever has these is said to be safe from all enemies. The bag has one further power: it holds the source of inspiration for all the poets of the land – these days perhaps 50,000 strong. Apart from your sword, which creates intrigue, you also had a war spear used for stirring up the raging ocean.

Your domination of the action of many stories fascinates me – how could you have travelled to so many places? It is surprising, for such a wanderer and god of action, that you have been immortalised standing still. Myths surround you; there are those who believe that mythology is history in disguise. Naturally in the best mythomaniac Celtic tradition, stories are embellished. By all accounts, you enjoyed your life on the ocean wave and now you live happily ever after in that land of Tir na nÓg. What, I frequently wonder, would you make of the Wild Atlantic Way and its ambassadors? A tourist gimmick, a money-grabbing exercise, exploitation of our heritage? You were the original ambassador.

I am sure you will not read this, so I do not expect that you will write back to me or answer me. Suffice to say, you live again; gods are immortal. You stand now as a triune figure of time:

Past, present, and future

Bibliography

Aldhouse-Green, M., *The Celtic Myths, A guide to the ancient gods and legends,* Thames & Hudson, 2015

Arnold, B., *Jack Yeats,* Yale University Press, 1998

Barrington, T. J., *Discovering Kerry, Its History, Heritage and Topography,* Blackwater Press, Dublin, 1976

Bourke, E. J., *Shipwrecks of the Irish Coast 1105–1993,* Dublin, 1994

Brooks, S., *Seahorses, Connemara and its Ponies,* Meredith Praed, 2006

Cabot, D., *Ireland,* Harper Collins, 1999

Chambers, A., *Granuaile, Grace O'Malley, Ireland's Pirate Queen,* Gill & Macmillan, 2014

Clements, P., *Irish Shores, A Journey Round the Rim of Ireland,* Greystone Books, 1993

— *The Height of Nonsense, The Ultimate Irish Road Trip,* The Collins Press, 2005

— *Burren Country, Travels through an Irish limestone landscape,* The Collins Press, 2011

Connolly, K., *Yeats and Sligo,* Brandon, 2010

Conroy, J., ed., *Connemara and Elsewhere,* Royal Irish Academy, 2014

Cooper, A., ed., *Lough Swilly, A living landscape,* Four Courts Press, 2011

Curran, B., *Complete Guide to Celtic Mythology,* Appletree Press, 2000

de Jubainville, H. d'Arbois, *Le cycle mythologique irlandais et la mytholgie celtique,* Paris, 1884, translated as *The Irish Mythological Cycle and Celtic Mythology,* Hodges, Figgis, 1903

Devaney, K., *The Drumcliffe Pilots,* Killynon House Books, 2009

Ellis, P. B., *Dictionary of Celtic Mythology,* Constable, 1992

Enright, D., *A Place Near Heaven, A Year in West Cork,* Gill & Macmillan, 2004

Feeley, T., *From Glack to Bunduff, A History of Kinlough Parish,* Original Writing, Dublin, 2013

Finucane, P. & A., *The Old Pier Union Hall,* Red Barn Publishing, Skibbereen, 2013

Fitzmaurice, G., ed., *The Kerry Anthology,* Marino, Dublin, 2000

Fitzpatrick, D., *Solitary and Wild, Frederick MacNeice and the Salvation of Ireland,* Lilliput Press, 2012

Galloway, I., *The Great Western Greenway,* Prospect, 2012

Gregory, A., *Lady Gregory's Complete Irish Mythology,* Bounty Books, 2012

Hayward, R., *In the Kingdom of Kerry,* Dundalgan Press, Dundalk, 1946

Healy, D., *A Fool's Errand,* Gallery Books, 2010

Heaney, M., *Over Nine Waves, A Book of Irish Legends,* Faber & Faber, 1994

Heather, A., *Errislannan,* Lilliput Press, 2002

Hopkin, A., *Eating Scenery,* The Collins Press, 2008

Houlihan, D., *Ballybunion, An Illustrated History,* History Press Ireland, 2011

Kavanagh, P. J., *Voices in Ireland, A Traveller's Literary Companion,* John Murray, 1994

Kinnafaela (T. C. McGinley), *The Cliff Scenery of South-Western Donegal,* Four Masters Press, Dublin, 2000

Lambert, J. & N., *Surf Café Living,* Orca Publications, 2014

Mac an Iomaire, S., *The Shores of Connemara,* Tir Eolas, 2000

McArdle, P., *The Irish Landscape: An All-Ireland Exploration through Science and Literature,* The Liffey Press, Dublin, 2015

MacCaig, N., *The Poems of Norman MacCaig,* Polygon, 2005

Mac Coitir, N., *Ireland's Birds, Myths, Legends and Folklore,* The Collins Press, 2015

McDonald, T., *Achill: 5000 BC to AD 1900 – Archaeology, History, Folklore,* Theresa McDonald, 1992

McGill, L., *In Conall's Footsteps,* Brandon, 1992

McGrath, B., *Landscape and Society in Contemporary Ireland,* Cork University Press, 2013

MacKillop, J., *Dictionary of Celtic Mythology,* Oxford University Press, 1998

— *Myths and Legends of the Celts,* Penguin, 2006

Mac Laughlin, J. & S. Beattie, eds, *An Historical, Environmental and Cultural Atlas of County Donegal,* Cork University Press, 2013

McMahon, S. & J. O'Donoghue, eds, *Brewer's Dictionary of Irish Phrase & Fable,* Weidenfeld & Nicolson, 2004

MacNeice, L., *Collected Poems,* Faber, 1979

Madigan, C., *Seasons, Species & Patterns of a North East Atlantic Rocky Shore,* Loop Head Summer Hedge School, 2014

— *The Wild Flowers of Loop Head,* Ennis, 2012

Maxwell, G., *Ring of Bright Water,* Penguin, 2001

Moriarty, J., *Nostos, An Autobiography,* Lilliput Press, 2001

— *Invoking Ireland,* Lilliput Press, 2005

Murphy, B. J., *County Kerry, 101 Interesting Facts,* Bloomhill Publishers, 2015

Nairn, R., *Ireland's Coastline, Exploring its Nature and Heritage*, The Collins Press, 2005

Nelson, C., *Wild Plants of Connemara and West Mayo*, Strawberry Tree, Dublin, 2001

Nelson, C. & W. Walsh, *The Burren: A companion to the wildflowers of an Irish limestone wilderness*, Boethius Press & the Conservancy of the Burren, 1991

Ó Cadhain, M., *Cré na Cille*, translated as *The Dirty Dust*, Yale University Press, 2015

Ó Crualaoich, G., *The Book of the Cailleach: Stories of the Wise-Woman Healer*, Cork University Press, 2003

O'Donoghue, R., *Heroic Landscapes, Irish Myth and Legend*, Londubh Books, 2011

Ó Dubhshláine, M., *Inisvickillane, A unique portrait of the Blasket island*, Brandon, 2009

Ó hÓgáin, D., *The Lore of Ireland, An Encyclopaedia of Myth, Legend and Romance*, The Collins Press, 2006

Pope Francis, *Laudato Si', On Care for our Common Home*, Veritas, Dublin, 2015

Praeger, R. L., *A Tourist's Flora of the West of Ireland*, Hodges, Figgis, 1909

— *The Way That I Went*, The Collins Press, 2014

Quinn, B., *The Atlantean Irish*, Lilliput Press, 2005

Robinson, T., *Connemara, Part 1: Introduction and Gazetteer*, Folding Landscapes, 1990

— *Connemara, The Last Pool of Darkness*, Penguin Ireland, 2008

— *Connemara, A Little Gaelic Kingdom*, Penguin Ireland, 2011

Simonds-Gooding, M., *A Retrospective*, Royal Hibernian Academy, Dublin, 2014

Stack, E., *Doolin, People, Place & Culture*, Tintaun, 2015

Stephens, J., *Insurrections*, Maunsel & Co., Dublin, 1909

The Three Best Things, An illustrated selection of Irish Triads, Appletree Press, 1993

Thomas, D., *The Collected Poems*, J. M. Dent & Sons, 1996

Thuillier, J. R., *History of Kinsale, A Field Study Approach*, 2006

— *Kinsale Harbour, A History*, The Collins Press, 2014

Tohill, J. J., *Donegal, An Exploration*, Portaferry, 1985

Uí Chonchubhair, M., *Flóra Chorca Dhuibhne, Aspects of the Flora of Corca Dhuibhne*, Oidhreacht Chorca Dhuibhne, 1995

Viney, M., *Wild Mayo*, Mayo County Council, 2009

Viney, M. & E., *Ireland's Ocean, A Natural History*, The Collins Press, 2008

Wall, E., *Writing the Irish West, Ecologies and Traditions*, University of Notre Dame Press, Indiana, 2011

Westropp, T.J., *Folklore of Clare*, Clasp Press, Ennis, 2003

Whilde, T., *The Natural History of Connemara*, Immel, 1994

Williams, G., *A Sea-grey House, The history of Renvyle house*, Renvyle House, 1995

Wilson, I., *Donegal Shipwrecks*, Impact, Coleraine, 1998

Winchester, S., *Atlantic, A Vast Ocean of a Million Stories*, Harper Press, 2010

Wyeth, A., *The Hidden World of Poetry, Unravelling Celtic Mythology in Contemporary Irish Poetry*, Salmon Poetry, 2013

Yeats, W. B., *The Poems*, Everyman's Library, 1992

Acknowledgements

I AM GRATEFUL TO ALL THE PEOPLE who helped me on my journey, provided transport and accommodation, or went out of their way to assist me. To those who gave generously of their time, agreed to be interviewed and are named in this book, I would like to express a collective thank-you. I wish to acknowledge the help of the following who guided me around, whether on foot, by boat, bike, on horseback or in the water: Peter Alexander, Michael Barry, Gretta Byrne, Seamas Caulfield, Paul Connaughton, Carmel Madigan, Geoff Magee, Eugene Maher, Kevin Naughton, Anne O'Carroll, John O'Donnell, J. J. O'Hara, Martin O'Malley, and Peter Williams.

With their inside knowledge, a triumvirate of Wild Atlantic Way ambassadors, Ronnie Counihan, Jim Kennedy and Auriel Robinson, provided additional advice and made useful suggestions. Many other people who supplied information, pointed me in the right direction, or facilitated meetings include Patricia Brennan, Stephanie Brooks, Emma Caffrey, Paddy Clarke, Edward Gaughan, Rosemarie Geraghty, Joe Grogan, Alannah Hopkin, Declan Mangan, Dennis Marshall, Darren McDermott, Eoghan Ó Curraighín, Irene O'Brien, Barry O'Kelly, Teresa O'Mahoney, Máire Ruain and Jacqui Uí Mhonacháin.

In tourism offices, heritage centres and museums, I drew on the invaluable local knowledge of staff, and thank Siobhán Kelly and Heidi Woods from Inishowen Tourism in Buncrana, Shane Smyth, Bundoran tourism officer, Rosemarie Mangan, tourism officer with Erris BEO, Tracy Kelly in Ballybunion tourist office, as well as staff in Fáilte Ireland offices in Letterkenny, Donegal town, Sligo, Westport, Clifden, Dingle and Kinsale. During on-location research I pored over the shelves of public libraries and owe thanks to the staff in Bundoran, Sligo, Clifden, Dingle and Kinsale who uncovered local history and heritage books or suggested contacts.

When I was cold and wet, many people poured coffee and tea into me, as well as stronger drinks and I wish to thank café owners, restaurateurs and publicans for their hospitality. Special appreciation is due to the following hoteliers and guesthouse owners who helped with accommodation: in Donegal, Michael Doherty at the Seaview Tavern, Ballygorman, Lorna Long at Rathmullan House, Mairead McClafferty at the Beach Hotel, Downings, John Yates at Woodhill House, Ardara, Marian Gaffney at the Bayview Hotel, Killybegs, and Audrey McEniff at the Holyrood Hotel, Bundoran; in Leitrim, Linda Brunetti at the Atlantic Seafront guesthouse, and J. J. O'Hara at Castle View B&B; in Sligo, staff of the Pier Head Hotel, Mullaghmore, the Clarion Hotel, Sligo town, and Waterfront House at Enniscrone; in Mayo, David Tyrrell at Broadhaven Bay Hotel, Belmullet, John and Elizabeth Barrett at the Bervie guesthouse, Achill Island, staff at the Hotel Newport, and Suzanne O'Brien at Knockranny House Hotel, Westport; in Galway, staff at Renvyle House Hotel, Lynn Hill at Anglers' Return, Toombeola, and Geraldine Linnane at Breacan Cottage, Doorus; in Clare, Declan O'Callaghan at Ballinalacken Castle Country House Hotel, Martina Sheedy at Sheedy's Country House Hotel, Lisdoonvarna, Kate Sweeney and Aidan McGrath at the Wild Honey Inn, Lisdoonvarna, Johnny Redmond, Strand Hotel, Kilkee; in Limerick, Elaina Fitzgerald Kane at the Fitzgeralds Woodlands House Hotel, Adare; in Kerry, Paula and Louise Huggard at the Butler Arms Hotel in Waterville, and Aoife Hickey at the Lake Hotel, Killarney; in Cork, Mona Best, Bridge House, Skibbereen, and Jimmie Conron at San Antonio in Kinsale.

I am immensely grateful to the team at The Collins Press. I am especially indebted to my agent Jonathan Williams for his sound advice and valuable comments, as well as meticulous proofreading.

I would like to thank the authors and poets from whose books I have quoted extracts. Every effort has been made to trace and contact copyright holders; any errors or omissions will be rectified at the earliest opportunity. Special thanks to Biddy Hughes of the marketing department of Westport House for the use of the photograph of the statue of Grace O'Malley; and to Clare Quinn, tourism development officer of the Causeway Coast and Glens Borough Council, for kindly supplying images of the statue of Manannán mac Lir.

The Arts Council of Northern Ireland provided generous funding under the Support for the Individual Artists Programme (SIAP) through its General Art Award Scheme and I am grateful for this. Their grant helped subsidise part of my trip and bought valuable time to complete the writing, editing, proofreading and indexing of the book. I wish to acknowledge in particular the encouragement of Damian Smyth, Head of Literature and Drama at the Arts Council.

Most of all, I would like to thank my wife Felicity and son Daniel who supported my wanderings along Ireland's Wild Atlantic Way which took me away from home on many western trips.

Index

Achill Island, 134–42, 147, 149
Achill Sound, 142, 147
Afternoon Club, 47–50, 299
Aghleam, 127–8
Alexander, Peter, 30–3
Allihies, 291–3
Allihies Copper Mine Museum, 292
Anascaul, 255
Anchor Tavern, 294–6
An Droithean Donn Bar, 188–90
Anglers' Return, 178–81
Antrim County, xi, 75
Aran Islands, 173, 183, 186–7, 190–1, 204, 213
Ardara, 27, 29, 33
Austies Bar, 76–80

Balfour, Arthur J., 282
Ballina, 107–9, 132
Ballinalacken, 204, 208
Ballybunion, 216, 232, 241–3
Ballycastle, 111–15
Ballyconneely, 170–1, 179
Ballycrovane, 287
Ballydehob, 296
Ballydonegan, 292–3
Ballygorman, 5
Ballyheigue, 241, 243
Ballyhillin, 8–10
Ballymastocker Bay, 17
Ballynahinch Castle, 179
Ballysadare, 94, 205
Ballyshannon, 10, 40–1, 43

Ballyvaughan, 200
Banba, 5, 89
Banba's Crown, 3, 5, 294
Bantry, 294–5
Barrett, John, 135–7, 141
Barry's Bar, 70–2
Bealbarnish Gap, 293
Beara Peninsula, 286–7, 290, 294
Begley, Seamus, 247–8
Belderg, 117, 119–21
Belfast, 33, 135, 158
Belmullet, 121–7, 132, 183
Ben Bulben, 69–70
Bervie guesthouse, 134–7, 140
Best, Mona, 298–9
Binevenagh Mountain, xi, 103
Black Head, 203
Blacksod Bay, 126–8, 130–1, 141
Blacksod Point Lighthouse, 132
Blasket Islands, 262–3
Blasket Sound, 262
Bloody Foreland, 27
Böll, Heinrich, 140
Bourke, Imelda, 219–20
Brandon Bay, 245–6
Brandon Mountain, 245–6
Broadhaven Bay, 126
Browne, Cheryl Cobern, 143–6
Browne, Jeremy (Earl of Altamont), 155
Browne, Lady Sheelyn, 151–7
Budd, Jamie, 296–7
Buncrana, 12, 21
Bundoran, 41–2, 44–50, 52, 299

Burns, May, 64–8
Burren, The, 191, 194, 200–4
Burren Way, 200–4
Byrne, Gretta, 117–18

Cahersiveen, 261, 269, 276–8, 281
Canada, coast of, 78, 229
Candlemas Day, 43–4, 50
Carndonagh, 10–11
Carrigart, 21, 24
Castlebar, 148, 158–9
Castlederg, 236
Castlegregory, 243–4, 246, 268
Castletownshend, 302–4
Catholic Church, 265–7, 283
Caulfield, Professor Seamus, 117,
    119–21
Céide Fields, 116–19
Chaplin, Charlie, 281–2, 284
Children of Lir, 88, 126–7, 220
Claddaghduff, 162
Clare County, 200–1, 203, 211,
    214, 219, 221, 227, 229,
    233–4, 236, 241
Clarke Harry, 264–5, 304
Clarke, Paddy, 35
Cleggan Peninsula, 161–2, 167
Clew Bay, 142, 146
Clifden, 160–2, 166, 170, 174–7,
    179
Cliffs of Dooneen, 232
Cliffs of Moher, 97, 204, 213–15,
    217, 236
climate change, 84–5, 265–6
Clíona's wave, 305–7, 309, 322
Clonakilty, 307–8, 317
coastal erosion, 84–5, 136–7, 166,
    174, 230, 232
coastal litter, 9, 64–8, 171–2, 302
coffee culture, 11–12, 15, 25–6,
    28, 35, 45–6, 91–3, 98–9, 107,

    114–15, 147, 150–1, 160, 186,
    215, 219–20, 238, 242, 253–4,
    276–8, 296–7, 311–12, 320
Coffey, Ella, 261–2
Collins, Michael, 37, 223
Collins, Tommy, 314–16
Commissioners of Irish Lights, 19
Coney Island, 76
Connacht Tribune, 181–2, 189
Connemara, 127, 160, 168, 170–1,
    174–82, 185–6, 188–91, 198,
    201, 203, 206, 216, 231
Connemara Gaeltacht, 181–2,
    185, 188–90
Connor, Breege, 48–50
Conor Pass, 246–7
Conron, Jimmie, 309–10
Coolera Peninsula, 91
Coomakista Pass, 284
Coomanaspic Pass, 280
Cooper, Michael, 153, 156
Cork city, 297, 300
Cork County, 3, 7, 41, 84, 218,
    285–7, 289, 293–4, 297, 300–
    3, 307–9, 312–13, 315–18
Corraun Peninsula, 141
Counihan, Ronnie, 169–70
Courthouse Bar, 247–8
Courtmacsherry Bay, 308–9
Coyne's Bar, 182–3
Crean, Tom, 255, 257–8
Croagh Patrick, 149–50, 157, 318
Cross Lough, 128
Curtin, Peter, 206–9

Dartry Mountains, 44, 57
de Cuellar, Francisco, Capt., 75, 77
Derry city, 5, 21
Derry County, xi
deserted village, Achill Island,
    138–40

de Valera, Éamon, 37
Devaney, Kieran, 77–80
Dicey Reilly's Bar, 41–3
Dingle, 244–5, 247–9, 252–6, 258, 260, 263–4, 267
Dingle Peninsula, 243–5, 258–9, 262–4, 279
Díseart Centre of Irish Spirituality and Culture, 264–5
Disney, Walt, 258, 282
Doherty, Michael, 5, 7–8
dolphin-watching, 171, 231–3, 293–4
Donegal Brewing Company, 42
Donegal County, 3–4, 6–8, 10–15, 18, 20–2, 24–31, 34–7, 40–4, 46–7, 49–50, 52, 58, 60–1, 108, 234, 299, 318
Donegal Democrat, 29
Donegal Gaeltacht, 30, 34
Donegal Post, 41
Donegal town, 28, 40
Dooks, 261
Doolin, 204–5, 211–14
Doolin Folk Festival, 205–6
Doo Lough, 157
Doorus Peninsula, 196
Downings, 21–4
Downpatrick Head, 115–16
Drowes Salmon Fishery, 60–3
Dublin, 3, 42, 77, 80, 92, 119, 135, 152, 164–5, 189, 194, 213, 236, 249, 260, 273, 283
Dunfanaghy, 5, 25–6
Dungloe, 28–9
Dunne, John, 175–7
Dunquin, 259–60, 262–3

Easkey, 94–6, 98–9
Egginton, Frank, 179–80
Elly Bay, 128

emigration from Ireland, 18, 130–2
Ennis, 222, 236
Enniscrone, 99–103
Erris Head, 128, 132–3
Erris Peninsula, 119, 121–2, 124–5, 130, 133
Errisbeg, 178

Fáilte Ireland, 14, 35, 52, 67, 77, 108
Falvey, Declan, 271–3
Falvey's Bar, 271–4
Fanad Head, 18–20
Fanad Peninsula, 14, 17–20
Fenit, 127, 279
fishing industry, 37–40, 193–6, 249–52
Flannery, Kevin, 248–52
Flight of the Earls, 16
Foxy John's Bar, 257–8
Foynes, 235
Foynes Flying Boat and Maritime Museum, 235–8
French, Percy, 219, 223
Fungie, 249, 252–3, 255

Gaeltacht Fhánada, 19
Gallagher, Pat, 38–40
Gallagher, Rory, 43
Gallagher, Shane, 60–3
Galway Bay, 185, 187, 193–5, 203
Galway city, 174, 192–5
Galway County, 30, 158, 161, 163, 169–71, 186, 191–3, 196, 236
Galway hookers, 175, 188, 198
Garrihy, Joe, 213–14
Garvin, Karen, 311–12
Glandore, 304–5
Glencolmcille, 30, 49
Glen Lough, 30–2

Glinsk, 181–2
global warming, 174, 265–7
Gogarty, Oliver St John, 168
Gooreenatinny, 162, 165
Grange, 69–70
Grant, Peter, 158
Great Western Greenway, 141–3,
    146–50
Grigson, Geoffrey, 32–3
Guevara, Ché, 220–3

Hag of Beara, 287–91
Hargadon's Bar, 81–4
Harry Blaney Bridge, 20, 23
Haughey, Charles, 255–6
Healy, Dermot, 69
Heaney, Seamus, 120
Heffernan, Anthony, 107
Henry, Grace and Paul, 134–6,
    138
Hill, Lynn, 178–81
Horn Head, 26–7
Houlihan, Danny, 241
Huggard, Paula, 281–3
Hy Brasil, 216

Inch Levels, 13–14
Inishbofin, 162, 166, 174
Inishglora, 126–7
Inishkea Islands, 126
Inishowen Peninsula, xi–xiii, 3–5,
    7, 13–14
Inishtrahull, xi, 5–6, 8, 18
Inisiciléan, 262
Irish civil war, 168
Irish coffee, 235–8
Irish Famine, 55, 108, 131, 139,
    143, 157, 165, 204, 230
Irish Times, The, 121, 179
Irish War of Independence, 34, 55
Iveragh Peninsula, 276, 278

Keel, 134–5, 138
Keem Bay, 138
Kelly, Diarmuid, 193–6
Kenmare, 284, 286
Kennedy, Jim, 306–7
Kerry County, 51, 127, 217,
    231–4, 241, 243–8, 250, 253,
    256, 259–60, 269–70, 272–4,
    276–81, 284–6, 294, 297, 305
Kerry Gaeltacht, 252
Kerryman, The, 277
Kilbeg, 34, 36
Kilcatherine Point, 287
Kilcullen, Edward, 101–3
Kilcullen's Bath House, 100–2
Kilkee, 216–24, 241
Kilkieran, 182, 184
Kilkieran Bay, 182–5,187
Killala, 108–11
Killala Bay, 100, 109
Killary Harbour, 136, 157–8, 167
Killeenaran, 194–6
Killimer, 233, 236
Killorglin, 261, 267–76
Killybegs, 34, 36–40
Kilstiffin, 216–17, 234, 241–2
Kincasslagh, 28–9
Kinsale, 307, 309–20
Kinvarra, 183, 193, 199–200
Kinvarra Bay, 196
Klimley, Dr Pete, 7
Knocknarea, 85, 91
Kruger's Bar, 262

Lahinch, 215
Lamberth, Jane, 92–3
Leitrim County, 51–3, 55, 57,
    59–63, 108
Leitrim Observer, 59
Letterkenny, 10, 14, 21
Lighthouse Tavern, 18–19

Limerick city, 210, 216, 218, 223

Limerick County, 234–6, 292

Linnane, Geraldine, 196–9

Lisdoonvarna, 206, 208–12

Lissadell beach, 69, 71

London, 5, 32–3, 144, 164, 195, 217, 294

Loop Head, 216–20, 224, 232–3

Lough Anaffrin, 32

Lough Foyle, xi–xii

Lough Gill, 243, 245

Lough Melvin, 59, 61–2

Lough Swilly, 12–13, 15–19, 21

Lowry's Whiskey Bar, 175–7

McCarthy, Vincent, 294–5

McDonnells Bar, 124–5

MacGillycuddy's Reeks, 261, 276, 292

mac Lir, Manannán
    affiliated with Tir na nÓg, 88, 324
    ale of immortality, 15
    anger, xi, 23, 127, 174
    appearance, xi, 38, 83–4, 321–2
    associated with Power of Three, 322
    assumes shape of heron, 111
    attention of newshounds, 321
    Catholic church view on, 267
    chief druid Gebann, 305
    cloak of concealment, 149, 322
    comparisons to Neptune, xi, 38, 174, 207, 322
    connection to Cliona's wave, 305–7, 309, 322
    connection to Cormac mac Airt, 203
    consort of Hag of Beara, 287–90
    crane bag treasures, 207–8, 323–4

    domination of action, 324
    dramatis personae, 322
    energy, 41, 127, 322
    euhemerised, 321
    feasting and love of food, 41, 321
    fondness for women, 267, 322–3
    fragarach or sword, xi, 89, 207, 324
    gifts to Tuatha Dé Danann, 149, 207–8, 322
    in folklore and legend, 111, 267, 278
    in the pantheon, 288
    kingdom of, 170, 174
    letter to, 321–4
    link to Mann Island, 182–5
    link to Skellig Michael, 89, 278
    lord of Tuatha Dé Danann, 88, 206–9, 321
    magical powers, 41, 322
    otherworldly kingdom, 15, 321
    philanderer, 322
    reference to in W. B. Yeats' 'Wanderings of Oisin,' 83
    relationship to Children of Lir, 88, 126–7
    relationship to Conmhaícne Mara, 174
    relevance today, 159, 209, 321
    retreat into seclusion, 89, 321
    riding Enbarr of the Flowing Mane, xi, 63, 89, 159, 203, 232, 312, 321–2
    ruler of Isle of Man, xii–xiii
    seahorses or caiple Mhanannáin, 27, 94, 267, 321
    sense of humour, 267
    shape–shifter, 41, 90, 127, 322

mac Lir, Manannán (*continued*)
    statues, Binevenagh, xi–xiii,
        theft of, 51–2, reward for
        information, 63–4, police
        search and appeal for
        return, 83–4, 321, recovery
        of, 103, mystery of motive
        for theft, 103, replacement
        of, 125–6; Castlebar statue,
        158–9; Mrs Man statue,
        144–6
    study of heavens, 50
    supernatural being, 322
    surrounded by myths, 324
    trickster, 90, 127, 209, 271, 322
    Wavesweeper chariot, 89,
        126–7, 144, 322–3
Madigan, Carmel, 225–30
Magan, Rita, 58
Magee, Geoff, 231–3
Magilligan, xi–xii
Maguire, Batt, 304–5
Maharees, 245–6
Malin Head, 3, 5–6, 10
Mamore, xi, 12
Mann Island, 182–5
Mannin Bay, 170–5
Mayo County, 18, 30, 35, 99, 108,
        112, 116, 118, 120, 129–32,
        138–9, 141, 145–6, 148, 154,
        157–9
Meath County, 85, 128
Men's Sheds, 268, 299–302
Mooney, Noel, 70–2
Moriarty, John, 181
Mullaghmore, 63–8, 75, 97
Mullaghmore Head, 54, 68
Mullet Peninsula, 126–33
Mulranny, 119, 142–6
Mulroy Bay, 20
Munnelly, Mary, 115

Murphy, Cillian, 216–18, 234
Murreagh, 259–60
Mweelrea Mountain, 157, 167–9

National Gallery, Dublin, 80
natterjack toads, 243–5
Natural History Museum,
    Dublin, 249
Naughton, Kevin, 182–5
Ned Natterjack's Bar, 243–5
Newfoundland, 173, 229, 237
Newport, 146–7, 149
Night of the Big Wind, 85, 166

O'Brien, Vincent, 243–5
Ó Cadhain, Máirtín, 189
O'Carroll, Anne, 288–91
Ó Criomhthain, Tomás, 260
O'Donnell, Bill, 294–5
O'Donnell, Daniel, 28–9
O'Donnell, John, 148–50
O'Dwyer, Mick, 281
Ó Fátharta, Máirtín, 188–90
Offaly County, 126
Ó Fiannachta, Monsignor
    Pádraig, 264–7
O'Grady, George, 112–14
O'Hara, Maureen, 235
Ó hEithir, Breandán, 190
O'Kane, Paul, 95–8
Old Head of Kinsale, 318
Old Irish Goat Society, 143–5
O'Malley, Ernie, 158–9
O'Malley, Grace (Granuaile),
    151–7
O'Malley, Martin, 172–5
Omey Island, 162–7
Ordnance Survey, 34, 137
O'Regan, Brendan, 236–7
O'Reilly, Brendan, 42–3
Osborne, Ian, 302

Ó Sé, Seán, 269
O'Shaughnessy, Margaret, 235–8
Oughtdarra, 204, 208

Parkmore pier, 196, 198
Pease, Nic, 300–2
Plantation of Ulster, 16, 56
Pope Francis, 47, 265–7
Portmagee, 278–80
Power of Three, 8, 14, 89, 100,
    161, 320, 322
Praeger, R. L., 26, 178
Puck Fair, 261, 268–76
Puckeroos, The, 273–4
Pye, Jerry, 55–7, 63

Quirke, Michael, 87–91

Raidió na Gaeltachta, 69, 188
Rathmullan, 15–16
Redbrae, 55–6
Redmond, Johnny, 222–4
Renvyle, 161, 167–70
Renvyle House Hotel, 168–70
Ring of Kerry, 276, 278, 284, 291
River Black Oak, 147
River Drowes, 52, 60–1
River Duff, 63
River Kenmare, 284, 287
River Owengrave, 146
River Shannon, 71, 236
Roadside Tavern, 206–7, 209
Robinson, Auriel, 85–7
Robinson, Mary, 114
Robinson, Tim, 170
Rosguill Peninsula, 20, 23–4
Ross beach, 225–31
Rosscarbery Bay, 307
Rosses Point, 76–80, 84
round towers, 110
Roundstone, 174, 177–9

Roundstone bog, 178–9
Royal Hibernian Academy, 260
RTÉ, 69, 77
Rusty Bar, 35–6
Ryan's Daughter, 263–4
Ryan-Purcell, Walter, 297–8

St Catherine, 38
St Deirbhile, 128–31
St Patrick, 58, 83, 109–10, 116,
    226, 267
Saldanha, HMS, 16
Saldanha Head, 17
Salthill, 190–3
Sardou, Michel, 175
Schull, 296–7
seaweed, 100–3, 183, 226–7
Shannon Airport, 222, 237
Shannon estuary, 216, 231, 233–6,
    241
Sheephaven Bay, 20, 22
Sheridan, Joe, 236–8
Simonds-Gooding, Maria, 260–4
Skellig Islands, 89, 278, 291–2
Skibbereen, 298–300, 302
Slieve Elva, 203
Slieve League, 34–5, 49
Slieve League Cultural Centre, 35
Slieve Miskish Mountains, 291
Slievemore Mountain, 138–40
Sligo Champion, 59
Sligo County, 3, 35, 60, 63–5, 71,
    73, 75–6, 79, 85–6, 90–1, 94,
    96, 99, 108, 155
Sligo town, 63, 76–7, 81–2, 84,
    87–8, 91
Spaniard Bar, 317–18
Spanish Armada, 69–70, 73–9,
    86–7, 89, 262
Spiddal, 186–90
Strandhill, 85, 91–4

...gh beach, 69–70, 72–6, 85–6
surfing, 44–7, 92, 95–8, 215, 244
Sutton, John Darren, 51

Tarbert, 233–4, 236
Thomas, Dylan, 30–3
Toombeola, 179
Tory Island, 18, 22
Tralee Bay, 243–5
Tuatha Dé Danann, 83, 88, 149, 206–9, 321–4
Tullaghan, 51–3, 58, 60–1
Tully Peninsula, 167
Tyrone County, 236
Tyrrell, David, 126–7

Union Hall, 305–6
Urris Hills, xi, 12, 17

Valentia Island, 278, 280
Varadkar, Leo, 30

Waldron, James, 18–19
Waterford County, 70
Waterville, 279–81, 283–4
Western People, 108–9
Westmeath County, 16
Westport, 141, 147–8, 150–2, 154, 157
Westport House, 151–7
Westropp, Thomas Johnson, 207–8
Whelan, Pascal, 162–7
White's Marsh, 307–8
Wicklow County, 93
Wild Atlantic salmon run, 61–3
Williams, Peter, 200–4
Wolfdog Tavern, 110–11
World's End, 311–16

Yates, John, 29–30
Yeats, Jack, 76, 79–80
Yeats, W. B., 76, 79–83, 87–8, 90, 169